SYMBOL AND EXISTENCE

MERCER UNIVERSITY

MERCER UNIVERSITY PRESS

Endowed by

TOM WATSON BROWN
and
THE WATSON-BROWN FOUNDATION, INC.

SYMBOL AND EXISTENCE

A Study in Meaning

Explorations of Human Nature

by

Walker Percy

Edited by
Kenneth Laine Ketner
Karey Lea Perkins
Rhonda Renee McDonnell
Scott Ross Cunningham
Institute for Studies in Pragmaticism
Texas Tech University

MERCER UNIVERSITY PRESS
Macon, Georgia
1979–2019
40 Years of Publishing Excellence

MUP/ H975

Published by Mercer University Press
1501 Mercer University Drive
Macon, Georgia 31207

9 8 7 6 5 4 3 2 1

Books published by Mercer University Press are printed on acid-free paper that meets the requirements of the American National Standard for Information Sciences—Permanence of Paper for Printed Library Materials.

Printed and bound in the United States.

Dust jacket design by Burt&Burt.

This book is set in Adobe Caslon Pro.

ISBN 978-0-88146-708-6
Cataloging-in-Publication Data is available from the Library of Congress

FOREWORD

Hello

As a greeting, it's plain and common, and the elements of it are simple: it requires at least two persons. One person says hello to another person.

What's happening here? Is it a clue? Is it concealing and revealing something significant?

Walker Percy says, "Yes!"

Such events are both basic and essential for human experience. Perhaps that claim surprises you. After all, a simple "hello" is just another everyday activity. But when the interaction succeeds, when one person *gives* the greeting and another person *receives* it, Percy sees two persons "co-celebrating" in life. The same celebration occurs in every act of naming our world, whether we name Fred or a lupin or Tay-Sachs disease.

Percy's exploration of this—our asserting, naming, co-celebration of life through language—gave him an important key in his lifelong search to understand symbol, existence, and meaning. This book records his exploration.

Perhaps you also are searching for meaning, for insights into what it is to *be* human. Many of Percy's readers share that quality with him, and through his novels, we often experience a joyful charge of recognition: "Oh! I'm a searcher too." That satisfaction often occurs when the conclusion is reached, and the protagonist is better off than before; the person who may have been in despair at the beginning of the novel, is, at the end, surrounded by a community and has learned to live through four o'clock on an ordinary Wednesday afternoon.

But what happened to the protagonist and to us, Percy's readers, in this experience? How is meaning found?

Percy's answer—or at least his search, which is moving him closer to answers—is here in *Symbol and Existence*. To encounter this book is to encounter a vigorous intelligence at work, pulling strands from the breadth of western thought into a new tapestry.

What is revealing in this encounter is his method of discovery, a scientific examination of life that requires neither laboratory building nor instrumental gadgetry. To learn Percy's method of conducting science is to learn how to examine humanity and our individual lives.

Such a possibility may be needed more today than when Percy first wrote (and revised and revised and revised) this volume; for, if we as a human species were in trouble in 1950, we are in even more danger now. In the shifting landscape of truth and reality as momentary whims of personal preference, Percy offers us an alternative: an objective open-minded scientific attitude equips us for our own search for understanding human life.

Again… Hello.

To continue the conversation about *Symbol and Existence*, other Percy projects, and Walker Percy himself, consult www.pragmaticism.net/Percy.

EDITORS' PREFACE

Search for a Radical Anthropology

Symbol and Existence: A Study in Meaning (S&E) is the foundation for the majority of Percy's writing, both fiction and nonfiction. It cogently assembles his answers to some of contemporary civilization's great unsettled questions regarding human nature. As the only systematic representation of Percy's general working theory, *S&E* gives an important framework for his diverse intellectual background—such as philosophy and psychology, medicine and anthropology, semiotic and zoology—creating what Percy calls his "radical anthropology," a well-rooted account of human nature.

Believing philosophical writing was his destiny, Percy invested serious and continuing efforts in this project early in his career. *S&E* is his original manuscript of that approach, his "radical anthropology." It was written and revised during the 1950s, then donated, along with hundreds of other Percy papers, to the University of North Carolina at Chapel Hill archives in four different drafts. The first two completed drafts were given by Percy himself in 1983. The third and fourth versions were added in 1994 and 2007 by the Percy estate after his death.

These multiple drafts and his 1950s correspondence with editors reveal his decade-long intent and attempt to publish *S&E*, but to no avail.[1] In the meantime, he was also writing novels, and eventually his third attempt, *The Moviegoer*, was published and won the National Book Award in 1962. Percy then deduced that his fortunes lay in fiction. His unpublished manuscript was fated to find its resting place

---

[1] See correspondence in UNC-Chapel Hill archives as well as Jay Tolson, *Pilgrim in the Ruins: A Life of Walker Percy* (New York: Simon & Schuster, 1992) and Patrick Samway, *Walker Percy: A Life* (New York: Farrar, Straus & Giroux, 1997).

buried in the Chapel Hill archives.

But Percy never abandoned philosophy itself, still considering at various times throughout his life that it was his true calling, even his identity. When asked what her father did, six-year-old Mary Pratt proclaimed: My daddy is a "silosopher."[2] While he never created another systematic book of philosophy like *S&E* again (though he many times expressed his intent to do so), he did publish philosophical essays. As early as the 1950s, Percy had already submitted some *S&E* chapters as stand-alone articles to various academic journals.[3] In 1975, *The Message in the Bottle (MB),* Percy's first published book length philosophical work, included some isolated chapters from *S&E*, but the book itself was quite different from *S&E*. Why? By that time, a discouraged Percy had come to the conclusion that few people were interested in or really wanted to read his philosophy.[4] *MB*, although a full book of Percy's philosophy, was hastily assembled and half-hearted as a result. No discernible pattern seems apparent to the arrangement of the *MB* chapters, some of which were merely photocopied from previous journal articles.[5] They were not in the order of their original source and in fact didn't seem to be in any order at all. These former *S&E* chapters were often substantially altered. Some fell victim to editorial intrusion; all were devoid of the context of his whole manuscript. All essays lost at least some of their original meaning. Some critics have said the piecemeal presentation in *MB* makes it more a collection of insights than a coherent theory.[6]

---

[2] Tolson, *Pilgrim,* 234.

[3] See pragmatism.net/Percy for a chronology of publication and for *S&E* correlations to other published work.

[4] Jay Tolson, ed., *The Correspondence of Shelby Foote and Walker Percy* (New York: W. W. Norton & Co., 1998) 213; Walker Percy, *The Message in the Bottle* (New York: Farrar, Straus & Giroux, 1975) 10; Samway, *Walker Percy*, 206; Tolson, *Pilgrim*, 262.

[5] Samway, *Walker Percy*, 313.

[6] William H. Poteat, "Reflections on Walker Percy's Theory of Language," in *The Art of Walker Percy: Strategems for Being,* ed. Panthea Reid Broughton (Baton Rouge: LSU Press, 1999) 193; Kieran Quinlan, *Walker*

Another book of Percy's essays appeared posthumously in 1991: *Signposts in a Strange Land*, a collection of independent essays divided into three general categories (life in the south; morality and religion; science, language and literature). Only one essay, "Naming and Being," is derived from his original *S&E* manuscript. A third non-fiction book, *Lost in the Cosmos*, contains a semiotic primer inside its self-help quiz, echoing many of the ideas in *S&E*, but without the full development of his philosophy seen here. *S&E* includes the original draft of these journal articles and book chapters that appear separately and randomly elsewhere throughout Percy's career, yet their later publication lacks the context and the coherent organization of Percy's philosophy that *S&E* has.

S&E corrects these problems. As a complete book of philosophy, *S&E* is methodical and systematic, something Percy critics had never attributed to his philosophy as presented in *MB*, nor to his more entertaining, less serious, later non-fiction works. *S&E* is the foundation for all of Percy's thinking, and without this foundation, his later philosophical works appear disconnected and fragmented. A study of *S&E* will prove fascinating to Percy scholars who wish to decipher Percy's authentic philosophical stance, as his thoughts are clarified in their original context; Percy's message can be re-viewed, re-imagined, and re-thought through *S&E*.

Moreover, because much of *S&E* is unique, it offers previously unknown insights from Percy. Well over half of this work is material never before seen or published. Of the 302 typewritten pages in the original *S&E* manuscript, 166 are new. The other 136 pages, published in 1950s journals or later books, are often third iterations of their original source in *S&E* and much revised by editors from Percy's original drafts.

Perhaps more surprisingly, although written over half a century ago, *S&E* is a prescient work that is relevant to philosophical trends

---

Percy: The Last Catholic Novelist (Baton Rouge: LSU Press, 1996) 147-151; Tolson, *Walker Percy*, 400-401. The "unsystematic" accusation has been unwisely advanced against a number of great thinkers: for example, one who influenced Percy, namely C. S. Peirce.

today. This work bristles with references encompassing a several hundred-year time span and a wide range of intellectual disciplines, including but not limited to philosophy, medicine, literature, anthropology, psychology, semiotic, biology, and sociology. Percy's use of these interdisciplinary sources contributes to his grand project of creating a new model for understanding humans, consciousness, language, and the meaning of life—one that resolves the dilemma between scientism and existentialism. Percy was influenced by the works of perennial scholars as well as leading academics in the mid-twentieth century, yet his studies are crucial for the twenty-first century.

During the time Percy wrote, rigid, cause-effect, hard determinist models were being revealed as inadequate. These models were slowly replaced by postmodernism in the latter part of that century, which embraced relativism, self-referentiality, and the conditionality of permanent values. The new paradigm rightly rejected the old modernist positivism, with its presumption to capture and summarize all of existence in grand narratives and theories. But the postmodern critique of modernism's flaws had its own problems. Anti-theorist philosophies don't create new theories. We see this in theoretical shortcomings in current semiotics.[7] The inadequacies of postmodernism's attempted correction of the positivist, determinist paradigm is evidenced in the fact that it essentially failed—as seen in the striking number of philosophical departments in universities today that have retreated into the strict analytical project, embracing the early twentieth century's tendency to accept that scientific experiments will answer the great philosophical questions, such as what it is to be a human being in the world. For Percy, it doesn't work. It didn't work then and it doesn't work now—and *S&E* explains why.

The chasm still exists between scientism, or the scientific method erroneously elevated to a worldview, and existentialism,

---

[7] Rhonda McDonnell, "Walker Percy's Intersubjectivity: An Existential Semiotic or 3 + 3 = 4," in *Walker Percy, Philosopher,* ed. Leslie Marsh (New York: Palgrave MacMillan, 2018).

which gets at human consciousness that the scientific method cannot explain. Alone, each theory is incomplete. One claims unbiased external objectivity without being able to account for human consciousness, and the other considers human consciousness yet wallows in an unverifiable and subjective solipsism. For Percy, both failed to adequately describe human beings and human consciousness. In contrast Percy acknowledges the chasm. He first rescues scientific method from the clutches of scientism, then presents a hypothesis that constructs a "tenuous bridge" between these two competing and ostensibly conflicting worldviews: it is in both symbol and existence, the human use of language, that the answer is found.

However, Percy's philosophy remains here, as later, a "thief" of his many diverse sources—he takes from them what he wants and lets the rest go.[8] With his language theory, he IS doing semiotic—yes—but it's not a Saussurean semiology or Morrisean semiotic, nor wholly Peircean semeiotic, nor does his triangle convey the same meaning as that of Ogden and Richards. Herein lies Percy's unique semiotic.[9] He's doing philosophy—yes—but not the kind of narrow analytic philosophy found in most American universities and modern academia today that lapses into the scientism of the past. His much broader philosophy—both existential, pragmatic, as well as scientific without being scientistic, without ill-founded and long disproven positivist flaws—resolves the paradigmatic dichotomy and void of philosophy today.

---

[8] Patrick Samway, ed., *A Thief of Peirce: The Letters of Kenneth Laine Ketner and Walker Percy* (Jackson, MS: University Press of Mississippi, 1995) 131.

[9] "Semeiotic" is the term Peirce used first for his nineteenth century studies as a continuation of the same terminology employed by earlier scientists such as Locke or even earlier physicians such as Galen; "semiotics" is a twentieth-century movement, quite eclectic with a flexible terminology, associated with behaviorists such as Morris, Saussure, and others; the term "semiotic" appears to be the label Percy preferred for his work because he wanted to separate his "improved" account of it from the account given by Morris and associates.

Percy uses the pragmatists as resources to reconcile these confusions and difficulties. Not only had postmodernism's critique of positivist flaws already been accomplished by the pragmatists, postmodernism's two great difficulties—finding objectivism in an epistemologically relative universe and ending the infinite loop of self-referentiality—had also already been solved by the pragmatists. Pragmatism undercuts cognitive relativism with a theory of truth and objectivity grounded in observation, experimental work, testing, and experience in a real world. Pragmatism kept the scientific method for inquiry, providing an objectivity Percy sought, without making the mistake of elevating it to an all-encompassing worldview that ignored some of the most important questions of philosophy: "who am I?" and "why am I here?" Richard Rorty says the pragmatists "were not only waiting at the end of the dialectical road which analytic philosophy traveled, but are waiting at the end of the road which, for example, Foucault and Deleuze are currently traveling."[10] At the end of that road, "pragmatism claims to discover a strain of human commonality that trumps the postmodern emphasis on difference and discontinuity."[11] Pragmatism had already advanced beyond the postmodernists, had already resolved problems they left unresolved—offering a postmodernism without the problems, or a post-postmodernism.

And it is to the pragmatists that Percy turns to support his philosophical hypothesis, his "radical anthropology." Pragmatism does not dismiss the existentialists' claim about empiricism's limitations when applied to human consciousness. *S&E* begins with the existentialists (Kierkegaard, Marcel, Heidegger) to note the flaws of the modernists, hard empiricists, and the first generation of semioticians—the structuralists. Then the pragmatists complete his system,

---

[10] Richard Rorty, *Consequences of Pragmatism* (Minneapolis: University of Minnesota Press, 1982) xviii.

[11] Larry A. Hickman, *Pragmatism as Post-Postmodernism: Lessons from John Dewey* (New York: Fordham University Press, 2007) 2.

specifically Charles Sanders Peirce,[12] by solving the problems of the second generation of semioticians—the relativists. Peirce's philosophy provided a source for the objectivity Percy sought that neither existentialism alone nor postmodernism offered. In fact, it has been argued that "pragmaticism[13] *is* an existentialism."[14]

S&E is a visionary and systemized response to the problems of the previous century's modernism and today's postmodernism (beginning to surface at the time Percy wrote) to propose a worldview that works, especially when it comes to the problem of human consciousness and the search for meaning. Percy's manuscript, written decades before postmodernism's dominion in philosophy and before its recognized problems, is a testament to his foresight. Current semiotics is just now beginning to discover the path that Percy laid out decades before. Recent studies present a new approach to semiotics, studying human behavior just as Percy did half a century earlier, using "a combination of Peircean semeiotic and existentialism, along with an eclectic mix of theorists from other disciplines... all of which ultimately concern how a person might live in the world."[15] Percy's philosophy echoes pragmatist claims and is an unnoticed forerunner of the emerging existential semiotics—or, more accurately, today's theories stand in Percy's tradition, correcting outdated ones and joining the

---

[12] Percy's employment of Peirce's research begins to appear near the conclusion of *S&E*. However that influence had entered Percy's thinking as early as 1947 (see Samway, *A Thief of Peirce*, x-xix). A manuscript essay *circa* 1959, entitled "Peirce and Modern Semiotic" probably is part of the intellectual nimbus of *S&E*. That essay has been published in Marsh, *Walker Percy, Philosopher*; reading it alongside the closing chapters of this volume is useful. Marsh's project also contains chapters by Cunningham, McDonnell, and Perkins that are relevant to this topic.

[13] "Pragmaticism" refers to Peirce's philosophy as distinguished from William James's "pragmatism."

[14] Kenneth Laine Ketner, "Pragmaticism Is an Existentialism?" in *Frontiers in American Philosophy* (Volume 2) ed. Robert W. Burch and Herman J. Saatkamp, Jr. (College Station: Texas A & M University Press, 1996), 105-110.

[15] McDonnell, "Walker Percy's Intersubjectivity," 115-132.

visionary 1950s Percy as part of a needed sea change for a new semiotic philosophy, for a twenty-first century post-postmodernism.

Few know that Percy said it first.

Kenneth Laine Ketner
Karey Lea Perkins
Rhonda Renee McDonnell
Scott Ross Cunningham
Institute for Studies in Pragmaticism
Texas Tech University

CONTENTS

SYMBOL AND EXISTENCE

by

Walker Percy

PREFACE

This book is the result of the collision of two worldviews in a single mind.

The first view hardly needs explaining. It is the native climate, with one or two exceptions, of the educated American mind. I shall refer to it in the sequel by several terms, "objective empiricism," "the objective point of view," "the scientific method elevated to a worldview," etc., because, as I explain later, no one word like "naturalism" or "empiricism" or "materialism" seems to express it satisfactorily. It is a decision about the nature of the world. To most of us it goes without saying that everything that happens in the world can be explained as coming about as a natural outgrowth of a preceding event. We believe every happening can be understood, as Whitehead expressed it, as an example of a general principle that it is the business of science to discover.

Let me state here and now that this book is not an attack on the scientific method. On the contrary. One of its premises is the validity, the immense value and efficacy, of the objective empirical method. All too often nowadays science comes under attack as the villain of modern man's alienation, who is allegedly bringing us ever closer to the test tube civilization of Huxley's *Brave New World.* The truth of the matter is that the true scientific spirit is, as Einstein called it, the tenderest little plant that needs all the encouragement it can get. Indeed there are even now signs that it is not flourishing. The danger is not that the scientific method will conquer the world but that it will be allowed to die out by a generation of consumers and technicians who, as Ortega (1952) has said, have not the slightest curiosity about the world or the products and techniques they use, who do not wish to contribute to knowledge or even to acknowledge a debt of gratitude to science but only to enjoy its fruits (59).

I shall draw a sharp distinction between the scientific method as a method, that razor sharp instrument of knowing and doing, and the scientific method elevated to an all-construing worldview, the other edge of the blade. This book offers a radical criticism of this latter tendency, a tendency which is widely prevalent in our society and which is apt to be held not so much by practicing scientists as by those at some distance from science, for whom the scientific method constitutes itself as a sort of magical formula. But it is a criticism that is undertaken with a full appreciation of the efficacy and beauty of the method. So many of the current attacks on science are disqualified by the failure of the attackers to appreciate the nobility, I would even say the sacredness, of the scientific calling. They speak of scientists treating the world as just a problem to be solved and raw material to be manipulated, but in leaving it at that they overlook the essential nature of the scientist's vocation, that peculiar joy of knowing and the endless susceptibility of his data to the act of knowing which binds a man to his laboratory for life. As Jaspers (1953) has said, the spirit of this age is the spirit of science, and it is impossible for anyone to criticize any age unless he has first participated in its spirit. To know the temptation of Science, one must first know her beauty; only her lovers may presume to name her shortcomings (81-96). I do not mean that one must be, or that I am, a research scientist. But one must have experienced, in some sense or other, the almost incomparable attractiveness of the scientific method, its truth, elegance, simplicity, hard-headedness, discipline, fruitfulness. To the current detractors of science, I say not less science, but more science. It is only when the Method is exhausted as a worldview, exploited to its farthest reaches, that its shortcomings—its limits, its marvelous efficacy as an instrument, its disastrous failure as a worldview—can be clearly seen.

One's first discovery of the scientific view of the world is always in the nature of a revelation—one might even use the word conversion. Again it was Einstein (1934) who compared the beauty of science with "everyday life with its painful crudity and hopeless dreariness" (2). It is nothing less than a conversion when a young man who has always lived in a sort of magic picture-book world of shoes and ships and sealing wax—see Rover, Rover is a dog, dogs eat meat because they are dogs; airplanes fly because they are airplanes; the sun will come up tomorrow because it will be another day; in America we have Democracy—when this young man discovers one day that behind all this seemingly arbitrary profusion, there are unifying principles and mechanical causes and field forces at work. What he discovers is that cabbages and kings are more alike than they are different, that both are organisms in an environment and behave accordingly. It is as if the young man—who all these years had been watching a puppet show in which Punch did this because he was Punch, and Judy did that because she was Judy—was granted a look behind the scenes and saw the wires that moved Punch. Yet this simile hardly does justice to the young man's discovery; it is much more exciting than this. For what he sees is not that real Punches and Judys are operated by a hidden personage pulling wires from above, but that they operate to a large degree of themselves, immanently and according to the same principles by which billiard balls ricochet around the table. (I do not mean to say that crude mechanism is now professed by scientific philosophers, but that mechanism is often one's introduction to science, and that in fact gross determinism still prevails at some levels despite probability and indeterminism at sub-atomic levels.) Renal cells do not secrete urine because it is their job to do this but because of an interplay of chemical and physical forces. Or so it seems to him. It may be true to say that mechanism or field forces eventually fall short as a total explanation. But they go a long way before they do so, and the going is good.

Again to those who say less mechanism, less immanentism, I say more. The shortcomings of mechanism only appear when mechanism is exhausted. The vitalist who opposes mechanism often does his cause little justice because he does not appreciate how far mechanism goes as an explanation. Occam's principle is surely valid here: in scientific thinking let us use the least hypothesis not the greatest.

It is a great mistake, I think, to draw a line somewhere ahead of science—usually a retreating front—and to say that beyond this mechanical principles do not work or to make room for God by squeezing him in here or there ("at least you can't explain bird migration, mental telepathy," etc.). No, once you have tasted of this apple, the delicious fruit of immanentism, there is nothing for it but to eat it all, to go with Haeckel as far as he can go, to out-Comte Comte. If religion and metaphysics are only to be provided for by certain esoteric physical findings, such as Heisenberg's Principle of Indeterminacy or Rhine's ESP or du Noüy's demonstration that life violates the Second Law of Thermodynamics—little loopholes in the great wall of immanentism—then the jig is up. For the wall is more beautiful than the loopholes. Perhaps the saddest sight of the day is the spectacle of people trying with all their might to squeeze through the loopholes, seizing upon the slightest rumor of occult phenomenon as their last hope of salvation. It is these people, paradoxically, who have fallen prey to scientism far more than scientists, who in their very despair assign an omnicompetence to science as a worldview which few scientists would claim for it.

Either objectivism, the scientific method elevated to an all-construing worldview, must be criticized far more radically than the loopholers do, or it needn't be criticized at all. Either there has been some colossal oversight in the scientific worldview—as great as the oversight of the king's subjects who thought the king had clothes on—or the loopholers are not worth bothering about. (I believe that there has been such an oversight, what Heidegger calls the loss of being or homelessness from being and Marcel calls the refusal of being.) There is something offensive about the current tendency to use as a weapon against science every mishap of science—like the fraud of the Piltdown Man—and to rejoice in anything that seems to "defy" science. It is as if some theists believed that scientific laws and the ordinary happenings that follow scientific laws are the work of the devil and that the only reason God works a miracle is to give evidence of himself against this overwhelming counter-evidence.

But let us be clear about one thing. There are indeed these irrational and anti-scientific currents abroad today. But what I shall be concerned with is a far subtler and far more pervasive tendency in those who regard themselves as scientifically minded. I do not refer to those who are acutely aware of the efficacy of science as a method of knowing and doing and who at the time retain a modesty and an openness to the inexhaustible world. I refer rather to the quite different penchant for extrapolating from a *method* of knowing to an all-construing *worldview*, a view, moreover, which is quite arrogant about what it claims for itself and what it refuses to others, a view, in short, which is no longer scientific but is covertly metaphysical and religious, yet at the same time is unwilling to examine or discuss its assumptions. The point is that for one who has in the course of "dreary everyday life" discovered the scientific method, there is always the temptation to elevate this elegant method to a totalitarian worldview. It is natural that it should be so. Any precision instrument is as dangerous as it is precise. But the only real danger is that one should be unaware of the danger.

This is the first point of view then—the conscious or unconscious elevation of the scientific method to a total all-construing worldview, the tacit conviction that *all* reality is an expression of certain underlying principles and relationships that are discoverable by the scientific method and that there is no remainder.

The second worldview comes later. I mean later in two senses: it has come later as a historical philosophy, and it generally comes later, I think, in one's own personal philosophy. In one's life, it is the coming to the end of a road, the beautiful road that lies open to a man when he first makes the turning Einstein speaks of—not the coming to the end of the scientific method but the coming to the end of scientism as a worldview. Nietzsche speaks of the tragic view that awaits the theoretical man when he comes to the limits of theory. It is not the discovery of a loophole here or there in the wall of immanentism; it is rather the coming upon the abyss. It is not the searching for and finding of a certain salient of data that resists scientific hypotheses; it is rather the yawning of the void of existence in him who searches.

Let me introduce the second view—which is quite as revolutionary as the first—by quoting a remark of Dr. Karl Stern (1954), the psychiatrist. He made the somewhat surprising observation that a great number of the neurotics he had seen were characterized by the positivist-objective attitude that they would not be taken in by anything, that they would not "swallow" anything that could not be proved. "I have also noticed that neurotic unbelievers in their fantasies endow the purely intellectual, nonintuitive and nonpoetic side of human thought (the sort of thinking which a logical positivist would claim to be the only proper mode of reason) with extraordinary, limitless power" (284). Dr. Stern appears to be saying that the neurotic of our time is not the man who has committed himself to some cultural or religious or metaphysical position—which the objective scientist would find, in varying degrees, illusory—but that the neurotic is none other than he who has embraced this objective point of view!

Again, I am aware of the danger of a misunderstanding, of appearing to suggest that one should therefore be less skeptical, less objective, that in short one should swallow religion because science, truth, is too bitter a dose for us. This counsel of despair appears indeed to be the advice of some philosophers and psychiatrists who say in so many words that myth and archetype may not be objectively "true" but that they are necessary for mental health, so you had better believe in them for your own good. But I am saying quite the reverse. Once one has set out on this high road of scientism, there is no turning back and no detouring. If the "enlightened objectivist" finds himself in anxiety he must not—indeed he cannot—turn aside into myth or archetype. To do so would betray both science and religion. He must press forward. The road must be travelled to the abyss.

Then what is the second discovery, which is at least as great a revelation as the first? It is the discovery of the existentialists that *something has been left out* of this first all-encompassing worldview. This is moreover a very extraordinary something. What has been left out is not a stray piece of datum nor an unexplored salient that science gradually narrows and finally explains. On the contrary. What is so queer about this leftover is that as the scientific worldview grows ever more efficacious, ever more encompassing of reality, this particular leftover also becomes ever greater, ever more glaring in its inaccessibility to the Method. More than that: not only is it inaccessible to the Method, but as the Method extends its competence, this leftover becomes ever more heterogeneous with the corpus of science. As time goes on, science has more and more to say about the other side of the moon. But as time goes on, science must say less and less about this leftover, because the more it tries to say, the greater becomes the leftover.

What is this leftover? It is nothing in the world before one, not shoes or ships or sealing wax, not the other side of the moon, not ESP or nuclear fusion.

The second worldview is the discovery of one's self as the stranger amid the data. As the city of science grows ever more imposing, it becomes ever more certain that a ghost is abroad in its streets. There is a someone there whom science has nothing to say about, whose dimensions and energies and needs are not the dimensions and energies and needs of science. This stranger makes his presence ever more insistent until, for some, the city vanishes and there remains nothing but one's self, a castaway upon a desolate shore where there are no signs, no science, only anguish.

It is the raw aching void of existence, one's own existence, which is the great leftover in the otherwise magnificent corpus of objective science.

As it happens, it is existence in *all* its manifestations which the objective worldview misses, but the oversight only becomes noticeable when it is one's own existence which is overlooked. It is all the same to a laboratory specimen of a paramecium or a cubic centimeter of water if its concrete act of existence is overlooked and if it is understood entirely as a manifestation of a particular evolutionary stage or as a specimen of a particular element. But it is not the same to me. Perhaps I am able to understand myself as an *example* of such and such a personality type or of such and such a cultural configuration or of such and such a libidinal dynamic. But after I have understood this, I must still live out this day and the next. The adherent of the first worldview, the passionate objectivist, finds himself in somewhat the same predicament as the young man Kierkegaard describes who was given the task of keeping busy all day and finished at noon.

It is for this reason that modern existentialism is almost entirely a subjective humanism since it takes account of only that painful left-over that science has most conspicuously missed: my own existence. Everything else is relegated to the realm of object, *en soi*, unknowable other, etc. Yet there are other acts of existence, and a true existentialism must take account not only of myself but also of you and of that which we see between us.

It is not merely another oversight of objective science which the existentialists have discovered, an oversight which a more radical science might now proceed to correct—rather is it the non-radical character of science itself in even its most radical reach. It is the discovery that the scientific project is mounted *within* a framework—a framework of spectatorship over against data—which it, science, can never get hold of, because this framework is the very condition of its getting hold of anything.

Therefore to those who say that objective science should be less radical, making concessions here and there to religious points of view, I say that science should be as radical as it possibly can be. For these concessions are usually just that, crumbs from the table of he who thinks that the feast is his—as in the *Look Magazine* article (Dean 1953), which announced that now we might believe in miracles because the Theory of Probability allowed that once in a great while bodies might fly up instead of falling down. It is only when the greatest reach of science is realized that its non-radical character can be ascertained and the door opened to a truly radical science, the science of being.

I do not think I am singling out a vague or an esoteric discovery as my second worldview. It is true that one is always in danger of being misunderstood, or, worse, of being thought to mean nothing at all, when one uses words like existence and being. (It is in fact one of the corollaries of this book that such words have become meaningless because Western man has become estranged from being, or as Maritain (1948a) would say, has lost his intuition of being.) But I can, if you like, be more specific. Let us avoid the word existence. I might say instead—and here is something on which we are far more likely to agree—that modern enlightened objective-minded man is in very great trouble. Something has gone wrong, and what is particularly alarming about this wrongness is that with every further attempt to grasp the world and himself by the scientific worldview, the wrongness does not diminish but rather increases. Far from it being the case that the objective worldview is bringing about, however gradually, an ever increasing adjustment and at-homeness in the world, it rather does the reverse: man finds himself ever more homeless and in fact in anxiety.

Yes, I have my all-encompassing scientific worldview. But what about myself? How am I going to live out this day? What does objective science have to say about the fact, the all-important fact, that I am not an expression of this or that scientific abstraction, but that I am myself, a concrete existing individual?

The second point of view, then, is the discovery of the existentialists that man's existence grows ever more heterogeneous with his scientific worldview.

The question that must be answered is this: How can these two points of view be reconciled? If we accept, on the one hand, the validity of the scientific method (which I do accept) and, on the other, the uniqueness of human existence (which I also accept), then what has one to do with the other? Shall we do as the scientists do and ignore existence, or shall we do as the existentialists do and ignore all other existences but myself? Is there a clue of some larger order under which the two may be brought into some kind of unity? Or are we faced with a fundamental dualism, a body of objective knowledge and a core of anguish?

I hasten to say that this book is not about existentialism nor about the philosophy of science. I do not intend to deal with man's homelessness in the modern world nor to suggest the direction where may be found his true home and his true happiness—though I might do this, but others have done it better. I do not intend to use one point of view to demolish the other, for I accept the validity of both. What I shall undertake is a very modest investigation indeed. It is neither a critique of science nor of existentialism but is of all things a study of *words*, those peculiar mouthy little sounds which we humans make—and a study of the extraordinary fact, which in my mind grows ever more extraordinary, that these words *mean* something, that they are symbols.

This little excursion into semantics may seem a far cry indeed from the great issues I have raised. It is a far cry. But it has not been my wish, or capacity, to add another book to the libraries written on the efficacy of the scientific method or on man's plight in the modern world. Instead I have hoped to explore the great dichotomy, science and existence, for some little point of intersection. I have assumed from the beginning that truth is one, and that there will not always be professors on this side of the ocean teaching various combinations of pragmatism and naturalism and sneering at existence, and café philosophers on the other side condemning science and enshrining a purely descriptive science of the concrete traits and exigencies of human existence.

In constructing this tenuous bridge, I should like to acknowledge an indebtedness to two books and two writers. One, Susanne Langer's *Philosophy in a New Key* (1951), gave me my clue. The second, James Collins's *The Existentialists* (1952), was nothing less than a revelation to one committed to the scientific worldview yet painfully aware of its shortcomings without at the same time being able to define them, let alone correct them. To anyone in the same position and who feels equally put off by modern existentialism as being too irrational and by textbook Thomism (which is also, or should be, an *Existenz-philosophie*) as being too rational, and who is willing to devote himself to some very closely written and closely reasoned prose, I can do no greater service than recommend Collins's book.

I mention Mrs. Langer's book at the risk of appearing disingenuous—for it is my aim to show that the vista she opens for us runs directly counter to her otherwise orthodox positivism. But it was she, not I, who said that the symbol was the new key, and this I truly believe it is—though not in quite the sense she intended.

PART I

INTRODUCTION

I. TOWARD A RADICAL SCIENCE OF MAN

1. The Schism in the West

The most remarkable thing about Western thought today is not its split into opposing schools of philosophy. This has always been the case. It is rather that the split is so great that the two sides no longer even have the means of arguing with each other. They occasionally shout across the abyss, but without a common ground of debate, the shout usually sounds like a curse and is replied to in kind.

I am not referring to the East-West ideological split in which, oddly enough, the issue is squarely joined—we know very well what communism is about and the communists understand capitalistic democracy no less well—but to a profounder division. It is the split between the objective scientific attitude which has been generally triumphant in the West since the Enlightenment and is still the prevalent intellectual climate in England and America and the subjective existentialist revolt in Europe of the past two generations.

To understand the seriousness of the existentialist revolt, it is first necessary to understand how radical it is. It is not to be confused with the older romantic revolt, or rather escape—for this is the difference. The romanticist fled the field of hardheaded science and took refuge in the spheres of emotion and experience. To the objective-minded man, this was as it should be. He was perfectly willing to allow the romanticist's claim to the realm of feeling and even have a go at it himself. Indeed, as Irving Babbitt said, the romanticist can only be understood as the bedfellow of the objective-minded man. Objective science prepares the way for a surrender to the emotions. Existentialism, however, is quite another matter—even though it has attracted romanticists, not to mention other fringe-lunatics. Existentialism is a direct challenge of the objective-minded man on the grounds of his objectivity. The existentialist does not leave the field; he assaults his opponent at his most vulnerable point. And here the opponent is vulnerable indeed. The existentialist accuses the scientist of knowing everything in the world except the one most important thing: what it is to be an existing human being.

Let us understand both the strength of the objective-minded man's position and the power of the challenge.

Let us also understand that the "objective point of view" is not to be limited to a particular school of philosophy, to naturalism, mechanism, materialism, empiricism—though it has kinship with all of these. Nor is it to be limited to those of us who "took" science and philosophy in school or who read Julian Huxley and *The Scientific American* afterwards. It is rather a fundamental way of looking at things, a native climate of thought, a "worldview," which is shared by the great majority who attended an American high school or college. The Chicago housewife, the Denver businessman, the Tulane sophomore is more apt than not to see the world in this particular perspective, even though they may not have the slightest interest in philosophy as such and would in fact deny that they saw the world in any perspective at all except the perspective of a hardheaded person of facts. It is a way of looking at things which has been described variously as tough minded, objective, factual, scientific, radical, hardheaded, inductive. It is, no one can doubt, a valuable and fruitful way of looking at the world. What is not so certain is whether this attitude is as "radical" as it is supposed to be. The question that must be raised is whether, in regarding itself as a radical all-construing view of the world, it does not overlook something—and whether the oversight may not be fatal.

Let us see how this worldview, which is so second nature to us that we are not even aware we have acquired a worldview—let us see how it works in practice. When we look at a thing or an event with a view to the understanding of it, how do we go about it? How do we go about explaining something to our own satisfaction, and, to ask the same question, how does the *Book of Knowledge* or *LIFE Magazine* or a college psychology textbook go about explaining it? If we see a solar eclipse or an earthquake or a puberty rite of the Hopis, or if we study the secretion of dog urine or the evolution of the horse's hoof, our method of approach is to see for ourselves or be told by someone else "how it works." What does this mean? It means that we are not satisfied to be told that a dog's kidney secretes urine because it is the business of the kidney to do this because "God put it there for this reason." We are not satisfied—or at least we *should* not be satisfied—until we know the physical and chemical and colloidal forces at work, the characteristics of the membranes involved, the various factors that issue in the secretion of urine. It is only when we discover that the filtration of urine in the glomerular space is a direct function of the blood pressure and the osmotic pressure of the plasma proteins that we feel we are beginning to understand the process. *Process* is indeed the key to our understanding. We understand a Thing *B* or Event *B* as the result of a previous state of affairs, Thing *A* or Event *A*. Of course we understand the whole process dynamically, not as a State *A* which suddenly snaps into State *B*, but as a dynamic succession of events which flow one into the other. We may argue about whether the process occurs by "mechanism," that is, as a result of bodies, atoms, planets, gases, colliding with each other, by energy exchanges, by field forces; but we would certainly agree on the fundamental nature of the process, a ceaseless and sequential action and interaction of the elements of the world upon each other.

If one had to pick out the single most valuable contribution of the past three hundred years, one could make a good case for the concentration on efficient cause rather than final cause, for the understanding of Event *B* in terms of Event *A* which preceded it. This idea of efficient causality is to be found not merely in the older theories of strict mechanism and determinism but also in the newer theory of probability, in which micro-state *B* is understood as following upon micro-state *A* as a result of a statistical distribution of elements. As Nagel (1953) reminds us, let us not imagine that the new probability approach alters our scientific view.

This way of looking at the world is both valid and valuable. Things are in interaction, and by learning how things interact, we can not only understand the process, we can interfere with it and even bring about the changes ourselves. We can not only learn a great deal about the world, as a result of our understanding, we can manipulate it. Indeed we have succeeded, in many cases, in making over our environment to suit ourselves.

It is the way a biologist watches a beehive. When he observes a bee discover a source of nectar and return to the hive and the other bees go straight to the spot, he is not willing to believe that the first bee "told" the other bees and let it go at that. He wants to know how it happens; that is to say, he wants to know the series of events by which the behavior of the first bee, Event A, ends in other bees going straight to nectar, Event Z. Each event, moreover, must arise from the preceding event inevitably and in a determined ratio. Thus Event B is a function of Event A, $B = f(A)$, $C = f(B)$.... $Z = f(Y)$. The objective inquiry into a process is not satisfied until each particular event is construed as an expression of a certain functional relation or pattern.

We try to understand events as expressions of, examples of, underlying principles. This is true not only of our approach to physical reality, molecules of a gas colliding with each other, stars acting upon each other through a continuum of field forces, and to biological reality, bees responding to other bees; it is also the way Arnold Toynbee (1954) looks at history: to search for the explanation of an event or a civilization in the pattern of which it is a particular instance. In fact, Toynbee's favorite phrase is that such and such an event is a "classical example of" such and such a historical process.

We may summarize by saying that the intelligent high school or college graduate is basically non-Aristotelian in his attitude toward the world. He does not believe that events happen because it is their nature to happen or because some being is trying to achieve a more perfect actuality, but because the event is mediated through an interaction of field forces, bodies, energy exchanges, etc. We may argue about the nature of the happening, whether it is a chance statistical happening or a gestalt distribution brought about by forces in a field, but in general we see the world as a process of dynamic interaction in which everything acts upon the world and the world upon it.

This view I would not hesitate to accept as correct as far as it goes, and not only correct but immensely valuable and productive both of knowledge about the world and of scientific products and services.

The fact remains, however, that something is wrong. And if I am correct in my assessment of the scientific method, what is wrong is not what the method commits but what it omits, what it has to omit through its inherent limitations. What is especially wrong, if this is true, is a religious extrapolation from the method in which it is made to do duty not merely as a method of knowing but as a total all-construing worldview.

Let us be clear about the question we are raising. It is not at all the objection one usually hears—that science is cold and impersonal and does not provide for the emotional life—an objection which has already tacitly awarded to science a total competence in the realm of real knowledge. Such an objection seems hardly worth making. The possibility I wish to explore is whether there are realities that can be known and that the scientific method cannot know, in other words, the possibility that the scientific method is not a radical method of knowing but a method undertaken entirely within a certain situation of observer and data, a situation which the method cannot transcend.

When I say something is wrong, I do not mean to bring an *a priori* objection to this way of looking at things, to say that it is "mechanistic," "materialistic," "godless," and so on. These charges may indeed be true of some religious extrapolations from the method, but even in these cases it probably does no good to make the charge because it is usually interpreted to mean that one must not look for intermediate causes and interactions. Rightly or wrongly, it is usually interpreted as calling for a retreat from the rigor of the scientific method.

The objection that must be raised is not raised on the grounds of some higher belief, some competing worldview. Indeed it need not be raised at all because it is forcing itself upon us. Even those who most passionately advocate the scientific method cannot fail to be aware of the objection.

The general objection is this: as objective science comes nearer its goal of including more and more phenomena under unifying generalizations, it has less and less to say about what it is to be an individual human being. And conversely: a person who is himself an objective-minded man living in the world, who the objective point of view tries to understand and manipulate—such a person finds himself increasingly isolated and estranged from the very world he understands and controls.

2. The Stranger amid the Data

It might be helpful to give a few examples of the other point of view—the view from the other side of the abyss. For what is important about this way of seeing things is not that the writer is attacking the scientific point of view as being godless or whatnot, but that he is describing a reality that the scientific method cannot get hold of. Indeed there is evidence that this predicament, which will be described, may have been brought about by the triumph of objective science. The writers cited below describe a predicament which is shared not only by the writers, by existentialists, but by the objective-minded man. When the existentialist and phenomenologist theorize about the world in the age-old philosophical fashion, the objective-minded man is not interested. But when the existentialist speaks in concrete terms about the *crisis* and *plight* in which a man finds himself in the modern world, the objective-minded man knows only too well what he means, and he cannot help listening. For it is none other than he, the objective-minded man, who is most apt to find himself in the very plight the existentialist describes.

An example or two will perhaps make clear the dilemma of the objective-minded Westerner who comes face to face with the power and deliverance of an existential insight. The first is taken from a phenomenological description of the *self* in Gabriel Marcel's (1951a) *Homo Viator:*

> I spoke of an enclosure, but it is an enclosure which moves, and what is even more essential, it is vulnerable: *a highly sensitive enclosure....* Actually, this susceptibility is rooted in anguish rather than in love. Burdened with myself, plunged in this disturbing world, sometimes threatening me, sometimes my accomplice, I keep an eager look-out for everything emanating from it which might either soothe or ulcerate the wound I bear within me, which is my *ego.* This state is strikingly analogous to that of a man who has an abscess at the root of his tooth and who experiments cautiously with heat and cold, acid and sugar, to get relief. What then is this anguish, this wound? The answer is that it is above all the experience of being torn by a contradiction between the all which I aspire to possess, to annex, or, still more absurd, to monopolize, and the obscure consciousness that after all I am nothing but an empty void; for, still, I can affirm nothing about myself which would be really myself; nothing, either, which would be permanent; nothing which would be secure against criticism and the passage of time. Hence the craving to be confirmed from outside, by another; this paradox, by virtue of which even the most self-centered among us looks to others and only to others for his final investiture. (16)

The second is taken from one of Kierkegaard's (1941) pseudonymous writings, *Repetition:*

> My life has been brought to an *impasse*, I loathe existence, it is without savor, lacking salt and sense. If I were hungrier than Pierrot, I should not be inclined to eat the explanation people offer. One sticks one's finger into the soil to tell by the smell what land one is in: I stick my finger into existence—it smells of nothing. Where am I? Who am I? How came I here? What is this thing called the world? What does this word mean? Who is it that has lured me into this thing and now leaves me there? Who am I? How did I come into this world? Why was I not consulted, why not made acquainted with its manners and customs but was thrust into the ranks as though I had been bought of a "soul-seller"? (104)

Can this state of man's dereliction in the world, illustrated in these two examples, the nothingness of self, the alienation, the boredom, the anguish, be disposed of as an individual malfunction, a tensional resultant of some particular drives and repressions? Is the existential predicament a pathology, an illness to be cured by appropriate objective-empirical techniques? Or is this state of dereliction an irreducible and *constituent trait* of human being in the world—to which our familiar method of inducing general causal principles somehow does not apply?

The third example is from Heidegger's *What is Metaphysics?*:

> What if the absence of Being abandoned man more and more exclusively to beings, leaving him forsaken and far from any involvement of Being in his Nature, while this forsakenness itself remained veiled? What if this were the case—and had been the case for a long time now? What if there were signs that this oblivion will become still more decisive in the future?
>
> Would there still be occasion for a thoughtful person to give himself arrogant airs in view of this fateful withdrawal with which Being presents us? Would there still be occasion, if this should still be our situation, to deceive ourselves with pleasant phantasms and to indulge of all things, in an artificially induced elation? If the oblivion of Being which has been described here should be real, would there not be occasion enough for a thinker who recalls Being to experience a genuine horror? What more can his thinking do than to endure in dread this fateful withdrawal while first of all facing up to the oblivion of Being: But how could thought achieve this as long as its fatefully granted dread seems to it nothing more than a mood of depression? *What does such dread, which is fated by Being, have to do with psychology or psychoanalysis?* [emphasis added] (quoted in Kauffman 1956, 213-14)

The stakes are very high. Either Heidegger is talking non-sense, as the positivists would say, when he speaks of Being and being, and man's loss of Being—or he is talking about the most important thing of all.

The question presents itself immediately: Are Marcel and Kierkegaard and Heidegger describing a distinctively human something, or are they at best setting forth in literary and emotive language entities and relations that (at best) could be more meaningfully expressed in terms of biological tensions and needs? The automatic response to these passages of one grounded in Freudian depth psychology, for example, is that this sort of writing represents either (1) an expression of an unconscious motivation on the part of the writer—one's attention goes immediately *behind* what is said to discover its hidden motivations—or (2) if it does by chance convey a "true" insight into the nature of things, it is a truth that could better be said in the prime terms of elementary drives and repressions and tensions.

It is not only the existentialists who have noticed—as who can fail to notice—that there is throughout the modern world an almost universal experience of estrangement, of uprootedness, of *homelessness*. Does anyone seriously believe that this sense of alienation is a passing symptom of the post-war years? Does anyone seriously believe that this is a malfunction of the individual organism, a medical symptom to be set right by an objective-empirical discipline, by unearthing a particular historical *cause*, by readjusting a subconscious tensional system? If there is such a thing as modern man's acute sense of homelessness—as existentialists from Pascal to Heidegger have said that there is—implying as it does an alienation from a true estate of human being, is not this alienation only worsened as the objective-empirical method redoubles its effort to claim man as its proper datum?

The open-minded empiricist's dilemma is this: he has on the one hand an unassailable faith in the method of his objective-empirical science, a faith justified by many things. The very world in which he lives is one great monument to the efficacious truth of empirical science. But more than that: if he himself is a scientist, he has first-hand knowledge of the credentials of his calling—the endless susceptibility of the data before him to a rendering by hypothetical causal principles, to test and verification, to the establishment for once and all of the inexpugnable fact, the unvarying correlation and the endless delight at which the human mind arrives, not to an ambiguous term such as being, which it seems to him may have a different meaning for anyone who hears it, but to a causal function that can be *proved* to everyone's satisfaction.

And yet, as he reflects over these striking analyses of the human predicament, he cannot fail to recognize a unique delineation of what it is to be a human being as being applicable not to his data but to *himself*. What the existentialists are setting forth, he begins to suspect, is not a dramatic expression of a time of discontent, a cultural manifestation, which will pass, but rather the perennial condition of human existence.

3. The Schism in the Sciences: The Antinomy of the Method

What is the meaning of this revolt against the objective method of the sciences? What is the meaning, that is, from the point of view of one who is interested, not in abandoning science for existentialism, but in discovering a radical science, a science that will take account of all realities? Is this revolt a lapse into irrationalism as it is often made out to be, especially by American philosophers? Does it testify only to an incapacity of man to live up to his own stern science? Or does it not tell a truth inaccessible to the scientific method and does it not testify to an inherent limitation of the scientific method, especially as it applies to man? Dr. Leslie Farber (1956) writes in a recent issue of *Psychiatry:* "Having used only the single mode of scientific knowledge for the past hundred years or so, we are uneasily aware that this was the wrong mode—the wrong viewpoint, the wrong terminology, and the wrong kind of knowledge—ever to explain the human being" (118). The terminology that Farber decides is the "right" terminology to explain human being is the I-Thou terminology of Martin Buber (1937). But this does not solve the problem, even if this is the "right" terminology. The objective scientist is still justified in asking, what is the relation between this I-Thou phenomenology and the great corpus of objective scientific knowledge? Is there no relation? If there is a larger unity under which the two can be brought into a methodological order, neither Farber nor the existentialists say what it is.

Let us accordingly shift our attention from the warfare between scientists and existentialists to a second difficulty, a peculiar and characteristic difficulty encountered within the sciences. It is a perennial confusion which arises whenever the scientific method is applied to man, not to the physiology and blood chemistry and knee jerks of man, but to man considered in his distinctive behavior as man. The reason I focus on this impasse of the method is not because I wish to give ammunition to the existentialists and other anti-scientists but because the only way to discover a radical science of man is to demonstrate the non-radical character of the objective method. It is only when the limitations of the objective method are clearly seen that one can begin to suggest remedies. Otherwise there is the danger that irrationalism will prevail and that the scientific method, the precious fruit of the past three hundred years, will be kicked out altogether.

There is no use, in other words, in continuing the purely philosophical quarrel between objective-empiricism and existentialism. Instead it would be more fruitful, I think, to stay within science and see where the method breaks down. We must focus on a particular moment of the method, the moment of objective-observer-confronting-data, in the particular situation when the "data" is the observer himself or men like him. All roads lead to man, to an anthropology in which scientists and philosophers can meet face to face. For it is only here, in the objective study of man as a real something in the world, that philosophers must use an approach congenial to the sciences and scientists must deal with the ultimately philosophical problem of how the organism that the sciences study can know the world—can be a scientist.

What is the difficulty which the scientific method encounters when it tries to get hold of man as man? Is it only a material difficulty due, as social scientists have been saying for a hundred years, to the complexity of the subject and the infancy of the science? Or is it a methodological difficulty due to an inherent limitation of the instrument?

Let us consider a single symptom of the difficulty, as an example of the sort of antinomy into which the method drives us. Let us see what happens when the method comes to deal with the most characteristic activity of man, his symbol-mongering, especially his language.

The symptom I wish to call attention to is the necessarily ambiguous attitude of objective scientists toward the phenomenon of myth. I choose myth from among several phenomena studied by the science we know as "anthropology"* because it illustrates very well what might be called the "antinomy of the method." The antinomy could be demonstrated as well among other cultural forms: language, art, science, religion—to use Cassirer's (1955) "symbolic forms" (217). I choose myth because the contradiction is particularly striking in much modern writing about "mental health" and the like. Kant (1929) defined a philosophical antinomy as the situation in which two apparently flawless trains of reasoning bring us into positions which are contradictory. In this case it is not pure reason which lands us in an antinomy but the scientific method. My point is that given the method and given a strict adherence to the method, the antinomy is inevitable. It is not a case of social scientists being more perverse or impious than physicists. It is rather the case that the scientific method must necessarily lead one, when the "datum" is man, into an antinomy in which the scientist claims for his data that which he denies for himself, although both he and the data are men. This is not an isolated miscarriage of the method, so that one might say with Anthony Standen (1950) that physicists and chemists are good fellows who apply the method neutrally but that social scientists are in bad faith. The fact is that it is the same method in both cases and the same sort

---

* What is known as anthropology in America is quite different from philosophical anthropology. The former is generally taken to mean either anthropometry, physical measurement, or ethnology, the study of cultural phenomena. It is only lately, as David Bidney (1954) has observed, that anthropologists have dealt with man as a personality affecting culture and being affected by culture. It would perhaps not be too much to say that anthropology in America has meant the study of everything about man (organism and culture) except man himself.

of men who apply it. The difference is that the method is an instrument fitted *par excellence* for the inorganic and almost to the same degree misadapted for the human behavior of human beings. Malinowski might conceivably have succeeded as well as Newton had he been concerned with the motions of planets; Newton would certainly have found himself in the same difficulties as Malinowski if he had applied the functional method to human symbolic phenomena.

How is the method driven into antinomy in the case of cultural phenomena? This happens because the implicit division of reality *within which* the scientific method is mounted, a division which is not incapacitating as long as the data is subhuman, is revealed when the sort of activity observed in the data is the same as the activity of the scientist-observer, namely, a true-or-false assertory activity, the asserting that such and such is the case. The division is revealed and becomes incapacitating because the scientist must understand this activity as he understands all other biological activity, as a natural phenomenon arising under certain conditions and serving certain biological or instrumental functions—and at the same time he is forced, since this new activity is a true-or-false assertory activity, to judge the assertion as he would judge his own or another scientist's assertions: as true or false. The result is an antinomy: assertory activity of the data is judged false and called false ("myth") and at the same time judged "true" for the data insofar as it serves the immanent purposes of the data.

Suppose, to give an example, an ethnologist is studying a particular culture. He will, if he is a faithful practitioner of the scientific method like Boas and Malinowski, regard culture as a phenomenon to be studied as any other phenomenon is studied. Just as an ornithologist observes the singing of male birds at nesting time and hypothesizes a functional reason for the survival of such behavior—that the bird sings to delimit its nesting area—so the objective ethnologist approaches the myths of a culture. What functional scheme provides for them? Various answers are given, Malinowski (1954, 87) saying that myths serve the social function of justifying cultural belief, Boas

(1938, 245-46) saying that myths have an explanatory function, Cassirer (1953a, 142-145) and Langer (1951, 176) saying that myths are a symbolic mode of world-envisagement. Sapir (1956) speaks of "genuine" and "spurious" culture accordingly as it does or does not satisfy the individual's desire for complete participation in his culture. By the same token a myth would be judged genuine (true) or spurious (false) accordingly as it satisfied the individual's need for "world-envisagement" or "cultural integration."

Yet Sapir would not, presumably, use the same criteria for his own evaluation. He would, presumably, judge a myth to be false, no matter how "meaningful" it was.

This double standard of truth, a scientific propositional standard for the scientist, a pragmatic or symbolic standard for the data, is to be found not only in "materialists" or "mechanists" or "positivists," but "idealists" as well, in short, in any theorist who, whatever his metaphysic, makes a distinction between his own truth-saying activity and the immanent activity of his "data." Thus, idealist Cassirer would agree with functionalist Malinowski in evaluating myth not according to a true-false scale but by its immanent role in integrating society, in conceiving the world.

This objective procedure of the method would seem to be reasonable enough, but the fact is that it has already driven us into an antinomy, which issues in the most bizarre consequences.

Let us observe a curious fact. It is that the word "myth" is, as David Bidney (1953) says, a "value-charged term" to begin with, signifying a decision of the scientist by his own true-false scale that these beliefs are false (296). Secondly, let us notice that this value-charged term is then used neutrally as it is applied to an activity of the data and judged by criteria proper to data. Myth, says Malinowski (1954), fills a universal human need (122). "Every society," says MacIver (1947), "is held together by a myth-system" (4). The objective social scientist is obliged to see myth as serving an immanent function within a cultural system, just as a biologist construes an activity of ants in an anthill.

But where is the antinomy? The antinomy lies in the circumstances that the very activity that the scientist-spectator rejects as false for himself, he regards as "true" for the culture under observation. He accepts two scales of truth which, under some circumstances, may be contradictory: one, a factual existential propositional scale by which he judges the truth value of assertions; the other, a biological or idealistic or otherwise immanent scale of truth by which he judges the behavior of his data.

This antinomy leads to the position so often encountered in the current sciences of man, whether it be ethnology or psychiatry, in which myth is prescribed as *such* for the ills of modern society. Myth is held to be "true," not in the plenary sense in which science is true, but in the Pickwickian sense that it satisfies a vital need. Thus Susanne Langer (1951) distinguishes two kinds of truth, a literal factual truth and a symbolic mythological truth (310). Our ills are due to a breakdown of our mythic symbols of world-envisagement: "the vital ideas embodied in it [myth] cannot be repudiated because someone discovers that the myth does not constitute a *fact*.... Some day when the vision is totally rationalized, the ideas exploited and exhausted, *there will be another vision, a new mythology* [emphasis added]" (164-65).

C. G. Jung (1959) makes a similar division and a similar prescription. Mental health depends upon a discovery and activation of our archetypes, the basic mythic forms of the collective unconscious. Under this division it becomes possible for Jung to prescribe for his patients a set of beliefs that he himself does not believe to be true in the same sense that his research is true. Jung's reasoning seems irreproachable. My research shows that in order to be happy a man must recover his mythic archetypes, says Jung. Yet such a position is not adequate scientifically and is unworkable as well. It is scientifically inadequate because it makes a division between scientist and data and presupposes two sorts of men: scientists who seek the truth and laymen who seek archetypes for mental health. It is unworkable because, as Bidney (1953) says, once a belief is considered a myth, it can hardly be believed thereafter—unless scientists make the division absolute and keep their discovery of myth secret. Jung approves the Catholic dogma of the Assumption of the Virgin on the basis of its Pickwickian truth as a good example of the anima archetype. Yet if there is one thing that ordinary Catholics and non-Catholics would agree on, it is surely this: if the Assumption did occur, then it should be believed; if it did not occur, then it should not be believed.

In sum, the antinomy into which the objective method is forced when it deals with religious and mythic belief must necessarily issue in the following advice, surely a counsel of despair: *it may not be true, but you had better believe it!*

The obvious lesson to be drawn is that there is, as Bidney (1953) says, a transcultural reality and an objective truth. Belief must be evaluated by an objective standard of truth as well as socio-cultural contexts (300). A belief is either true or false and must be so accepted or rejected. It cannot be held false by the scientist and prescribed as "true" for the layman. For the layman is, as much as the scientist, a man and, as much as the scientist, lives by the truth. We remember the prophetic words of Nietzsche (1927) about the Theoretical Man and his longing for myth: "And now the mythless man remains eternally hungering amid the past, and digs and grubs for roots, though he have to dig for them even among the remotest antiquities" (1078). It is surely a sign of the desperate crisis of our own culture that responsible social scientists and psychiatrists should feel obliged to prescribe the very antinomy in which their method has landed them: myth!

We should note in passing that the issue is more than academic. The antinomy of the method in the sciences of man is not only unproductive of theoretical results and practical remedies for the current crisis; it is also dangerous. For it renders science helpless in the face of modern tyrannies, or worse, it even tends in some cases to ally science with the tyrant. An ethnologist who holds a purely objective-functional or symbolic-idealist view of culture cannot make a serious objection *on the basis of his science* against the Nazi or Communist state. On the contrary: if he judges myth by its social efficacy in integrating culture, it is hard to see how he can withhold approval of the myth of racism or the myth of inevitable class conflict. For, judged objectively, both myths are quite effective in their integrative function. One of the more peculiar phenomena of the twentieth century is the professor who in his classroom teaches an objective-immanent theory of man in which man is regarded as an organism or culture member or libidinal dynamic, and who outside his classroom is a sincere and passionate defender of human rights, intellectual freedom and so on. Dr. Victor Frankl (1955) suggests that it was not the Teutonic gods who prepared the gas chambers of Dachau—it was the professors (xxi).

But in speaking of myth, it is not my purpose to attack the scientific method in the name of an unscientific humanism. On the contrary, I believe that our best hope lies in a broad empirical approach to the world, an approach that recognizes a public realm of real things and real relations that can be in some degree known and about which statements can be made and evidence advanced. Toward this end I wish to call attention to this inherent limitation of the objective scientific method. As it moves along the scale of reality, it is extraordinarily fruitful at the subhuman level, so much so that it recommends itself as a total all-construing organon of reality. In this connection we might even speak of the temptation of science. When it passes man, however, and as ethnology and social science deals with characteristically human manifestations, rite, institutions, myth, belief, propositions, it is driven into an antinomy. This happens as we have seen because the objective scientific method has no means of taking account of those peculiar activities of man which are oriented on a true-false axis. The scientific method is itself one of these peculiar activities, a true-or-false activity; it says that such and such is the case and sets out to prove it or disprove it. But it cannot deal with true-or-false activities in the data. It can verify or reject statements about data: the earth is flat, a falling body accelerates at 32 feet per second-per-second, but when these statements are themselves the data, the method is in an antinomy: a statement may be false by the scientist's standards of verification but "true" by data standards of immanent efficacy.

In short, the objective sciences of man are non-radical sciences since they are able to consider man only in the partial aspect of an interacting element in a larger dynamic system: a biological milieu, society, culture, etc.

4. A Radical Anthropology: The Objective Science of Man as an Asserting Animal

The critical area of reality that cries out for study, therefore, is not the subhuman level where the method works so well, or the superorganic level of culture, the activities of man considered in themselves, where the method issues in an antinomy—but man himself, the asserting animal. A radical anthropology must treat as its primary datum, not man as a responding organism—though this treatment is a legitimate science—and not man as an element of a larger reality, society or culture—though this treatment is a legitimate science—but man as the organism who makes assertions, who makes a society and a culture possible. What is needed is an anthropology that will embrace man in his most universal trait, not merely the totemist tribesman with his fetishes and magic but the scientist-observer as well with his hypotheses and verifications.

The science that is presently called anthropology is really culturology, an objective non-radical science mounted within the same framework as any other objective science. The hypothesis that the culturologist induces from his survey of cultures is not meant to apply to him, the scientist. This is easy enough to demonstrate. Ruth Benedict (1946), for example, understands cultures as conforming to certain ideal patterns, i.e., the Dionysian and Apollonian. The cultural products, language, art, mythology, of a particular culture member are examples of such and such a pattern, the culture of the Plains Indian exemplifying the Dionysian ethos, the Pueblo Indian the Apollonian, etc. But she would not presumably wish to have her own work understood as an example of a certain type of mid-Manhattan culture. She would presumably wish to have her work evaluated on the grounds of its claim: the assertion that such and such is the case. The objective scientist expects his own assertory behavior judged, not as an example of such and such a pattern or principle, but by a true-false scale. Freud would not presumably wish us to understand his theories of the unconscious as expressions of his own instinctive drives but rather as stating what is actually the case. Here again, it is not a case of Freud the physician being in bad faith—compared with other physicians like Harvey and Semmelweis. Freud's antinomy is the result, not of his being unlike Harvey, but of his being too much like Harvey. Freud was merely trying to use the scientific method of medicine to bring some order to the welter of conscious and unconscious assertory life of man: compulsions, delusions, beliefs, taboos and so on. But the objective scientific method is applied within a spectator-data structure and its conclusions are not meant to apply to the activity of the scientist. The ultimate goal of the objective method, to unite a variety of events under a single functional relation, is wholly inapplicable to the assertory behavior of the scientist, his declaring that *S* is *P* and his understanding of his fellow scientist's declaration, *S* is *P*. A purely objective culturology or psychology is therefore a non-radical science since it must exempt a sector of reality from its scope.

How will a radical anthropology differ from a purely objective science in which the truth-telling scientist stands above his interacting data? Does this mean that we must abandon the scientific posture, that of a real observer looking at a real world and trying to make some sense of it? Does this mean that we must retreat to a pure phenomenology or some other kind of transcendentalism in which the mind studies its own consciousness? No, it means only that we study man as we study anything else: to see what sense can be made of him. But we do not limit the sense to the sense of physico-mathematical function. This method differs from a purely objective science in one respect: It does not decree that the data shall be limited to one form of activity, interaction. It does not propose to study man only as a responding organism or as a unit of a superorganic culture, but rather man as that organism who makes statements, tells stories, has beliefs, in short, carries out an assertory behavior which can only be judged on the grounds of its own claim—as true or false.

We have empirical sciences which study man as a responding organism (psychology), as a culture member (ethnology), and as a personality dynamism (psychoanalysis). We also have logical sciences which are primarily concerned with the assertions of man (symbolic logic, mathematics). *But we do not have an empirical science which studies man as that organism who makes assertions.*

We wish to stand outside the observer-data structure and bring under our gaze not merely the data but, and more especially, the observer. We know a great deal about Kwakiutls and Trobriand Islanders; we know very little about that remarkable creature, our fellow Western man, who abandons his own hearth and culture and spends his life among them. He makes great personal sacrifice, undergoes much inconvenience, devotes a great part of his life to observation, and the rest of it to theorizing, passionately attacking other theories and advancing evidence to support his own. Yet with all the hardships, he is the happiest of men because his joy is the purest of all joys, the joy of knowing what was not known—and asserting it. We too are fascinated by his "findings," by the primitive folkways of today and the artifacts of bygone days. But even more fascinating is that selfless and single-minded creature himself who goes picking through the rubble-heaps of the world, seizing upon a potsherd as though it were the grail. We can only share the wonder of the local "culture members," the bemused Bedouins who stare open-mouthed at our fellow Westerner.

A radical anthropology, then, must deal primarily with man as the creature who is not only capable of believing the most preposterous myths and practicing the most bizarre rites but capable also of hypothesizing and verifying, in short, with man as the organism who makes assertions. Do we propose then to convert anthropology into a sort of logic, to make a single science, a *characteristica universalis*, of all the assertions of man? No, the primary datum of a radical anthropology is neither assertions themselves nor biological behavior itself. The great question which all sciences of man have managed so far to dodge and which must sooner or later be faced, is this: How does it happen that an organism which can be otherwise understood as a biological system interacting with its environment through the mediation of signs, how does it happen that this organism also names things, makes propositions about things, theorizes, guesses, has beliefs, constructs mathematical formulae? How does it happen that a responding organism *asserts* of a thing that such and such is the case? How does it happen that the "organism" the scientist studies may also be a symbolic logician who asserts *S* is *P*? As Ernst Cassirer (1953a) declared, no positive science has ever succeeded in jumping the gap between the organism who responds with a cry and the organism who makes propositions (150).

Such an anthropology must deal not only with man as an organism *in* an environment or as a culture member who inherits a set of beliefs *about* his environment—it must aim directly at the intersection of the two activities. What sort of event takes place the consequence of which is that an organism makes an assertion? We must not pretend that the gap does not exist—as do many psychologists and linguists. Nor must we, on the other hand, be content to accept as a scientific explanation that man has a soul and that it is the soul that makes assertions. We cannot, in other words, summon up a soul as a *deus ex machina* to account for something else. If we encounter a "mind" or "soul," it must be because the encounter is empirically unavoidable, because our investigation has brought it to pass. It must be possible to ask the usual questions: How do we know this? What takes place? How does it take place? Nor shall we admit defeat by accepting a dichotomy of mind and body, a *res extensa* that interacts with the world and a *res cogitans* that thinks and is conscious and makes statements. There is nothing mysterious about such an anthropology; we seek only to understand what takes place before our eyes: that a thing in the world not only reacts with the world; it also stands apart from the world, is conscious of the world, and makes statements about the world.

5. The New Key

Our aim must be to make a beginning in an anthropology which preserves the virtues of the objective scientific method and at the same time retains a sensitivity and openness to the peculiarly human realities described in the existentialist writings quoted above. This means that we must steer clear of the extremes of a behavioristic psychology and a subjective existentialist phenomenology while taking account of both. Is this an impossible task? Are we faced with an indefeasible either/or: Must we either regard man from the stance of the objective psychologist as an organism in an environment or from the stance of an ego-consciousness examining its own acts? Must we choose between Watson and Freud, Mead and Husserl, Morris and Cassirer, Dewey and Heidegger?

But suppose we approach our subject not with a conviction that he is one or the other, either a reacting organism or a locus of consciousness, but rather in the certitude that he is both and with a burning curiosity as to how this has come about. How does it happen, first, that the objective scientific method approaches the enigma, man, with the best possible credentials and the highest confidence—and emerges on the other side much the worse for wear, an instrument of dubious efficacy? What we wish to know, what cries out to be known, is not what happens on the inorganic-organic side nor the socio-cultural side—these we have heard a great deal about—what we wish to know is what happens in the dark wood in between. If the organism goes into the wood as a responding organism and emerges as an asserting acculturated organism, then we may be sure that something extraordinary has happened in the interval. Our excitement derives from our feeling that at least we are closing in on our quarry—for it must be that somewhere in the wood we are bound to encounter a unique happening, a happening which is neither "material" nor "mental" but both.

I am making an assumption which needs to be confessed at the outset. It is that our anthropology, if it is to keep in touch with the objective method of the sciences, must approach man from "below," that is, from the subhuman organic level. There is no use, as I shall attempt to show later, in making an "apodictic" starting point within my own consciousness. Once I start with my own ego-consciousness, my *cogito*, as did Descartes and Husserl—and Sartre—I have already built the prison from which I cannot escape. It may be possible to travel from things and organisms to consciousness, as we shall see, but it is not possible to make the return trip, to start with a solitary consciousness and its contents and break out to a real world.

Our starting point is not hard to find. It is already implicit in our posing of the problem as the change that takes place when an organism responding to *signs* begins to make *statements*. For what we shall begin with is not consciousness nor thoughts nor ideas nor moods, the *entia rationis* which the method can't get hold of, but *symbols* and the use man makes of them, and in particular, *language*. Symbols are real things, sounds that tremble in the air, gestures that can be seen, but they are also "mental" in the peculiar use that is made of them. Man is the creature who uses symbols. Even in the nineteenth century when biologists were trying their hardest to fill in the gaps between man and the rest of the animals, the best that Darwin could do with language was to cite the Paraguay monkey that was observed to utter "six distinct sounds." Yet even Darwin (1936) did not attempt to show that these grunts of the *Cebus azarae* were symbols (41). Nowadays most biologists are franker to admit man's peculiar gift of tongues.

When man speaks, names, asserts, spins a yarn, worships, calculates, theorizes, and even thinks, he does so by means of symbols. The point of intersection we spoke of, between man the responding organism and man the culture-member, is the symbol and man's use of it. To call man the rational animal, the culture-member, may be true enough, but such titles have not been very helpful in clarifying man's place in the world from the point of view of a scientific anthropology. It is surely in Cassirer's (1953a) new title, *animal symbolicum* (44), that we find the clue to a radical anthropology, a science of man which can speak of behaving and asserting without becoming incoherent. The symbol is truly the "new key," as Susanne Langer (1951) called it.

In focusing upon man's use of symbol, we are hardly blazing a new trail. Rather we are joining the crowd. From the most diverse directions, the most contrary points of view, approaches converge upon the symbol. To give two examples: The positivists have joined forces with pragmatists and logicians to form the new "metascience" of "semiotic," the science of signs, as the basis of a unified philosophy of science. The culmination of German idealism in modern times is Ernst Cassirer's *The Philosophy of Symbolic Forms* (1953b, 1955). It is not a philosophy of the idea or the world spirit or the will, but a philosophy which seeks to discover a unity in the characteristic activities of man, his language, art, religion, myth, science—a unity which is forthcoming because each is a "symbolic form." Even the existentialists in their preoccupation with the moods and structures of consciousness are not unaware of the importance of the symbol, especially language. Heidegger (1953) cites *Rede*, speech, as one of the modes of *Existenz*. Marcel (1951b) suggests that an understanding of language will clarify the mysterious theme of intersubjectivity which lies at the very heart of his metaphysics.

Here again, however, we encounter the same split. There are semioticists like Morris and Carnap who see men only as organisms and symbols only as signs, things in interaction in an environment. There are philosophers of the *Geist* like Cassirer and W. M. Urban who see the symbol as a Kantian activity of the consciousness through which the world is not merely construed, but constituted. The symbol remains nevertheless, indeed for this very reason, the point of intersection. Assuredly we are closing in on our quarry, for it is both things at once, a veritable something in the world that an empiricist can get hold of and at the same time a vehicle of conception through which we understand the world. Here at least we have found common ground upon which the existentialist and scientist, idealist and materialist, can debate with some confidence that they are talking about the same thing. Here at least we are not eternally at cross purposes with one side talking about things and things interacting with things, and the other side talking about *ideas* of things. For we are all talking about *words*, the little grunts and hisses and explosions that one man utters and another man somehow understands to "mean" something else.

What follows is neither a critique of an idealist philosophy of language nor a naturalist philosophy of language. Nor is it a fully developed philosophy of language in its own right. It is an investigation of language in its homeliest aspect, the ordinary exchange of ordinary words, with the hope of shedding some light on man's place in the world. How does it happen that I understand the word you speak, and what does it mean for our thinking about man, for a radical anthropology? It is my conviction that even a modest investigation of the homeliest interchange of language can reveal more of the nature of man, of the nature of the relations between man and man, man and his environment, than the most heroic culturology or positive psychology.

The event in which you speak a sentence and I understand it conceals by its very everydayness a phenomenon utterly unlike anything else in space and time.

PART II

SYMBOL AND SIGN

CHAPTER I

SIGN AND SYMBOL

The simplest exchange of language is an extremely mysterious phenomenon. By mysterious I do not mean that the brain events that take place during an exchange of language are very complex and little understood—though this is true, too. I mean rather that language, which at first sight seems to be the most familiar *sort* of occurrence (however complex the mechanism), an occurrence that takes its place among other occurrences in the world—billiard balls hitting other billiard balls, sunrises and rainfalls, barkings of dogs, crying of babies—is in reality utterly different from these events. The simplest act of naming, in which you call this flower a "lupin" and I understand that "lupin" shall be its name, is qualitatively different from other natural events.

What is the nature of language?

This question does not at first sight seem to present any serious problems. If one is an average educated American or Englishman or Pole, or anyone else acquainted with the scientific temper of the last two hundred years, one can answer the question readily, or at least one knows the kind of answer that should be given. The answer is apt to be expressed in some such terms as follows.

Here is what happens (one might well reply) when one person speaks a word or sentence and a second person understands him. I utter a series of peculiar little sounds by which I mean to convey to you the meaning I have in mind. The sounds leave my mouth and travel through the air as waves. The waves strike the tympanic membrane of your outer ear and the motion of the membrane is carried to the inner ear where it is transformed into electrical impulses in the auditory nerve. This nerve impulse is transmitted to your brain where a very complex series of events takes place, the upshot of which is that you "understand" the words; that is, you either respond to the words in a way I had hoped you would, or the words arouse in you the same idea or expectation or fear I had in mind. Your understanding of my sounds depends upon your hearing them before: upon a common language. As a result of your hearing the word *ball* in association with the thing ball, there occurs a change in your brain of such a character that when I say *ball* you understand me to "mean" ball.

This is hardly, of course, an acceptable explanation of language to a linguist or a psychologist, but it is the *sort* of explanation one would give. The linguist's or psychologist's definition will not differ in kind. It is the sort of explanation one will find in the *Book of Knowledge* and in a college psychology textbook—and in a book about semiotics. It may be less technical or a great deal more technical—and no doubt modern philosophers of meaning would prefer the term "response" to "idea" in speaking of your understanding of my words—but technical or not, it is generally accepted that something of the kind takes place. The essence of the process is a sequence of events in space-time: muscular events in the mouth, wave events in the air, electro-colloidal events in the nerve and brain.

In short, one is not apt to see any particular difficulty in answering the question about the nature of language. To put it as simply as possible: one person utters words, and the words arouse in a second person's brain the appropriate ideas and responses.

The trouble is that this explanation of language completely misses the essential character of language. It is not merely an oversimplified explanation; it is not merely an incomplete or one-sided explanation. It has nothing to do with language considered as language. Language is not this sort of thing at all.

All these space-time events we have mentioned do occur, and without them there would be no language. But language is something else besides these events.

What I wish to call attention to is not a new discovery, a new piece of research in psycholinguistics, which revolutionizes our concept of language, as the Michelson-Morley experiment revolutionized modern physics. It is rather the extraordinary sort of thing language is and which our theoretical view of the world completely obscures. This extraordinary character of language does not depend for its being known on a piece of research but is there under our noses for all to see. The difficulty is that it is under our noses; it is too close and too familiar. Language, symbolization, is the very stuff of which our knowledge and awareness of the world is made, the very medium through which we see the world. Trying to see it is like trying to see the mirror by which we see everything else.

There is another difficulty. It is that language cannot be explained in the ordinary terminology of explanations. Anyone who has the slightest acquaintance with the scientific temper of the past two hundred years knows what I mean by the terminology of explanations. This is the native attitude of the modern mind toward that which it does not understand—and it is its most admirable trait. The attitude is briefly this: Here is a phenomenon; how does it work? The answer is given as a series of space-time events: this is how *C* works: you see, this state of affairs *A* leads to this state of affairs *B* and *B* leads to *C*. This attitude goes a long way toward an understanding of billiards, of cellular growth, of anthills and sunrises. But it cannot get hold of language.

This does not mean that language cannot be understood or that what happens in language is not a natural event. It is a natural event, but it is not a sequential causal event. It therefore requires a frame of reference different from the familiar functional schema by which science expresses causal relationships. This new terminology is apt to sound vague and metaphysical since it does not deal with the usual sequence of space-time events with which we are familiar. One does not like to be vague or metaphysical—especially when "metaphysical" is used as synonymous with "vague." But when one encounters a phenomenon which does not lend itself to our everyday terminology of explanations, then we have to use the words we have, however unsatisfactory these words may be.

The importance of a study of language—as opposed to a scientific study of a space-time event like a solar eclipse or rat behavior—

is that as soon as one scratches the surface of the familiar and comes face to face with the nature of language, one also finds himself face to face with the nature of man. The subject matter of a radical anthropology is man as an asserting or symbolizing animal. If one studies man at a so to speak sub-language level, one studies him as one studies anything else: as a phenomenon which is susceptible of explanatory hypotheses. A psychologist timing human responses moves about in the same familiar world of observer and data-to-be-explained as the physiologist and the physicist. But as soon as one deals with language, not as a sequence of stimuli and responses, not as a science of phonetics or comparative linguistics, but as the *sort* of thing language is, one finds himself immediately in uncharted territory. You can study language and meaning as an affair of stimuli and responses if you want to. But, as we shall presently see, you will find yourself in a notorious difficulty for which there is no remedy.

1. Cassirer's Unbridgeable Gap: Responding Man and Asserting Man

Let us look a little more closely at the objective explanation of the sort of thing language is, not merely the off-hand account of the average educated man but the explanations of the philosophers and scientists of language.

It runs something like this. All organisms, men included, respond to their environment and communicate with each other by means of signs. Through processes of adaptation, organisms have acquired mechanisms by which they respond to signs in a biologically learned fashion. These signs include not only signs in nature, like smoke signifying fire, thunder signifying rain, but signs from fellow organisms. Male moths respond to the faintest odor by seeking out the female. Male birds respond to another male's song by staying out of his nesting area. Further, responses may be conditioned. Through an association of a sign with a biological need-satisfaction, any organism, man included, can be trained to respond to an artificial sign. Man has acquired another refinement of sign communication. As semanticists like Alfred Korzybski (1952) have expressed it, both dogs and men know pencils, but only man assigns a label to the pencil (392). Some empiricists, like John Locke (1824), would also say that men apply signs to ideas:

> Man, though he has great variety of thoughts, and such from which others as well as himself, might receive profit and delight; yet they are all within his own breast, invisible and hidden from others, nor can of themselves be made to appear. The comfort and advantage of society not being to be had without communication of thoughts, it was necessary that man should find out some external sensible signs, whereof those invisible ideas which his thoughts are made up of, might be made known to others. (48)

But modern philosophers of language prefer to avoid subjective entities like *thought* and *idea*, not necessarily because they do not believe there are such things but because it is hard to be scientific about things and happenings which cannot be seen and tested. The distinguished linguist Leonard Bloomfield (1955) expresses a current attitude toward language. He speaks of the *biophysical* aspect of language, the tongue movements, sound waves, vibration of ear drums, etc., and the *biosocial* aspect: "persons in a community have been trained to produce these sounds in certain situations and to respond to them by appropriate actions" (227).

But in addition to uttering and responding to signs and assigning signs to things as names, men also group signs into sentences that, as the scientific philosopher Reichenbach (1956) expresses it, "correspond to states of affairs of the physical world" (256).

Such is the usual objective attitude toward the phenomenon of language. Man's use of language is still understood as a development, albeit a marvelous one, of the sign language of animals. Positivists profess to see no qualitative difference between the language of the *Cebus azarea* monkey Darwin (1936) spoke of, "which utters at least six distinct sounds, which excite in other monkeys similar emotions"

(41), and human language—no difference, that is, except man's perverse habit of confusing words with things, a penchant that Stuart Chase contrasts with the more sensible sign behavior of his famous cat Hobie Baker. Even to sophisticated philosophers of language, the "semioticists," it goes without saying that man's behavior as the creature who makes assertions is a development *in continuo* from the behavior of the animal who responds to signs. One does not say how this takes place; one merely speaks in the same breath of these three activities: (1) men responding to each other by means of signs (the science of behavioristics), (2) men applying signs to things as names (the science of semantics), (3) men analyzing the relations between signs (the science of syntax or symbolic logic).

The attitude of the objective-minded man toward language, from the high school psychology student to the linguist, from Locke to Bloomfield, may therefore be summarized as follows: language is a system of signs to which one learns to respond meaningfully; man also applies signs to things as their names and arranges signs in sentences, which refer to a state of affairs in the world.

It is the purpose of this book to say two things about the view of language professed by the objective-empiricist since the time of Locke. One, it represents either the most monumental naïveté in the history of scientific thought or the most willful omission of everything that one's theory can't explain. Two, the phenomenon that is left out is absolutely central to an understanding of language and, more importantly, absolutely central to an understanding of man.

To say that words are signs to which one responds, and to add casually that one also "applies" signs to things as their names and "arranges" signs in sentences about the world, and to believe that one has remained within the realm of responding organisms within the old corpus of scientific knowledge is certainly a heroic example of one or the other lapse, of naïveté or of blind allegiance to theory. Such a view of man's behavior amounts to an admission that a near miraculous event has occurred—as well as a refusal to recognize it. Reichenbach (1956) admits that the organism that responds to the world also *knows* the world, expresses truths about the world in sentences that can be verified. But instead of telling us about this extraordinary state of affairs, Reichenbach is content to return to his old theme, that hardheaded science has replaced metaphysics (252-261). Semanticists and positivists insist that all happenings can be analyzed into a series of space-time functions which scientific formulae can express. They also insist that man knows the world, can assert truths about the world, and verify them. He "knows" a thing first (cats and men "know" a pencil), then names it. But how does a responding organism know and name? The answer is not forthcoming. What is left out is the central phenomenon Cassirer (1953a) speaks of in which a thing is known *through* its name, the act of symbolization (41-44).

This unbridgeable gap—one might better call it an abyss—is the same gap Cassirer spoke of when he observed that no amount of biological theorizing can bridge the gap between biological response-utterance and proposition (150). What the positivist leaves out of his theory of human meaning is nothing less than that one activity which makes a man human, what Cassirer (1955) called the spontaneous creation of the human spirit—the symbolic forms (217).

Yet one cannot but admire the agility and cool nerve with which modern scientific philosophers hop back and forth between natural science and logic, responses and propositions, without noticing the abyss between. To speak in the same breath of responses and naming-giving and syntax and to believe that in so doing one has created a "unified science" may be a *tour de force* of a sort, but it is hardly in the best tradition of scientific thought that strives, not for unity at any price, but for a clear look at what is not understood and for an understanding of it.

The abyss remains whether one notices it or not, and sooner or later, we must look down. It is a legitimate movement of the scientific method to understand man as far as possible as a something in the world in interaction with the world and with other men, to study man's behavior for empirical regularities that can be expressed by general laws, to see the objective science of man as all of a piece with the corpus of scientific knowledge—and the method should be followed as far as it will lead us. It is also a legitimate movement of the scientific method to study the assertions of man in order to determine their internal consistency (logic) and their correspondence with the world (verification). But to pretend that one of these two sorts of activities flows into the other without further explanation—as anatomy flows into physiology, to use the example of a semioticist (Morris 1955, 121)—is to close one's eyes and jump the abyss. It is one thing when creatures are in interaction with each other. It is something else when a creature tells the truth or tells lies about creatures in interaction.

What takes place in the abyss? What is the nature of the real event that happens before our very eyes when a twenty-three month old baby (the usual age at which it happens) who had up to now been a good organism with sensible needs and a good sign-apparatus for satisfying them, what happens when this child suddenly discovers that this sound father utters is the *name* of the thing he holds?

2. Buber's Man: He Who Sets the World at a Distance

The nature of the problem may be expressed diagrammatically. Objective science looks upon the world as a dynamic interaction from which science induces underlying principles and patterns of interaction. Everything in the world, man included, acts upon the world and is in turn acted upon by the world. This state of affairs may be expressed as several elements in interaction, each with all the others.

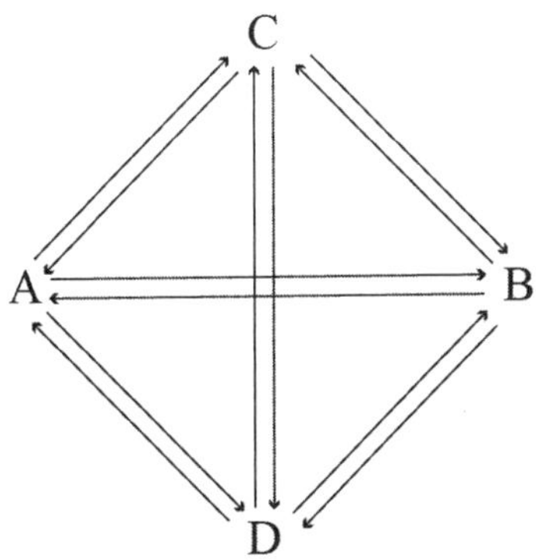

But when man appears and names something *water* and asserts of it that *water is cool*, a new state of affairs has come into being. The elements are still in interaction; man remains an organism who gets thirsty and responds to signs of water by drinking water. But another relation appears. The new element man *M* stands apart from the interaction of the world and asserts that one element of the interaction *A* "is" another element *B* (this stuff water is this word *water*); he asserts also that *S* is *P* (the water is cool).

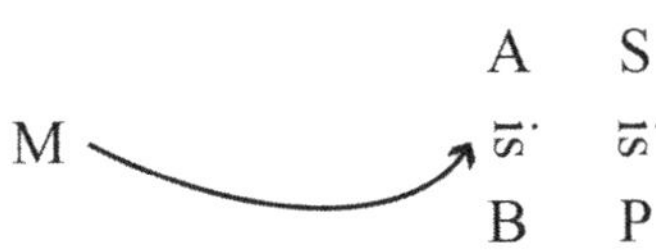

Martin Buber (1957) speaks of this relation as "the primal setting at a distance" and designates it as one of the twofold principles of human life (97).

Unhappily, the objective scientific method is unable to grasp this relation—*for the scientific method is itself a mode of this relation!* Yet this limitation of the method does not mean that it lies beyond our power to understand how it comes about that an organism "sets itself at a distance" and makes assertions, and to understand also what are the consequences of an understanding of this event for our basic thinking about man.

3. Sign and Symbol

What is the difference, if any, between sign and symbol? Between the communication of animals, by which one organism interprets the sign of another and acts upon it, and the language of men? Is the symbol a uniquely human creation, radically and generically different from the biological sign, or is it merely an evolutionary refinement of the sign? The question is of the utmost importance. A whole literature has sprung up in advocacy of the thesis that most of our difficulties stem from our failure to recognize the true nature of language, from our penchant for short-circuiting the proper causal order of sign communication and imputing a nonexistent bond between name and thing.

The situation is one of confusion at least twice compounded. For not only do people use either word, sign or symbol, to mean quite different things, and introduce a third word "signal," but there is also genuine disagreement as to the relation between the two functions. We can only hope to avoid total obscurity by defining our terms as clearly as possible. We will use the word "sign" as synonymous with Morris's "signal." There would perhaps be little disagreement between behaviorist and Thomist, Carnap and St. Augustine, in asserting that there exists a meaning situation in which an element performs the function of directing the attention of the organism to something else. This element we will call a "sign." The sign provokes a learned response toward the signified depending upon previous experience. Thunder announces rain to man or beast; the buzzer announces food to Pavlov's dog; the scrape of a match announces the imminence of a flame.

What is a symbol? Here we come to the parting of the ways. One's definition seems to depend on one's particular theoretical allegiance. Instead of defining the symbol, with its peculiar property of re-presenting something rather than announcing it, or as the scholastics would say, of containing *within itself*, in another mode of existence, that which is symbolized (John of St. Thomas quoted and translated by Maritain 1948b, 220), it would perhaps be better to examine empirically the way in which the function of symbolization arises from the function of signification.

What is particularly to be noticed is that the sign function fits admirably into our empirical conception of organism-in-an-environment. The determinate response of the organism to the sign depends upon the previous reception of the sign and the establishment of a residual trace or engram in the brain. Thus the first time I hear thunder, it does not announce anything at all. But having experienced the sequence thunder-rain several times, there occurs in my brain a physical or electro-colloidal change of such a nature that upon hearing thunder again, I expect rain. The phenomenon of conditioning is recognized as being universally operative for all higher organic life, man included. It is a sequence of space-time events occurring in a causal order and mediated through physical structures. Thus, sign (any sensible: sound, sight, smell, gesture) *leads to* sensory reception at appropriate afferent sense organ (eye, ear, skin) *leads to* electrical impulse in afferent nerve *leads to* excitation of engram in central nervous system *leads to* electrical impulse in efferent nerve *leads to* appropriate response (muscular, glandular, etc.).

It was inevitable that the sign function, which is clearly the elementary form of intelligence in animals and man, should offer itself as the prototype of all meaning structure. For it possesses the incomparable virtue of being explicable in terms of structure and function; it conforms to established causal principles and observable energy exchanges, and so is continuous with all other processes in the universe; it is verifiable; it is, and surely no one would disagree, a matter of fact. A great deal of human behavior can be understood as a response to signs. Pavlov's dog can be conditioned and so can man.

Nothing seemed more desirable from the empirical point of view, therefore, than the application of this admirably simple schema to the realm of communication in man—with every expectation that it would yield the same fruitful results as the application of experimental animal physiology to man. Enormous energy has been expended by the psychogeneticists in the attempt to explicate human meaning as an outgrowth and refinement of the sign function. The whole edifice of behaviorism is erected on no other premise than that intelligence is understandable in terms of learned responses to sign stimuli.

Once the sign function is established as the basis of all knowledge and communication, the symbol must be conceived as a kind of sign, and symbolic meaning, involving words and thoughts, is seen as a refinement of the causal order of signification. The semioticist, Charles Morris (1946), defines a symbol as "a sign produced by its interpreter which acts as a substitute for some other sign with which it is synonymous" (25). This is not a distinctively human relation: "So if a symbol operates in the dog's behavior, the symbol could take the place in the control of behavior which the buzzer formerly exercised: hunger cramps for instance might themselves come to be a sign (that is, a symbol) of food at the customary place" (25). In lieu of the buzzer, hunger cramps become a symbol—of food! If such a definition of symbol seems strange, it must be pointed out in all fairness that Morris's avowed purpose is to construct a science of meaning, to confine himself to a public and sequential order of events, a behavioral succession of stimulus and response. Nevertheless, the question remains as to whether the relation of hunger cramps to food has anything at all to do with symbolization.

Ogden and Richards (1953), who would not go as far as the behaviorists in excluding *thought* from a science of meaning, nevertheless retain causation, sequential reaction, as the basis of meaning. Their famous triangle is a schema of a causal relation:

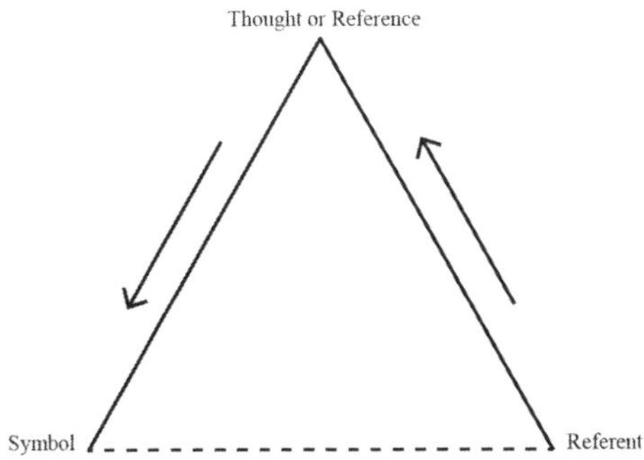

> Between a thought and a symbol causal relations hold. When we speak, the symbolism we employ is caused partly by the reference we are making and partly by social and psychological factors.... When we hear what is said, the symbols both cause us to perform an act of reference and to assume an attitude which will, according to circumstances, be more or less similar to the act and the attitude of the speaker (10-11).

There is no direct relation between the symbol and the referent. "Symbol and Referent, that is to say, are not connected directly (and when, for grammatical reasons, we imply such a relation, it will merely be an imputed, as opposed to a real, relation)" (11-12).

Stuart Chase (1938) stresses that the triangle has no base. "Yet human beings are constantly leaping from word to thing, identifying word with thing. [As Ogden and Richards say,] 'The most prolific fallacy of human intercourse is that the base of the triangle is filled in.' Try as you may, you cannot eat the word 'oyster'" (98).

Yet when we speak of the symbol, the word, as a kind of sign that "causes" or "announces" the presence of an idea, are we doing justice to the peculiar property of the symbol—that of standing for something else? As Mrs. Langer (1951) points out, it may be quite justified in a sense to speak of the symbol as an artificial sign that announces the presence of a certain idea. "Yet it strikes a strained and unnatural note, which is usually a fair warning that the attempted interpretation misses the most important feature in its material" (51).

4. The Relation of Denotation

What is completely left out of the behavioral or causal rendering of the symbol is the obvious but nonetheless extraordinary property of naming: the language symbol, above all, denotes something.

A sign is a term in a causative schema directing the organism to an object. Signification is a sequential action that is explicable in terms of physical structures and energy transformations. Denotation is a peculiar relation that the symbol bears directly to the object—the symbol is the *name* of the object. It is precisely this imputed relation between symbol and object which is deplored by Chase and others because it cannot be explicated in physical terms. But explicable or not, a name denotes a thing, names it, and is not merely the signal that calls it forth.

It is the function of denotation that is radically different from any kind of signification. There is a basic confusion on this point. Dogs are said to understand names and they do. When I say "James" to James's dog, he *looks* for his master. He responds intelligently to a word-sign. But when I say "James" to you, James's friend, you say, "What about him?" You *think* about James. What the dog will never, never know is that "James," the queer little sound, is the *name* of his master. "Signification is the only meaning a name can have for him" (Langer 1951, 50). The dog lives in a pure stimulus-response milieu: sign *leads* to thing. No matter what marvels of signification he can perform—so that to his audience he will appear "to know as much as people"—the one thing that will never dawn in his *mind* is that the word "ball," a peculiar mouthy little explosion, is the name of the round rubber thing, or, in the sense which so scandalizes the positivists: that *is* a ball.

It is the unique, the absolutely unprecedented, character of naming which escapes us. Far and away the most important natural event that has ever occurred, whether we are speaking historically or ontogenetically, it does not even strike us as remarkable. Our thinking is of its very nature so through-and-through symbolic—because it is by the symbol that we construe the world—that any attempt to see the symbol function for what it is, is like trying to look at a mirror.

Perhaps the best opportunity to grasp the significance of naming is afforded us by the accounts of the deaf-mutes and other unfortunates who did not discover the use of language until a comparatively late date—late enough to recall it.

When Miss Sullivan, Helen Keller's companion, tried to teach her pupil words by spelling them into her hand, she encountered a characteristic difficulty. Helen "learned" the word d-o-l-l quickly enough, but as a trick to show off to her mother—"I didn't know that I was spelling a word or even that words existed" (Keller 1928, 22). Also she *understood* the word "water" as having something to do with the mug or fetching water or drinking water, and so on. *She understood signs perfectly well:* when Miss Sullivan brought Helen her hat, she knew she was going for a walk. But what she did not know and could not seem to learn was that the word "water" was the *name* of the liquid, that *this is water*. And the more we reflect on it, the more extraordinary the simplest act of naming becomes. Giving a thing a name is an extremely mysterious business.

But the great moment did at last come. As the water flowed over one hand, Miss Sullivan spelled w-a-t-e-r into the other, first slowly, then rapidly. "I stood still, my whole attention fixed upon the motions of her fingers. Suddenly I felt a misty consciousness as of something forgotten—a thrill of returning thought; and somehow the mystery of language was revealed to me. I knew then that 'w-a-t-e-r' *meant* [emphasis added] the wonderful cool something that was flowing over my hand. That living word awakened my soul, gave it light, … set it free!" (23).

The case of Victor, the savage of Aveyron, is even more to the point. It seems to be one of the few authenticated cases of the capture of wild children, children who have managed to survive somehow their abandonment in the wilderness. Dr. Itard, who undertook to teach Victor language, operated on the theory that Victor, like any other animal, would use a word as a *sign* of a want. He withheld water and tried to make Victor use the word "*eau*" as a sign that he wanted water. But this attempt failed, and Victor used every sign but the vocal one. Victor did succeed in learning the word "*lait*," but with unforeseen—and to Dr. Itard, disappointing—results. Victor spoke the word "*lait*," but not as a sign of a want. Itard says:

> It was not till the moment, when, despairing of a happy result, I actually poured the milk into the cup which he presented to me, the word *lait* escaped him again, with evident demonstrations of joy; and it was not till after I had poured it out a second time, by way of reward, that he repeated the expression. It is evident from hence, that the result of the experiment was far from accomplishing my intentions; the word pronounced, instead of being the sign of a want, it appeared, from the time in which it was articulated, to be merely an exclamation of joy. If this word had been uttered before the thing that he desired had been granted, my object would have been nearly accomplished: then the true sense of speech would have been soon acquired by Victor. (quoted in Langer 1951, 97)

Dr. Itard considered that he had failed to teach Victor the "true sense of speech," that is, a sign communication by words. Actually, of course, the good doctor taught better than he knew. For what Victor had discovered, not because of but despite Dr. Itard's theoretical efforts, was something far more extraordinary than word-significance. He had hit upon the symbol—the sudden incalculable inkling that the sound "*lait*" *is* the white liquid in the glass.

What attitude shall we as empiricists take toward this evident discovery of Helen Keller and Victor? Shall we deplore it as a "wrongly imputed relation," ignore it as failing to conform to our canons of meaning? The behavior of the objective-empiricist in the face of this situation is revealing: every instinct within him moves him to disqualify this queer relation of quasi-identity as "wrong" and to elect instead for the causal function, to throw out *A* "is" *B* with its treacherous little copula and save *A leads to B*. But is this doctrinaire preference, a saying which *ought* to be the case, faithful to the true empirical enterprise of seeing what *is* the case? Should we not rather explore this strange *non-causal* relation for what relevance it might have for cognition and consciousness?

An empirical element common to both cases is the excitement and joy that attend the discovery, a joy which, unlike all previous pleasure, is unrelated to the economy of biological needs and satisfactions. It is a joy which is the index of a sudden access of understanding, a meeting of minds, and an affirmation. A relation that was intended by the teacher is, by some happy conjunction of circumstance, grasped in a flash of insight. At once the simplest and the most mysterious of relations, it is an insight which cannot be approached by the most refined propaedeutic of sign education: a chimpanzee cannot grasp it (Yerkes and Yerkes 1945, 309). Once grasped, it cannot be relinquished: it is and remains the irreversible condition of our knowing anything at all. Helen Keller, once she knew what water *was*, had only one burning desire: to know what everything else *was*.

The advent of symbolization can be studied, not only in the extraordinary cases of human beings cut off in one way or another from the social context in which language ordinarily arises, but ontogenetically, as it is acquired in the maturation of the normal child. The child who holds up a ball and says "ball" is not necessarily voicing the signal of a want; he is not asking or answering—rather is he celebrating for perhaps the thousandth time the remarkable circumstance that this "is" a ball. As Ernest Schachtel (1954) puts it, "man's grasp of reality is not merely based on his wish to satisfy primary, biological needs—is not merely, as Freud assumed, a detour on the path to wish fulfillment—but… it also has as a prerequisite an *autonomous* [emphasis added] interest in the environment" (309). There is, then, a prime cognitive relation between man and object, which has nothing to do with the categories of need-satisfaction. What are we to make of it? Will it suffice simply to label it as "autonomous focal interest," a "need of symbolization"?

It is surely evident, whether in the case of the deaf-mute, the wild boy, the normal child (to all but those who are more interested in saving theory than in discovering what is the case), that there has occurred a profound re-orientation in the meaning relation which existed between the organism and the object. A symbol is radically and generically different from a sign—for which distinction we should be grateful to Mrs. Langer. Any attempt to reduce one to the other will either issue in a fragmentary account of meaning, in which the heart of the matter is simply left out, or, what is more extraordinary, provoke a chronic ill-temper whose only recourse is to scold man for obstinately refusing to treat words as good biological signs—a truly remarkable attitude for an allegedly empirical-minded man.

5. The Unprecedented Character of Symbolization

Our task is clear. Instead of trying to force this extraordinary relation into a biological mold—whatever the cost of distortion and omission—we must see it for what it is. We must pursue the consequences which flow from it—instead of discrediting them when they do not fit our biological standards.

What did it entail when the first man on earth (for the first man who spoke was, almost by minimal empirical definition, the first man), under a set of circumstances which, for the purposes of an empirical study, it is futile even to guess at, first discovered that a sound he made with his mouth was the *name* of an object before him? One is accustomed to think of this event as but one of many such events in an evolutionary ascent: sexual reproduction, emergence of the lungs and warm-bloodedness, standing erect, binocular vision, apposition of thumb, language.... Yet if we think about it, we will soon realize that there is something about language which is not only quite different from any other organic accomplishment, but is absolutely unprecedented *in kind* in all of natural history. We may agree with the apostles of continuity that all, or nearly all, events, whether organic or inorganic, can be conceived as occurring under the same dispensation of causal instrumentality. Whether one is speaking of the motion of the planets or of a solution of electrolytes, the response of an amoeba to light or the response of Pavlov's dog to a buzzer—we think naturally and fruitfully in the instrumental terms: *A* leads to *B* in a determined ratio, or, in other words, *B* is a function of *A*. Data lends itself inevitably to this interpretation. But language is different. For the essence of naming is not a relation of cause but a relation of identification. There occurs, not a sequence of elements, but their apposition—a pairing and fusion. What Helen Keller (1928) finally "caught on to"—and there are no other words except this or "revelation" or "awakening" to characterize Helen's experience—was that the gesture in her hand *was* the water (23).

At this point we can avoid a lot of trouble and all the bootless arguments about whether it is "right" or "wrong" to say "This is water," by not insisting on the copula "is." For it does not matter whether we express the relation as *This is water*, or, *This object we shall label by the word water*, or simply a pointing and naming, This: *water*. What is common to all three, what actually occurs in each case is the *pairing* of two elements, the gesture and the thing, under the relation of identification. The essence of this pairing is an affirmation: it is affirmed of one that it *is* the other. Here, of course, is where the confusion starts—with the semioticists' deploring the imputing of any such relation between the thing and its symbol. But perhaps a great deal of this confusion can be avoided, as Professor Veatch (1953) suggests, and as we shall later see in a discussion of intentionality, by distinguishing between the structure of the *intending instrument*, the symbolic quasi-identification, *this is water*, and the *intended object*, the water as being what it is (188).

But right or wrong, deplorable or not, the advent of symbolization is incalculable in its significance. In the entire inorganic cosmos and in the entire subhuman scale of life, the event of identification, to the best of our empirical knowledge, has never before occurred. For the first time, Something *A* does not simply become Something *B* through an orderly change: instead Something *A* is *affirmed* as being what it is by means of its identification with its symbol. *It is*, we begin to realize, *the first event in natural history which transcends the order of causality.*

The Promethean moment in man's history was not the capture of fire but the awesome moment when he gave the first name to a creature, and thereby knew the world and affirmed it. "*And the Lord God having formed out of the ground all the beasts of the earth, and all the fowls of the air, brought them to Adam to see what he would call them: for whatsoever Adam called any living creature, the same is its name*" (Gen. 2:19 Douay-Rheims).

6. The Structure of the Symbol Meaning Relation

Once we have realized the unprecedented character of the symbolic meaning-situation, and once we have clearly seen that any attempt to formulate it in a traditional causal schema will inevitably leave out its salient property, a valid empirical method of inquiry becomes available to us. We must first examine symbolic meaning for its essential structure, leaving our theoretical formulations to follow upon and accommodate things as they are rather than to precede and condition them. We must give it a *minimal* characterization, delineating only those terms and relations that are indispensable and that are verifiable by common experiential insight. We must make no premature commitments about *being*—and here we part company with the strict phenomenologist—either in the bracketing of it or in the opting for the "absolute priority of consciousness," etc., but rather retain an abiding sensitivity to causal implications in the ontological realm.

We can schematize the relation of signification very simply as a triad of elements related in a causal sequential order:

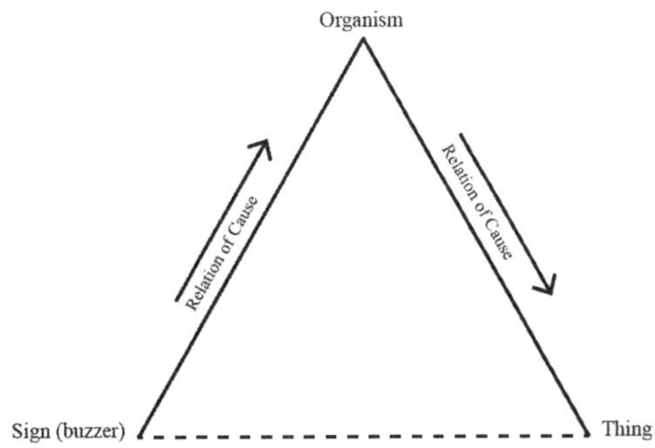

Whether the sign be natural or contrived, thunder or buzzer, whether the organism be animal or man, the principle of operation is exactly the same. A sensible (sight, sound, etc.) is transmitted to an organism where it activates a previously conditioned electro-colloidal system in the central nervous system, which issues in discriminate behavior with respect to thing. This behavior can take many forms: action toward, withdrawal from, expectation of, fear of, hunger for, etc. There is no necessary direct relation between sign and thing, save only the obvious one of association in time and space. Thunder, as it happens, bears a certain relation to rain, but the artificial sign, the buzzer, is unrelated to food: signification only requires that the elements, sign and thing, be related in time sufficiently often so that neurological conditioning may occur.

One other thing should be noticed. The sign can be *any* environmental element, and its operation as a sign depends on nothing else than its temporal and habitual association with that for which it is a sign. That is to say, it does not in the least matter whether the sign is a gesture from another organism or a physical element in the environment: the relation of signification is the same. Words as signs are no different from any other signs. A word from me, "Fire!," can be interpreted by you in the same generic mode as the roar of a lion or the splintering sound of a toppling tree. A colony of bees operates by the most complex and refined interchange of signs: by the bee dance, one bee can actually direct another to a distance and in a direction. But signification occurs equally well in the interaction between a *single* organism and its environment. The interpretation by the solitary polar bear of the sound of splitting ice is of precisely the same order as the communication of one bee with another.*

The minimal requirement of signification is that there be *one* organism in an environment.

If we examine the minimal structure of symbolization, however—prescinding for the present from the vexed question of thoughts, ideas, representations, images, connotation, and taking account only of those physical elements in the empirical situation which are both indispensable and indisputable—we immediately perceive a striking difference. The action of symbolization requires as an indefeasible condition of its operation the presence of *two* organisms—and two very special kinds of organisms: one, O_1, the subject organism, the organism of the sign situation; but also and necessarily, O_2, the organism from whom the symbol is received as meaning what it does. The critical moment in the advent of symbolization is the moment when Helen Keller suddenly perceives that the symbol is intended *by her teacher* to denote water. Only a moment's reflection is required to realize that in the sign situation of organism-in-environment, *symbolization cannot possibly occur.* No amount of complex sign interpretation can ever issue in the simplest name-giving because there is no name-giver, or else no one for whom the name shall be intended as meaningful. The objection immediately arises: but I symbolize perfectly well alone; in fact, it is only when I am alone that I create new meaning, by the making of the art symbol, by the naming of new species, by the formulation of a scientific hypothesis. *True, but the irreducible condition of every symbolic act, and the very essence of the truly*

* We are not concerned here with determining which responses are acquired by conditioning and which are determined by innate response mechanisms (the "IRM" of John Bowlby 1953) since both occur in the same physico-causal order.

creative effort, is the rendering intelligible, that is, the formulation of experience for a real or an implied someone else. If a Robinson Crusoe is able to formulate the experience of twenty years alone, it is because he has already learned the social trick of symbolizing, that is, of rendering public his experience. The simplest or the most complex symbolization, a pointing at a thing and a naming, or the sudden apprehension of a great line of poetry, requires as a minimal condition of its operation, the *Two*—a Namer and a Hearer, whether real or posited. In order that a language symbol, a name, denote anything at all, it must denote it for at least two of us. The condition of denotation is more-than-one.

We have, therefore, as the minimal structure of symbolization, a tetrad of elements instead of the triad of signification:

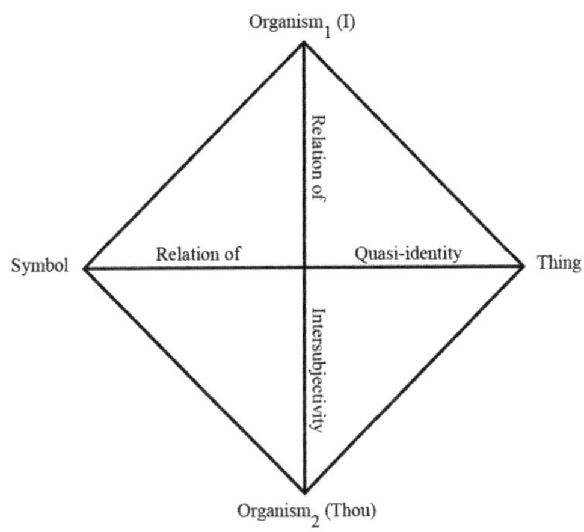

But it is in the *relations* of the terms of the triad of signification that the most extraordinary change has occurred. As we have seen, the action of signification can be explicated in its *entirety* as a sequence of events occurring in and mediated by physical structures. It occurs in the causal order which is universally valid for the world around us. Every event, from the motion of molecules to the motions of the planets, from the chemistry of the cell to the behavior of the larger anthropoids, lends itself admirably to this schematization. But what is one to make of the symbolic relation: the sudden inkling that *this is milk?* We may deplore it with Korzybski or celebrate it with Cassirer but we cannot dismiss it.

7. The Relation of Quasi-Identity

The bottom of Ogden and Richards's triangle is closed by the imputed relation of quasi-identity. When Ogden and Richards and the others rule out a direct relation between name and thing, when Korzybski deplores identification, they do so solely on the dogmatic grounds that the only "real" relations are causal relations. They simply discard the relation of denotation as "wrong." Having set out with signification as the only basis of meaning, and discerning no causal relation between symbol and thing, they pronounce them unrelated excepting only as the symbol "calls up" the reference in the mind.

If the positivists (Ogden and Richards, Chase, Korzybski) are saying merely that primitives often make the mistake of confusing word with thing and that we too are prone to hypostasize such words as "democracy," "communism," "virtue," without bothering to look for a real referent, who can disagree with them?—though this hardly strikes one as a particularly seminal insight. We gladly accept their counsel of putting ourselves on guard against primitive word magic—although it would seem to me a more rewarding pursuit to inquire *why* the primitive should do this. But the epistemological naïveté of the positivists lies in their proclaiming in one breath a purely causal *sign* theory of knowledge and engaging in the next in endless preachments about the *wrong* use of *symbols* or labels—the abuse of a function which is not even provided for in their theory. They are both reductionists and miraculists about the same thing. Knowing is nothing but a stimulus-response context. Yet knowing is also a private autonomous awareness in which we somehow know things and then distribute labels among them. (The heroic exception is George H.

Mead who clearly saw that mind, language, and consciousness are inseparable from the social context.) (See Part III, Chapter I.) Consciousness of things as things, awareness of a tree as a tree, is apparently accepted uncritically as a sort of magic given, tacked onto the original sign situation. Stuart Chase's ingenuousness is characteristic. Following Korzybski's abstractive scale, he speaks of the difference between animal knowing and human knowing. Both he and his cat, he says, "recognize" a pencil. But only he gives it a label (Chase 1938, 84). Now apart from the fact that "giving a thing a label" is not here explicated at all in terms of semiotic science, there is the extraordinary assumption that both of us, my cat and myself, "know" and "recognize" the pencil entirely independently of formulation under the auspices of the symbol. Naming is viewed as a sort of option, a semantic convenience. There is left out the whole epochal event in which the organism apprehends something as and only as it is associated with the symbol that is given him and that he in turn can produce. Knowing is no passive reception or reaction to a thing but the active creation of meaning through the production and mediation of the symbol—the subjective component which is so indispensable that Cassirer, in his discovery of it, went to the opposite extreme, dismissed the thing as noumenon, and pronounced the symbol the whole knowable reality.

8. The Relation of Intersubjectivity

If we choose to rule out the imputed relation of quasi-identity as it occurs in symbolization as "wrong" and limit ourselves to a physicalistic science of meaning, our conclusions will be valid as far as they go—we are, after all, animals, and we can be conditioned like any other animal. But what we will omit is that in the natural order, which makes us distinctively human, there is an orientation to the world that is so characteristic and all-pervasive that Cassirer (1953a) is justified in defining man as "*animal symbolicum*"(44).

But there exists among the elements of the symbolic tetrad another relation which is at least as extraordinary as that of denotation (and inseparable from it and even more deserving of our attention because it has entirely escaped the notice—and unquestionably the condemnation—of the semioticists).

We have seen that from a purely objective-empirical point of view, there must be, in distinction to signification, at least two organisms in the symbol relation: a Namer and a Hearer, one who makes the symbol and one for whom the symbol is intended as meaningful. The condition of symbolization is that there be two of us, real or posited. But it is not this objective minimum of twoness which constitutes its unique importance—it is rather the nature of the bond by which the two are oriented toward the object. Here again we encounter the characteristic difficulty of formulating a non-causal relation in the empirical language which we have traditionally applied to external events in the world. This peculiar relation is quite inexpressible in sequential "response" language, yet it is both irreducible and indispensable to the symbolic function. It can only be expressed—unsatisfactorily perhaps—by some such terms as "intersubjectivity" or "mutuality." The occurrence of symbolization—whether it be my creation of a symbol which shall be intelligible for you: that is, stand for, re-present, the same thing for you as it does for me, or whether it be my receiving a symbol from you—is a flash of *affirmation*, the sudden advent of a *mutuality* toward the thing intended. The delight of the wild boy of Aveyron when it suddenly dawned on him that the sound "*lait*" *meant* the milk—the rare pleasure with which one suddenly understands an obscure painting or poem, understands what the artist *means*—are both unmistakably associated with the coming into being or the extension of a zone of intersubjectivity. It, the pleasure, is even the index of the extent of intersubjectivity. The two organisms, you and I, come to be related in an entirely unprecedented fashion—a bond which we shall be interested in comparing with the favorite existential theme of intersubjectivity, the "I-Thou" bond, and its loss with the theme of alienation, the "one-other" bond. Previously we had existed in an adaptive stimulus-response milieu, in a complex conversation of gesture, admirably set forth by Mead's (1952) example of the two dogs or the two boxers (42 ff.). The relation is specified by a biologically relevant orientation—whether hostile, friendly, maternal, sexual, and so on. An object may be implicated, as a bone between the two dogs or Helen's doll, but the relation is a pure sequential interchange, and the pleasure or hostility manifested is invariably an index of the biological relevance of the object. The dog's delight at the buzzer, Helen's delight at the feel of her hat, are interpretable in a context of biological relevance. But the symbolization has a totally different orientation—it is the co-intending of the object by its symbol. It is always the fathoming of an intent, an "Oh! I see what you mean!" Its characteristic tone is affirmatory, a "Yes! Yes! I understand!" It is in no wise a reaction, but a sharing, a participation. Thus, in the symbol tetrad, the you and the I are related by an indefeasible bond, that of intersubjectivity.

It may be interesting at this point to compare an existential-phenomenological view of intersubjectivity, arrived at by a much broader empirical method than that to which we have restricted ourselves—from "above" rather than "below":

> But it is apparent by definition that what I may call the intersubjective nexus cannot be given to me, since I am myself in some way involved in it. It may not perhaps be inaccurate to say that this nexus is in fact the necessary condition for anything being given to me.... Without doubt the intersubjective nexus cannot be in any way asserted: it can only be acknowledged. Here again we meet an idea which has already taken up much of our attention. This recognition must assuredly be patient of translation into an expressible affirmation. At the same time we should be careful to remember that the affirmation should possess a special character.... *I should readily agree that it is the mysterious root of language* [emphasis added].... One might say that the intelligible milieu or medium is only the projection on an ideal plane of what existentially speaking presents itself to us as the intersubjective nexus. (Marcel 1951b, 10-11)

As American empiricists, we are apt to feel an impatience with Marcel's cultivated vagueness and his erection of mystery as a category. But what is so exciting is that he has hit upon something which has been overlooked and something the importance of which it is impossible to exaggerate—and hit upon it empirically, that is, by an experiential inquiry in which we can take part. We can't help feeling, however, that as it stands, Marcel's intersubjectivity is "in the air"—especially when he considers at some length whether or not "being *is* intersubjectivity" (16)—and that such an insight can be grounded, without necessarily being reduced, in the solid bedrock of our empirical science.

9. Who Is the Namer?

I shall conclude this chapter by calling attention to one last element of the symbolic orientation. I hesitate to do more than mention it—not because it does not deserve attention. On the contrary. Its implications are so momentous for our thinking about man and project us so immediately into an issue about which one is apt to have the strongest prejudices, that if I did more than advert to it in passing, there would be no space for anything else. I shall mention it then, at the risk of offending my objective-empirical reader, but no more than mention it. No conclusions will be drawn from it, and it will not be used as a premise for metaphysical deductions.

Who is the Namer? The question must sooner or later force itself upon us as we consider the implications of the central act of symbolization.* We have seen that it entails the relation of quasi-identity, that peculiar state of affairs that comes about when the symbol is identified with the thing and when a predicate is identified with a subject—when one asserts *S* is *P*.

* The simple truth of it is that this question (and answer) only occurred to me after the book was written, and is added as an afterthought. This business of the pairing of the symbol and object had bothered me for a long time. What was one to make of it? It was a case of not even knowing what kind of question to ask—for the question was too obvious to be seen. Once the right question was asked, the answer followed immediately.

But there is entailed more than a relation. The symbol and the thing, the subject and predicate, do not merely stand in a certain relation to each other, as a father stands to a son. Something is being done to them; they are paired. Their relation depends entirely on their being related by a relater. That is to say, they are brought into this relation by an operation that is performed by an agent. I am not multiplying entities here. Symbol and thing stand in a relationship that is quite different from all (genetically) preceding relationships. The relation depends entirely on the continuing intention of the relater. There is no such relation between sign and thing signified. I am multiplying entities if I say that the relation of signification requires a signifier and an act of signifying. It is far simpler to regard signification as a simple material sequence: buzzer sounds, dog responds by salivating, etc. But we cannot say this about a symbol and the thing symbolized. For the symbol and thing are identified; they are paired. Who does the pairing? Obviously the Namer. Who is the Namer? Is he identical with his organism? Is the one who names with the symbol the same as the one who responds to the sign? Is he merely the organism that has achieved a higher level of function—just as the pigeon that has learned to fly is the same organism as before? Does the question, *who is the Namer?*, mean no more than the question, *who is the flyer?* And is it to be answered in the same way: that the flyer or Namer is no more or less than the same organism who could not fly or name and who now can?

No, the Namer is not the same as the organism.

This becomes evident as soon as we realize that the act of naming is generically different from the *act* of flying, the *act* of fertilization, the *act* of mitosis, the *act* of responding.

The biologist would probably object, and properly, to the use of such terms as "acts" and "actors" in describing any sort of behavior, whether it be an amoeba's response to light or a child's learning to speak. It would not appear fruitful to him to multiply entities and to distinguish parts in the dynamic totality of an organic response. What is to be gained by separating the organism from its behavior, when each is specified by the other and neither can be understood without the other? The triumph of biology is rather that it has been able to interrelate structure and function under the single canon of adaptive behavior. One does not understand behavior as the actions of an actor but rather as the adaptive responses of an organic system to an environment.

But we may not so consider the pairing of symbolization.

In any other action, whether it be an inorganic change or animal behavior, any one event or status may be fruitfully considered as a function of a prior event or status. Thus a stellar explosion is a function of an energy state before the explosion; urine secretion is a function of the state of the glomerular membrane and the plasma osmotic pressure; a flourishing shrub is a function of soil conditions, climate, etc. This rclation, expressed traditionally by the notion of cause, may also be expressed by saying that a variable state *A* leads to a variable state *B* in an invariable ratio, or that state *B* is a function of state *A*:

$$B = f(A)$$

As we apply this relation to inorganic and organic change, it means that even complex animal behavior can be at least partially understood as a dynamic and determined succession of events. Even the "thinking" of primates—as when a chimpanzee in a cage grasps the possibility of putting two sticks together to reach a banana outside the cage—even this complex behavior is understandable as such a succession: state *A*, chimpanzee plus banana-out-of-reach plus potential gestalt of two-sticks-making-one-long-stick; state *B*, the synthesis of this gestalt in the chimpanzee's brain leading to the recovery of banana. The entire sequence is specified by a fundamental adaptive drive for food, which is possessed by any organism-in-an-environment.

The act of symbolization is quite different. It is not a succession of physiological events at all but an immaterial operation performed upon two objects otherwise unrelated, an operation by which they are brought into a certain relation, that of quasi-identity.

The only relation between *S* and *O*, the word "ball" and the thing ball, is the intended relation, *S* = *O*. The state of symbolization which follows upon the state of non-symbolization is not to be understood in terms of physiology or behavior at all since it is the grasping by the Hearer of the intended relation of the Namer, *S* = *O*.

What sort of relation is this between symbol and object? It is not a material relation since neither symbol nor object is changed by the act of symbolization—the word "ball" and the thing ball remain the same whether one is understood to mean the other or not, whether they are identified or not; nor are they brought into a material relationship—as one billiard ball is brought into a material relation with another billiard ball when they collide.

It is for this reason that the constant attempts of genetic psychologists to explain language as a kind of behavior strikes such a strained note—for one leaves out the most important feature. For example, Malinowski (1953) tries to support Ogden and Richards's contextual or sign theory of language by citing the language of South Pacific islanders while fishing together, the constant interchange of words as signals for appropriate behavior: "Pull in," "Let go," "Shift further," "Lift the net," etc. And indeed one could hardly have selected a situation more similar to the sign behavior of animals or more explicable in these terms. But what sort of behavioral sense can be made of another sort of language activity carried out by these same islanders later in the day, when, as they sit around a fire, one native spins out a good yarn and others, listening, understand him. To say that such an activity serves a "social and emotive function" may indeed be true, but it hardly does justice to that extraordinary situation in which one man utters some sounds and another man, listening to him, does not respond to these sounds as signals but rather takes the meaning of the speaker, understands what these sounds re-present.

What sort of agent is it that intends this immaterial relation? It is not the organism, not the complex biological system which interacts with its environment—for such a system can only change the environment or itself undergo a change. The agent who performs the act of symbolization—he who names—must be an immaterial agent, since the action it performs is an immaterial action. It is not my organism, my body, who names; it is I.

Who is this "I"? Do I mean to imply a ghost inhabiting the organism?

I imply no such thing and am in fact convinced that the case is otherwise, that whatever its nature, the immaterial symbolizer is not a Somebody Else but is rather the living man himself considered in those acts which are most characteristically human. Perhaps the Aristotelian notion of the soul as the highest principle of operation, the "substantial form," of the body could be fruitfully applied here.

My aim here is to pursue the direct consequences of the act of symbolization. One such consequence is the necessity of recognizing a Namer who is not identical with his organism considered as a biological system responding to an environment. But since this brings us at once into the ancient and sterile battleground of mind *versus* matter, soul *versus* body, and since I am more anxious to develop fresh insights than to wage traditional warfare, I will say no more about this mysterious Namer.

We shall be concerned in the sequel with the direct consequences of the symbolic relation, for the empirical light which it sheds on such perennial quarrels as the nature of consciousness, truth and error, cult and magic—those peculiar properties and activities which set man apart from the rest of the animals and make him such an unsatisfactory specimen for an objectizing inquiry. In the next chapter we shall examine perhaps the strangest of all metamorphoses, the process by which the sensible, the gesture, the word, becomes the vehicle of meaning, how the word "becomes" the thing through an intentional change: the symbolic transformation.

In this chapter, to summarize, it has been our purpose to delineate the symbolic relation in its minimal structure, to identify those elements which are indispensable and those relations which are irreducible. In contrast to the sign, which, as we have seen, is a term in a causal relation mediated by physical structures and existing between an organism and its environment, we may tentatively define a language symbol as follows: a symbol is that sensible (spoken word, written word, gesture) which comes into a relation of quasi-identity with the thing through the co-intending of the Namer and Hearer and through whose auspices the thing is known as it is intended by the symbol.

CHAPTER II

THE SYMBOLIC TRANSFORMATION

The unique property of the symbol, as philosophers as different as Susanne K. Langer and John of St. Thomas have set forth, is that it in some sense comes to contain within itself that which is symbolized. "*Quid est illud in signato conjuctum signo, et praesens in signo praeter ipsum signum et entitatem ejus? Respondetur esse ipsummet signatum in alio esse*.... What may be that element of the signified which is joined to the sign and present in it as distinct from the sign itself and its own entity? I answer: No other element than the very signified itself in another mode of Existence" (John of St. Thomas quoted and translated by Maritain 1948b, 220). Mrs. Langer's (1951) interpretation is undoubtedly more congenial to the modern understanding: "Symbols... are *vehicles for the conceptions of objects*" (49).

When we say that a symbol "stands for," or "represents" something else, what, exactly, do we mean? In the popular conception, symbols are ordinarily thought of as a flag standing for a country or a lion standing for courage. In the mathematical or positivist sense, symbols are convenient proxies for unwieldy concepts: let *x* equal an unknown, let *p* equal a proposition, etc. Another common example is the iconic symbol: a statue of Hermes representing Hermes—and in this instance we might be willing to admit that Hermes is in a sense "present" in the statue—though it does not strike one as a particularly fruitful notion. All three of these are indeed examples of symbol formation, but, as we shall see, they are marginal or even misleading instances of something which is far more radical in its operation than any of these would indicate. None of these popular notions of what a symbol is illustrates the unique and characteristic property of the true symbol—a property which both Cassirer and Freud converged on from different directions—that it does not merely stand proxy for something, but that it organizes and construes experience or, in Freud's word, renders it *darstellbar* (not "presentable" as Brill translated it with its unfortunate connotation of propriety, but *formulable* (Langer 1953, 241)).

What we are interested in is not how the iconic or "like" symbol comes to represent the thing that it copies, how a statue of Hermes represents Hermes—this seems obvious enough—nor how the mathematical symbol stands proxy for something it does not resemble—but how the "unlike" symbol, the word, the gesture, the ambiguous art form, comes somehow to contain within itself, to be "like" that which it symbolizes. It is here in the language symbol, in the relation of word to thing, that the almost miraculous action of the symbolic transformation is best revealed. It is here that all the trouble starts—for here stirs for the first time the beginning of the idea and so truth (Maritain 1948b, 221n), and, at exactly the same moment as the reverse side of the process, the first manifestations of word magic and the absurdities of primitive life and thought. The price of truth is error.

What do we mean by a symbolic transformation? Is it true that the language symbol is actually changed, that it comes to be something other than what it was? Mrs. Langer speaks of the "symbolic transformation of experience," of the brain as a great transformer which is incessantly engaged in translating experience into symbols. But she never specifies the nature of the transformation. What exactly is changed and into what? How does the change take place? The symbolic transformation is by no means obvious and needs to be firmly established before it can be used as a basis of theorizing.

The easiest way to demonstrate the change is to begin with those words in our language that, as Professor Richards (1950) puts it, "are variously called expressive, symbolic, or simulative—words which 'somehow illustrate the meaning more immediately than do ordinary speech forms,' to quote Leonard Bloomfield" (57). It is this "somehow" which is the sole object of our investigation.

Richards gives the example of the morpheme of "slime," "slip," "slobber," "slide," "slither." It is unquestionably true that the "smoothly wet" series—or single words like "shaggy" or "limber"—seem to imitate the thing or quality or action which they denote. So much so, indeed, that one's reaction is apt to be: "What's the problem? These words are onomatopoetic—they imitate the thing in question. 'Shaggy' just naturally sounds shaggy!" In fact, in the first memorable argument about the question of whether names are naturally suitable or purely conventional, in Plato's *Cratylus* (1892) Socrates admitted that in this sort of word, *"olisthanein"* (to slip), there is a "liquid movement of the l, in the pronunciation of which the tongue slips, and in this he (the imposer of names) finds the expression of smoothness" (277). Aristotle, on the other hand, declared that there can be no natural connection between the sound of language and the thing signified.

Actually this apparent likeness is an illusion. In *olisthanein* the tongue does not slip. The word "slippery" is no more "smoothly wet" than any other word; there is nothing shaggy about the sound of "shaggy"; there is nothing fuzzy about the word "fuzzy"; and that we should think so is the best of all testimonies to the pervasiveness of this extraordinary transformation. What, after all, has the mouthy little sound "fuzzy," or "furry," got to do with a texture? There is, nearly all modern linguists would agree, no connection between these words and their meaning, or at least no such obvious connection as is popularly imputed to them. (As to the possibility of another relation besides likeness or isomorphism, we shall inquire in a moment.) These words are examples of false onomatopoeia. It is easy to satisfy oneself of this: repeat one of these words often enough—"fuzzy, fuzzy, fuzzy," etc.—and a queer thing will happen: all at once the word will lose its magic guise of symbol, its "fuzziness," and becomes what it really is, a drab little vocable, an odd little series of grunts and hisses.

Richards (1950) offers the explanation "that these expressions or symbolic words get their feeling of being peculiarly fitting from the other words sharing the morpheme which support them in the background of the mind" (62). Perhaps this is true—though it does not seem to explain why words with allied meanings should share the same vocal group (sl-) in the first place. Certainly the transformation is mediated through an "association," though it is not necessarily one reinforced by a series. Take the word "glass." I call attention to the remarkable fact that the word "glass" *sounds like* the thing glass. It will not suffice to say that the sound "glass," through a habitual association, calls up the idea or image of glass—though this may be true enough. We are not so much interested in the venerable quarrels about image and idea, abstraction and representation, concept and conception, which are "called up," "associated with," "abstracted from," the sensory impression—as with the more immediate apprehension of meaning *as it comes to be articulated in the symbol itself*. Beyond question, the word "glass," a sound gestalt which is nothing like glass, has somehow come to contain *within itself* the characteristic sensory configuration of the substance glass—the slick surface, the sharpness of the edge, perhaps above all the brittleness. Max Picard (1951) gives a revealing account of the intimate relation of word to conception, revealing because he is speaking of German words, and so the English-speaking reader is afforded an unobstructed glimpse into the extraordinary articulation of word to thing. He speaks of how perfectly the words "*Baum*" and "*Himmel*" contain within themselves and so express the conceptions of tree and sky:

> The soul of the word shapes the body of the word, selecting the vowels and consonants and joining them together in such a way that the body of the word acquires a face; and this face comes to resemble the face of the thing denoted by the word. Certain words are darlings of the word-soul, which has taken special pains over them, and one can plainly recognize the face of the thing in the face of the word. For example, in the word *Baum*, the b, which suddenly springs from the ground of the shut mouth through the small round of the lips, resembles the trunk of a tree thrusting itself through a round opening in the ground. Until the tree, like the b of the word, burst, a little surprisingly, out of the earth, the earth was everywhere sealed and shut. Then there is a pause between the b and the au; the au does not immediately connect with the b; there is a short gap like the interval of waiting in which one waits to watch the trunk of the tree growing upward... or there is the word *Himmel*. The mouth opens wide and as it breaths the letter H, it aspires to the summit of the heavens. (103)

To the non-German, to whom the words appear as what they are and not as transformed symbols, all this is apt to seem the merest fancy. In truth, he can hardly imagine two words *less* likely to transmit their respective conceptions. "*Baum*" and "*Himmel*" seem more suited to convey a connotation of sausages and *The Katzenjammer Kids*.

The question arises at once as to whether one's figuration of a word is private and unique with each person, or whether there is not in a national or cultural group some minimal element of configuration held in common—a question which, important as it is, does not directly concern us. Suffice it to say that it is hard to see how there could be a national poetry if everyone had a totally different figuration of a great metaphor of Shakespeare.

Now we are at the heart of that extraordinary process, the symbolic transformation. What is perhaps most extraordinary of all is that it should have gone totally unnoticed by the objective-empirical study of language. Indeed, so far as I know, only one philosopher of language has ever clearly perceived that a *change* has taken place. Professor R. A. Wilson (1948) writes in *The Miraculous Birth of Language:* "The natural sound element has been taken up into and practically disappears from our consciousness in its significant symbolic connotation. In other words, the natural sounds have been completely transmuted into conventional sound-symbols" (220). A temporal pattern, sound, comes to represent a spatial configuration—"the most momentous and fruitful single achievement of the human intellect" (241).

1. How Does the Symbolic Transformation Occur?

The great question which gradually takes form in our minds, the question which more than any other fascinated Cassirer (1953b), is this: How can a particular sensory content, a mouthy little sound, become the vehicle of an intellectual meaning? (91-92). How can one thing mean another? (And later: Is this the very condition of our knowing anything at all—that it be known in and through *something else*?)

One or two other examples may be revealing before we even make a guess about the inner workings of this transformation. Speculation about the figurations of particular words is to an undetermined degree a private and individual project—such a problem is perhaps susceptible of an empirical inquiry, by comparing the figurations of a single word undertaken by a group of subjects—but they represent at the very least the *sort* of process that goes on.

It is evident that the original root of a word does not necessarily exercise a control over the meaning pattern of the word. If, for example, we look up the history of the word "hideous," we discover that the early forms are *hisdos* and *hidous*, and that the third syllable, hid-*e*-ous, was not added until the sixteenth century. Yet the meaning of "hideous" for one is ineluctably bound up with, makes use of, the pattern of rhythm, the sound gestalt, which this all important extra syllable gives to the word: the quick beat of tongue against teeth and the resulting stop-and-explosion of air allows itself to be constituted as the very act of revulsion. It is not conceivable that the two-syllable words, *hisdos* or *hidous*, could have articulated quite the same meaning.

All parts of the structure of the sensuous word, spoken or written, are seized upon and utilized in the articulation of meaning within the word. Hence the perverse resistance of language to spelling reform. In the Shavian view, since a name is only a conventional label for a thing, there is no reason why cumbersome and irrational spellings should be retained. In the word "knife," for example, why not drop the *k* and the *e*? The answer is that the visual *k* plays an integral part in the organization of the meaning "knife." (I speculate that in my case my powers of formulation have construed the visual *k* as the handle of a knife with folding blades, etc.) The Shavian reformer who asks us to write "nif" instead of "knife" is not just dropping superfluous letters as he supposes: *he is asking us to reorganize our conception of knife!*

Of all words, proper names are perhaps the most intricately and irrevocably transfigured—because they are tailored not to the common features of a class of things but to an individual in all his uniqueness. We are familiar with those cases in which a name is so saturated with the personality of a boyhood friend or figure of literature that it is positively disqualified for any other use—"Elmer," "Maggie," "Barney." The first Ralph I know forever articulates the name "Ralph"—so that in a really extraordinary fashion the sound "Ralph" comes to represent a special quality of lankiness, of blond bumbling good nature, etc.

(But, one is apt to protest, this is all simply a matter of association! These names simply evoke certain recollections which have been habitually associated with them. This is undoubtedly true. But something else has happened. I am not concerned here with the process of association. I am concerned with the *change* in the word that has occurred in one's consciousness though this change may very well have come about through association. A metamorphosis has taken place. *The word itself has undergone a change in one's consciousness.* The original sound pattern has been totally lost to sight through its reorganization by meaning.)

An instructive example of the symbolic transformation is afforded by the evolution of the new, often compound, words of our technical era. When an entirely new invention comes along, what shall we call it? We are in the same position as Helen Keller after she had "caught on" to the symbolic orientation. In pre-symbolic cognition—animal sentience—the object which has no biological relevance for the organism—being neither food, nor enemy, nor sex object—is simply passed by and not known. But once Helen knew *what water was*, she had to know *what everything else was.* Herder contrasts the case of the man and the animal who are confronted with the biologically indifferent object—say a lamb passes before the eyes of a non-lamb-eating or a non-lamb-fearing animal—he would let it glide vaguely past because his instincts are not involved:

> But with man, not so! As soon as he is in a position to become acquainted with the lamb, there is no instinct to interfere with him... White, gentle, wooly—his mind in its conscious exercise seeks a characteristic for it—the lamb bleats! He has found the

> differentia. His inner sense is activated.... "Ah! You are the bleating one!" ...he feels that he has recognized in it *humanly*, has interpreted it, in that he knows it by a property.... By a property, then? And is that anything but by an inward *denoting* word? The sound of bleating, thus apprehended by a human being as the character of the sheep, became, through the medium of reflection, the *name* of the sheep, even though his tongue had never attempted to utter it. (quoted in Cassirer 1946, 29-30)

What shall we call the four-wheel thing that goes by itself? "Auto-mobile": self-goer. It is certainly true, as both Herder and Cassirer emphasize, that at first we know the thing by a particular property. But the question which remains is whether or not, once we have gained access to the thing through the instrument of the property and named it by a particular aspect, we continue to know it as such—or whether the name, no matter how arrived at or by what property, *then undergoes a total transformation*. For this crude and limping approximation—"auto-mobile" self-goer—is gradually impregnated and transformed until the two original symbols are fused into a single whole which comes to contain within itself the re-presented reality of the object (for whom does "automobile" still mean self-goer?). Once the lamb is named, by whatever limping device, once there is introduced into the cognitive tension the tiniest grain of fixed attribute, there will crystallize about it the whole sensuous reality of the object. (Compare "tele-vision" and "butter-fly" in which the original contributing symbols are "lost." Also compare "pocket-book": in its erroneous use to mean wallet, the "book" is totally submerged—it is with a slight shock that one comes to realize that "book" is part of the word.)

So also with holy words and obscene words: the word actually seems to merge with the thing—a state of affairs which Chase (1938) characteristically finds not interesting but reprehensible (63).

2. The Symbol Must Be *Unlike* the Thing

As we examine the conditions under which the symbolic transformation occurs, a remarkable fact comes to light. In order that a thing be known under the auspices of the symbol, it is necessary that it be *unlike* the symbol! One of the older theories of the origin of language was the imitative theory: that man first named things by uttering sounds that were *like* the object he saw. This is not only untrue but represents the one state of affairs under which symbolization could not occur. Language, as Sapir (1953) says, is what it is essentially, not because of its admirable expressive power but in spite of it (159-160). In Cassirer's (1953) words, "The aim of repetition lies in identity—the aim of linguistic designation lies in difference.... The more the sound resembles what it expresses; the more it continues to 'be' the other, the less it can 'signify' that other" (189).

The necessity of *unlikeness* becomes clearer when we consider the case of the wild boy Victor. The problem was to teach Victor to symbolize the glass of milk under the auspices of another sensuous content. Suppose Dr. Itard had used the perfect iconic symbol—a reproduction, a picture, a painted sculpture of the glass of milk—and apposed it in Victor's sight with the real thing. Now unquestionably Victor would have "seen" the similarity—it would presumably have been clear to him as it would in a fashion to a dog or a chimpanzee, that the two sensuous objects were "alike." But the imputed relation of quasi-identity would not have occurred—the glass of milk and its copy are and remain *two* things: the limit-situation which isomorphic symbolization tends to approach is *two* glasses of milk. One condition, among others, of Victor's sudden perception that this milk is *lait*, is that the sensuous *lait* be *different* from the milk.

An isomorphic copy cannot be transformed. It remains a copy. It is for this reason that the isomorphic symbol, the statue of Hermes, the univocal re-producing of Hermes feature by feature, is not only a poor example of symbol-formation but as such even inhibits the symbolic change.

Is this a clue to the ancient riddle about the conventionality or suitability of names? Is it not only the case that primary root names are conventional but that they *must* be conventional, that is, naturally *unlike* the thing named? The argument of the *Cratylus* seems to have been decided in modern linguistics in favor of the sophist Hermogenes who held that names are purely conventional (Plato

1892, paragraph 384)—though Jespersen (1949, 19) says that the question remains open. (See also Gray 1939, 14; Sapir 1921, 10.)

Cassirer (1953b), however, in his encyclopedic grasp of linguistic research, has called attention to the fact that in the most diverse language groups, certain phonemes, vowels and consonants, are used with great regularity to express certain qualities and relations. "Almost always *a, o, u* designate the greater distance, *e* and *i* the lesser.... In the same way certain consonants and consonantal groups are used as 'natural phonetic metaphors' to which a similar or identical significatory function attaches in nearly all language groups—e.g., with striking regularity the resonant labials indicate direction toward the speaker and the explosive linguals direction away from the speaker, so that the former appear as a 'natural' expression of the 'I', the latter of the 'Thou'" (193).

Is there, then, a possible third relation between symbol and thing, which is expressed neither by the category *like* nor *unlike*?

3. The Relation of Analogy

"Despite all change," remarks Curtius with regard to the Indo-Germanic languages:

> a conservative instinct is discernible in language. All the peoples of our family from the Ganges to the Atlantic designate the notion of standing by the phonetic group *sta*; in all of them the notion of flowing is linked with the group *plu*, with only slight modifications. This cannot be an accident. Assuredly the same notion has remained associated with the same sounds through all the millennia, because the peoples felt a certain *inner connection* [emphasis added] between the two, i.e., because of an instinct to express this notion by these particular sounds. The assertion that the oldest words presuppose some relation between sounds and the representations they designate has often been ridiculed. It is difficult, however, to explain the origin of language without such assumptions. In any case, the representation lives like a soul even in the words of far more advanced periods. (quoted in Cassirer 1953b, 191)

There arises, then, the possibility of a third relation—analogy, analogy in the classic sense as being something quite apart from similarity. The sound "sta-" is in no imaginable sense a re-presenting of the *act* of standing still—there could hardly be two things more different. Yet there must exist the possibility of an attributable analogy between the two which is not to be found between standing still and "plu-." The relation is similar to the psychological phenomenon of synesthesia, the trans-sensory analogy, in which, for example, certain colors are characteristically related to certain sounds. Could the color blue ever be denoted by the sound "yellow" or yellow by "blue"?

Perhaps it is possible tentatively to formulate one condition of symbolization—that the symbol be isomorphically unlike, yet retain the possibility of an attributed analogy.

What sort of analogical structures within the word are seized upon by the transforming power to articulate its meaning? It is impossible by the very nature of the process to do more than approximate it descriptively; but in the case of the adjective "limber," for example, one speculates: How does "limber" mean limber? One has the inkling that the two syllables are extremely important—they are the two segments into which the limber thing is divided by the bend. The *b*? This is the very point of the bending, the muted explosion of the *b* lending itself to resiliency, the *action* of the bend (the sharper explosion of a *p* would approach disjunction and breakage), etc. (Compare Max Picard's (1951) analysis (above) of *Baum* and *Himmel* with our tree and heaven (103).)

There suddenly opens before us the whole vast field of the operation of the symbol in art (see Part IV); in poetry, for example, the inefficacy of the isomorphic or dead metaphor in which the symbol is so thoroughly informed by the thing that its use is tautologous: "babbling brook," "flecks of foam"; the powerful effect of the unlike-but-analogous symbol, Empsons's ambiguous metaphor, which presents no clear univocal likeness yet offers vistas of possible analogies: "fiery floods," "thrilling region of thick-ribbed ice," "bushes of foam."

To dwell another moment in the region of metaphor—which at this point, admittedly, raises more questions than it answers—we may agree with Professor Richards (1950) that "the mind is a *connecting organ* [emphasis added]" (125). Its favorite task is the discernment of analogies. And its most fruitful accomplishment is the apposing of two things that are neither entirely alike nor entirely different, a tensional union in which new meaning is engendered. If they are univocally alike, we have the sterile coupling of thing and its copy from which no meaning can issue. On the other hand, if they are absolutely different, only bafflement can result. "As the two things put together are more remote, the tension created is, of course, greater. That tension is the spring of the bow, the source of the energy of the shot, but we ought not to mistake the strength of the bow for the excellence of the shooting; or the strain for the aim. And bafflement is an experience of which we soon tire, and rightly" (125).

To return to the aboriginal naming act: what we are particularly concerned with is the peculiar need and the peculiar satisfaction associated with linguistic symbolization. As Marcel (1951b) said, when I ask *what is that flower?* I am not really satisfied to be given a scientific classification of the flower—which seems to evade my question and to reduce the flower to something else. I am only satisfied to be told it is a lupin—even though the sound "lupin" may explain nothing at all about the flower—for now the singular existence of this particular flower seems to be validated (13). I would add: *especially* if the word "lupin" *explained* nothing. (We prescind for the moment from the decision as to whether this satisfaction is a remnant of word-magic or something else, that is, whether it is "legitimate" or "illegitimate.") What happens when the child asks *what is that?*, and upon being told, occupies himself endlessly in regarding the object and naming it: *ball?* He too is engaged in the mind's favorite task of determining *how* this object can "be" this sound "ball," in the search for the analogies between the one and the other and the articulation of the one to the other on the basis of the analogies. The task is consummated when the word is articulated by its meaning—when, as they are for us, "glass," "daisy," "green," are thoroughly informed by what they denote. The miracle of language is that, the semanticists to the contrary notwithstanding, the word does, in a sense to be determined, "become" the thing.

The three relations of likeness, unlikeness, and analogy may be represented diagrammatically.

LIKE

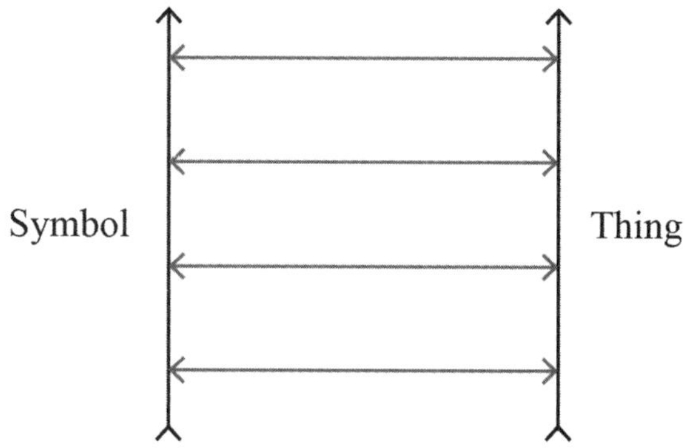

With the symbol and thing perfectly apposed, each feature of the thing finds its like in the symbol and the only semantic result is duplication. The wild boy Victor, confronted by a symbolic likeness of a glass of milk, sees *two* glasses of milk—

DIFFERENT

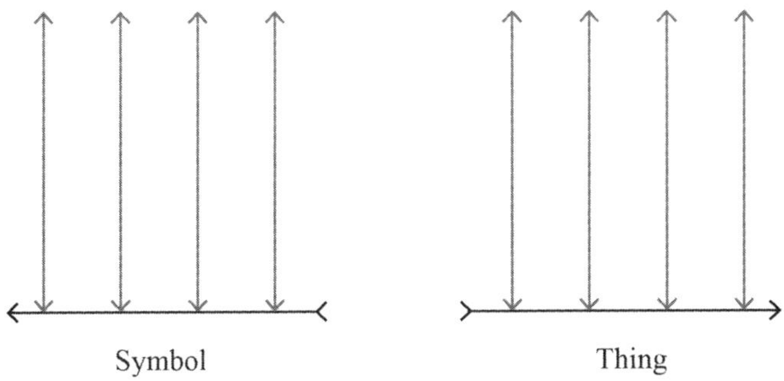

When symbol and thing are absolutely different, there is no opportunity for an interaction of experience radiations.

If I read *flesh is grass*, different as is flesh from grass, the mind casts about and hits on one or more possible analogies. But if you say *grass is buttons*, the result is apt to be bafflement (though not necessarily, for the mind's resources are almost infinite, and the most unlikely appositions can, under the influence of context, yield a rich harvest of meaning—see Richards's (1950) example of "bread" and "house" (126).)

One may call a tree a great many different things, as Gray (1939) points out, *Baum, arbor, dendron, crann, medis, kuoks, darakht,* etc. (14), but is it justifiable to conclude from this variety that names are purely conventional? As long as each one contains a possible analogy—and admittedly this allows a very large field—the symbol can be transformed. One may say *it rains* or *il pleut*, but the crucial question is whether one could ever say *it stans* and mean the same thing.*

* There are two levels of analogy in operation here. At the metaphorical level, *flesh is grass*, we are comparing two meanings. At the primitive naming level, however, *this is water*, we are apposing a sound to a percept.

ANALOGOUS

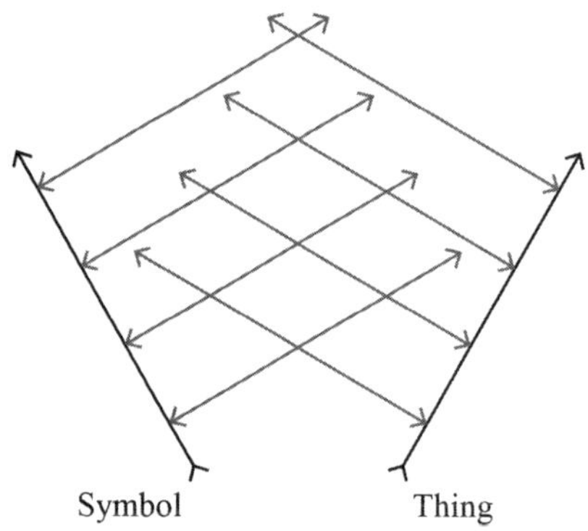

In the case of the true analogy, the mind is afforded space to articulate meaning. There is an interaction in which correspondencies are attributed. In lieu of space, in the apposition of likes, only reduplication can occur. With too much space, an absolute disassociation, nothing can occur.

4. The Vocable: The Perfect Symbolic Material

We have yet to treat, however, that peculiar property of the vocable, which makes it the perfect symbolic material. Anything can, under the proper conditions, become a symbol: a gesture, a written word, a public object such as a flag. But in each case, the symbol is perceived first as what it is in itself and only thereafter, and more or less laboriously, transformed into a symbol. The vocable, however, possesses the unique trait of being, like the others, a sensuous thing and yet at the same time a thing extremely difficult of characterization *in itself*. As Mrs. Langer (1953) points out, the more barren and indifferent the symbol, the greater its semantic power—a peach makes a very poor symbol (59-60). A word is itself utterly trivial. It is a naked structure of polarities and heterogeneities—a skeleton waiting to be fleshed. A phoneme is extremely difficult to isolate and examine. This elusiveness is undoubtedly due in part to its mode of generation: I utter it—it is literally under my nose—so close to me that I cannot, so to speak, get a good look at it. It possesses, if I may use a chemical figure, a very high combining power and is rarely found in its elemental state. Take the phoneme *rr* as in "berry." It is almost impossible to know this peculiar little sound for what it is by itself. We can isolate it from the word and try to examine it—but as soon as we do so, it takes refuge in the visual configuration—*rr* or *R*. It is only by peeling off these various guises, repeating it, studying the tongue positions, that one can get at this powerful little symbolific element and see it for what it is—hardly anything at all.

It is this naked structure of temporal polarities and heterogeneities which lends itself so readily to symbolic change. In primitive languages, the simple polarity of *reduplication* is susceptible to any number of meaning constructions. In Kwakiutl, reduplication can convey the diminutive, the idea of a playful performance of an activity, the endeavor to perform an action. Thus *gweg* is whale, *gwagwegim*, little whale, *gwagwek!a*, to endeavor to get a whale (Boas 1911).

It is illuminating to observe how one sensuous content can be differently transformed by different meanings, as, for example, the English word "stick": (1) the verb "stick," as to stick on: the vocable is informed by stickiness, the gluey side of adhesive tape; (2) the verb "stick," as to puncture: the vocable is informed by the action of point-insertion; (3) the noun "stick," as a stick of wood: vocable informed by hardness, brittleness, dryness, etc. It may even be surprising to realize that the three are one and the same word—in each case, the word has seemed rather specially suited to convey its meaning. (The relation of quasi-identity and the intentional transformation expressed in the proposition *this is a stick* will be compared below with the magic cognition of totemistic tribes who would say, for example, that *this nurtunja is an emu*, or *I am a parakeet*).

In the vocable, then, the transforming power of the symbolific function is provided a framework of polarities and heterogeneities in which it can detect analogies and on which it can deposit the living flesh of the word.

5. The Constituting Power of the Symbol

We have dealt thus far only with the organizing power of the thing, or rather one's conception of the thing, as it operates to transfigure the plastic material of the symbol. The question that remains to be asked is whether this is a unilateral action or whether the symbol itself makes a contribution.

The constituting power of the symbol is, of course, one of Cassirer's major themes:

> When, for example, we link a given intuition or idea with an arbitrary linguistic sound, we seem, at first sight, to have added nothing whatever to its content. And yet, on closer scrutiny, the content itself takes on a different "character" for consciousness through the creation of the linguistic sign: it becomes more definite. Its sharp and clear intellectual "reproduction" proves to be inseparable from the act of linguistic "production." For the function of language is not merely to *repeat* definitions and distinctions which are already present in the mind, but to formulate them and make them intelligible as such. Thus in every sphere, it is through the freedom of spiritual action that the chaos of sensory impressions begins to clear and take on fixed form for us. The fluid impression assumes form and duration for us *only when we mould it by symbolic action* [emphasis added]... All these spheres [the symbolic] have this in common: that *the product of their activity in no way resembles the mere material with which they began* [emphasis added]. (Cassirer 1953b, 106-7)

However much the word (or any other symbol) lends itself to an intentional transformation by our impression of the thing, the process is still a mutual interpenetration of symbol and impression. It remains a condition of symbolization that the impression must be re-presented within the confines of the word-gestalt. The meaning takes on an aspect of wholeness, separateness, autonomy—in short, thingness—which is at once the glory and the despair of human knowing.

For Cassirer (1953b), of course, the contribution of the symbol is decisive—it is the structure of the word, the art form, the rite, the scientific hypothesis, which imposes itself on the otherwise unknowable reality and makes it meaningful. The "symbolic transformation" is the rendering of the noumenon by the symbol. All of man's characteristic activities are symbolic constructions of the world. "Thus, with all their inner diversity, the various products of culture—language, scientific knowledge, myth, art, religion—become parts of a single great problem-complex: they become multiple efforts, all directed toward the one goal of transforming the passive world of mere *impressions*, in which the spirit seems at first imprisoned, into a world that is pure *expression* of the human spirit" (80-1). In the end, Cassirer takes his place as the last of the great Kantians.

Without pretending to offer a critique of Cassirer's idealism, I think it would not be presumptuous to say that the whole direction of Cassirer's effort lies in his analysis of the ways in which the *a priori* structure of the symbol informs that which is symbolized. In asking his crucial question, "How can a finite and particular sensory content be made into the vehicle of a general spiritual 'meaning'?" (93), and in replying in effect that it cannot—unless it, the symbol, itself *constitutes* the meaning—it seems to me that Cassirer has overlooked or disqualified the almost miraculous metamorphosis by which the symbol is informed by the impression. In Cassirer's view, the interpenetration of symbol and thing is almost entirely a one-way street; the thing is specified by the constituting power of the symbol. Cassirer thought that any alternative to his idealism must lead to skepticism because no matter how much the symbol is "like" the thing, it remains a copy and the best we can know is a copy. But what is not taken into account is that the transformation is above all *intentional*. The symbol is always a symbol *of* something and what we know is not the symbol but something *through* the symbol (an intentionality which even the Bantu recognizes: he would never try to drink the word "water," whatever other magic properties he may impute to it). In order to extend the Kantian *a priori* to the whole domain of man's symbolic activities, one is obliged to rule out the most extraordinary of all empirical findings: the process by which I reorganize the gesture into an intentional species of the thing. In Cassirer's view, nothing is actually *trans*formed: an unknown and unknowable something is merely given its *first* formulation. What Cassirer has left out, it seems inescapable to conclude, is nothing less than the symbolic transformation.

The relation of symbol to thing is, therefore, one of mutual articulation and interpenetration. The sensuous symbol offers itself as the vehicle of meaning and at the same time imposes its own unity and distinctness.

There emerges a reciprocating relationship of contributions, a polar scale of meanings in which, as one component diminishes, the other increases. At one extreme—in the small linguistic area to which we have limited ourselves—is the concrete word with its adequate and familiar reference "glass," in which there is a wonderful re-presentation of the thing by its symbol. (Here we are dealing, of course, with the singular *conception*, not with the universal definatory *concept*; the relation between the symbol and the idea, the higher abstractive process, we have deliberately avoided.) At the other extreme is the word which symbolizes a remote or an obscure or a complex or an abstract or a nonexistent referent—and here one cannot fail to agree with Chase, Ogden and Richards, Ritchie and all the other prosecutors of human stupidity—words such as "democracy," "Christianity," "Classicism," "Chinese," "leprosy," all too often operate not as miraculous vehicles of meaning but as dense impenetrable husks, the "simulacra" of Marcel. For, referent or no referent, the symbol will organize itself, and in lieu of adequate referential data, it will make use willy-nilly of anything at all, suck in any available adventitia [medicine: corrective tissue], to construct its meaning.

6. Man's Knowledge Is neither Angelic nor Behavioral, but Symbolic

The great vista which begins to open before us is the inkling that we know nothing directly and of itself—the "angelic knowledge" of Maritain—but only through the mirrors of *something else*. "The representation of one content in and through another is an essential premise for the structure and formal unity of consciousness" (Cassirer 1953b, 105). An analysis of symbolic meaning illustrates how, at even its most primitive level, man's orientation to the world is both sacramental and anagogic—that when he knows, he knows through the mediation of sensibles, things; that he knows higher things through lower things.

The positivists' warfare against "identification" results from a confusion of the orders of epistemology and logic, or rather from an ignorance of the former. At the propositional level, as Veatch (1953) points out there is a "confusion of the structure of the intended object with [that] of the intending instrument" (188). *That is a daffodil* expresses an identification and a transformation: this is "wrong" if it be taken to mean that the word is the same as the thing (though who on earth ever took it so?); it is right if it be taken—as who can fail to take it—as an instrument through which the object daffodil is intended to be what it is. The human way of knowing, of possessing things in an intentional mode, *in alio esse*, is one of identification. "What precisely is the nature of an intentional relation? The answer we would like to suggest, albeit with some diffidence, is that this relation is always a relation of identity" (186).

In Allen Tate's (1953) words, "the symbolic imagination takes rise from a definite limitation of human rationality which was recognized in the West until the 17th Century; in this view the intellect cannot have direct knowledge of essences" (37).

[The empiricist error] is the magic epistemology from Locke to Korzybski—in which one is presumed somehow to have conscious thoughts and later to assign them labels. "Man, though he has a great variety of thoughts, and such from which others, as well as himself, might receive profit and delight; yet they are all within his own breast, invisible and hidden from others, nor can of themselves be made to appear. The comfort and advantage of society not being to be had without communication of thoughts, it was necessary that man should find out some external sensible signs, whereof those invisible ideas which his thoughts are made up of, might be made known to others" (Locke 1824, 48). Korzybski (1950) remarks "Fido abstracts objects from events, and... if his nervous system is similar to ours, his lower order abstractions are similar to ours" (395). Moreover he notes "that Fido does abstract from events, at any rate, in lower orders, 'has objects' (O_a) which he can recognize" (392). Both Locke and Korzybski would have us believe that we somehow know what things are, are conscious of them, that we know, think, recognize—and only as a matter of convenience apply words and use language.

This approach is typical of the positivist technique of playing both ends against the middle. We are dealing at one moment with a behaviorist science of meaning in which the organism is studied in a causal-adaptive nexus—on the other, we suddenly find ourselves studying conscious humans who know what things are, recognize them, distribute labels among them, and commit enormous follies in so doing.

There is another alternative besides the adaptive sign "knowledge" of pragmatics and the immediate knowledge of the angels (and semanticists)—and it is not necessarily the private dreams of idealism. The great gap in the middle—the genesis and development of symbolization—is ignored, in the hope that, by the one or the other approach, it can be conjured away. It is the purely human way of knowing which is bound to the senses and yet oriented to truth—in which "nature offers... clearly denotable objects in depth and in the round, which yield analogies to the higher syntheses" (Tate 1953, 38).

CHAPTER III

MAGIC COGNITION I: FORMATION OF THE SIMULACRUM

Most textbooks of logic distinguish two mental processes: one, the operation of the reason by which exact definatory concepts are arrived at and combined in propositional form; two, a more or less marginal activity, referred to variously as sensible representation, image, conception, and so on. The former is considered to be the instrument of our thinking. It is by abstraction and discursive combination that we arrive at universal concepts, make judgments about them, and communicate them to others. The latter is generally looked upon as a sort of private phantasmagoria, a vague and fleeting imagery that is evoked by word and thought and that varies from person to person. Nearly always described in pictorial language, it is usually regarded as at most an aid, a very dubious aid, to reason.

The discovery of the all-pervasive character of the symbolic transformation, however, sheds a new light on this latter "representational" component—or rather suggests a third mode of cognition that is representational in character but that is bound up with meaning in a far more intimate and radical fashion than is indicated by the usual descriptions of "evocation of fleeting images." It is undeniable that by the abstractive and discursive process we arrive at exact definatory concepts and propositions by which our meaning can be communicated to others. It is also undeniable that words "call up" imaginal elements, which are likely to be peculiar to us and changeable. But the possibility now arises whether there is not also configured intentionally in the word itself (and in the proposition, as we shall see in the next chapter) a species of meaning that—unlike the purely discursive understanding, an operation that is optional and effortful, really an exercise—is *immediately, passively,* and *necessarily* transmitted with every exchange of symbols.

Figurational meaning must be considered under two aspects. One, what light does it shed on error, that is, the magic cognition of both primitive and modern? Two, what is its role, if any, in the highest operations of the intellect, in the attainment of *truth*? Is it the stepsister of reason, a primitive remnant—and the sooner gotten rid of, the better? Or is it the means, the indispensable means, by which we approach being in the existential judgment?

In view of our almost involuntary splitting of the life of the mind into its rational ("true") components and its imaginative (more or less "untrue") components, it is interesting to note that St. Thomas (Aquinas 1922), following Aristotle, declared unequivocally that it is impossible for our intellect to understand anything except by turning to "phantasms." Modern Thomists, moreover, are increasingly aware that the purely rationalistic metaphysics of Christian Wolff is alien to the teaching of the Common Doctor. Frederick Wilhelmsen (1954) writes: "Existence is attained immediately in the judgment; but the judgments necessarily entail the use of phantasms, and, except in direct judgments of existing material things, the phantasms employed are symbolic. The philosopher must go through the phantasm to reach being" (41). What remains to be determined, however, is the relation of the phantasm to symbolic figuration and its precise role in meaning. Is it a sort of crutch to which one has recourse in difficulties, or is it the very soul and life of the human way of knowing? Moreover, what interests us immediately is a subject with which St. Thomas did not, characteristically, concern himself: the anatomy of error. Can a study of the symbolic function lead to a systematization of that most unsystematic of all things: untruth? In this connection, Father George Klubertanz (1953) has opened a promising avenue of investigation by suggesting, if I understand him correctly, that understanding through pure "symbolic phantasms" as occurs, for example, in unintelligent memorizing, constitutes a definite, if inferior, *mode* of knowing (193).

1. The Figured Meaning within the Word

But to return to the homely example of the linguistic symbol. We have seen that in at least some words—Picard's "darlings of the word-soul" (1951, 103)—there is configured *within the word* a certain characteristic pattern of the thing which is symbolized. In the words "grass," "plum," "peak," "book," "girl," "sheet," for example, by a sort of rude and involuntary abstraction, I divine within a typical class member, a certain sensible essence, which I articulate within the symbol. "Girl" sounds like girl. It is, moreover, a *common sensible*, comprising elements contributed by more than one sense: in the case of "plum," I utilize a texture, slickness-over-plumpness, a color, a convexity, etc.—all of which are united organically in the symbol "plum." In the case of the proper name "Ralph," some indefinable but perfectly definite quality, a mysterious individual essence, as it were, is extracted from the manifold of sensory impressions which make up my experience of Ralph, and sustained almost like a living thing within the medium of his name. In the class name, "grass," certain qualities possessed in common (by the grasses I have known) are abstracted and the individual variations omitted. But symbolic abstraction is quite different from conceptual abstraction. My figuration of the word "grass"—which is involuntary and inescapable, be it noted: I have a conception of grass, *despite* myself—is apt to be quite different, if I live in Santa Fe, from your figuration of grass if you have always lived in Kentucky. So that when we talk casually about grass, we do not have quite the same thing in mind. If, however, a New Mexican and Kentuckian botanist speak together of grass, they will have defined their terms so that the class name "grass" will denote exactly the same thing. We will have established a plant class on the basis of structural and physiological considerations—a grouping, moreover, which may well include some bamboo-like plants, which are quite ungrasslike. We will agree to include these latter, even though one may experience a figurative dislocation in so doing: "but this is not grass!" (though later it shall be—by a gradual articulation I shall at last be able to conceive bamboo as grass; the bamboo will receive a new formulation and so will the symbol "grass").

2. The All-or-None Law of Symbolic Meaning

We could dwell endlessly on the mysterious and elusive, but nonetheless real, process by which the sensible symbol becomes transformed by its meaning—in those cases of "adequate" reference when there is actually grass within our experience from which a common sensible can be abstracted. But what of those symbols that denote something complex or obscure or remote or abstract or even nonexistent, instances in which no common sensible is available to articulate the meaning? Does the symbolic transformation wait upon an adequate reference, or is the symbol transformed willy-nilly, reference or no reference? If so, what principles govern this transformation? Is it possible to discern *a priori* categories of symbolic meaning, constitutive principles of formulation to which the name *a priori* could be given with far more justification than to the canons of discursive thought? It shall be possible, as we shall see, to enunciate first of all a general all-or-none law of symbolic construction. Everything in the world is either construed as something or is simply not known, passed over—and all symbols become totally organized or they are not symbols. The scientist by a considerable effort may delineate certain areas where his knowledge is defective—he may become aware of his own ignorance—but in the child, in the primitive, and in our everyday mode of knowing, the world is *totally* formulated; the symbols we exchange are totally organized. The organization of the symbol will not be postponed until adequate referential data is available, but proceeds irrepressibly under the presiding influence of context and similarity.*

* A good example of this is the willy-nilly construing by the old-type (and perhaps stereotyped) Negro of all expressions beyond his immediate ken. It is related that during the First World War an officer came upon a small group of Negro soldiers taking their ease under a shady tree:

"What are you men supposed to be doing?"

"We's a liais'n [liaison] detail," one replied.

The French genetic psychologist Jean Piaget (1955) has shown that when children are given a sentence with an unknown word, they are not aware that they do not know the word. Instead they simply construe it according to the context of the sentence (164). It is taken to fill whatever gap that remains to be filled and is transformed accordingly. *There are no gaps in figuration.*

The question is this: How can one and the same process, the uniquely human symbolic function, be both the indispensable means of arriving at the truth and also the snare by which we fall prey to error? We have alluded in passing to the possible role of figurational meaning in discursive thought. The laws of discursive thought have been under intensive study for more than two thousand years. What are the laws of figurative "thought"?

It is possible to distinguish at least three moments in the development of symbolic awareness. In pre-symbolic sentience, as so dramatically set forth by Helen Keller and more learnedly by the German philosopher Herder, one does not, humanly speaking, "know" that which is not symbolized. One is oriented to the world in the mode of biological adaptation. That which is biologically relevant one responds to discriminately, and the joy-fear manifestation is taken to be a reliable index of the biological significance of the thing for the organism; that which is not biologically relevant is simply passed by, not even "known" by the ordinary signification reaction of animals.

The advent of symbolic awareness introduces, as we have seen (Part II, Chapter I), new elements into the cognitive structure. There is a sudden awareness of something *as* something. And an indispensable condition of this new awareness is the coming into being of a relation that we have called intersubjectivity. Associated with this unprecedented state of affairs is an equally unprecedented joy, which no longer stands in a relation to the biological significance of that which

---

"Then why don't you get to it?"
"That's what we's doin'—just liais'n around."

is symbolized but is rather associated with the joint discovery and affirmation of the thing, its co-celebration as being what it is under the auspices of the symbol.

What happens to this aboriginal intersubjective-awareness-in-joy? Does the world around continue to be enjoyed as a sort of preternatural garden of delights, in which the homeliest thing remains as it was when we first knew it, an inexhaustible source of wonder and communion? Or in a more properly empirical language: what happens to the "autonomous... object interest" which Schachtel (1954) observed in children (318)?

That it does not last is, sadly, a fact which need not detain us. What rather concerns us is the tracing out of the change in the triadic communion of I, Thou, and Thing. What happens, phenomenologically speaking, in the deterioration of the aboriginal symbolic awareness? What is the term of the deterioration? This line of inquiry leads directly into a consideration of that peculiarly human trait, the dark companion of intersubjective joy: boredom. It is a favorite theme of the existentialists, but we shall be less interested in phenomenological mood descriptions than in a study of the structural changes that take place among the elements of the meaning situation.

It will be revealing to reconsider the extraordinary question *what is that?*—which, as Marcel saw, takes us straight to the mysterious heart of language. What, exactly, is the meaning of this question? What do I really want to know when, under certain circumstances, I put this question rather sharply to my companion? What is the origin of my need and the source of its satisfaction?

To vary Marcel's figure slightly: Let us suppose that one has developed an interest in birds and finds it a pleasant pastime to watch several common species feed at a window station, say cardinals, sparrows, and jays. Then one day a newcomer arrives, an unknown species. One thing is to be noticed at once: *there is a powerful tendency to construe the stranger as one of the familiar species.* If he bears any resemblance at all to a jay, it will be probably seen as a jay—albeit with varying degrees of dissatisfaction. What is almost impossible of human achievement is to see something strange as what it is in itself.

Even the wildest approximation-by-construction is more tolerable than the direct confrontation of the totally new—witness the variety of versions of a strange sea-creature; it is easier to see it as a mermaid than what it actually is. But suppose that the new bird is sufficiently unlike one of the others so that, to the interested observer, it simply cannot pass as one of them. Something peculiar happens. There arises in the beholder a remarkable malaise. It is a disability-before-the-thing which in the case of bird watching is a very small thing indeed but which, in other circumstances, can amount to acute anxiety: the uncanny feeling one experiences when confronted with something which is absolutely unconstruable. (Here is clearly exemplified the all-or-none law of symbolic construction: the new thing is either known, if it is a sparrow or jay or cardinal, or not known. Unless it is startlingly different, it simply disappears into the nearest symbolic category. Similarly, the native, when questioned by the botanist about the most varied plant life, replies, "Oh, that's a bush"—unless it yields a drug or a poison, etc.—because he does in fact see all bushes as alike. It is when the strange thing cannot be so disposed of or ignored that the potent all-or-none law is thwarted, and anxiety ensues.)

It is at this point that the bird-watcher puts the mysterious question and puts it rather importunately: *what is that bird?* What does he want to know? He will be impatient with certain kinds of answers, even though these answers are "right." If his ornithologist friend should, by way of a reply, give him an exact classification of the bird based on anatomical structure, etc., the bird-watcher will be disappointed. He is likely to repeat his question: "Yes, yes. Very interesting. But *what is it?*" Suppose now that his friend gives him a name, but a descriptive name, one denoting certain obvious traits. "It's a blue-gray gnatcatcher." The fact is that the bird-watcher will still be impatient. He will probably accept the name—what else can he do?—but his abiding protest, if he dared to speak it aloud, might be: "Any fool can see that it is blue-gray and that it catches gnats. What I want to know is—*what is it?*" What does he really hope to hear? The source of his dissatisfaction is that these proximate names do not seem to do the bird the same justice as the splendid names "sparrow," "jay." If his friend should reply, however, "That's a towhee," the situation is different. "A what?" "A towhee—T-O-W-H-E-E." "Ah, so that's what it is," replies the bird-watcher, ruminating, "towhee." (It is better at this point not to tell him that the mysterious name towhee is only an inept approximation of the bird's call.) There is then set in motion the mind's favorite project, that of connecting: one's task now—and it is what one wanted to do all along—is to see *how* this bird can be a "towhee." The bird, for the first time, is sanctioned and by the apposition of its symbol provided the space and the structure within which it may articulate itself.

The mania for naming among all sorts of collectors has often been observed and usually referred to in disparaging terms—as though one knew any more about the bird for having named it! And especially in the case of an uninformative name! But in a sense one does know more, and *especially* in the case of the uninformative or obscure name! For one has been given an obscure *something*, which he can set up alongside the obscure bird, enabling an interaction to occur. The various "unknown" features of the bird are given a means of formulation. As Wilhelmsen (1954) writes: we don't grasp being directly—we sidle up to it (40). We make casts in its direction with the symbol. Most important of all, the symbol must occupy the same ontological status as the bird. It is not a modifier of the bird but is a something with which the bird can be intentionally identified. To say that the bird is a blue-gray gnatcatcher is to say no more than that the bird is blue-gray and catches gnats. Only a color and a habit of the bird are affirmed. But to say *that bird is a towhee*—a "wrong" identification—is to affirm the being of the bird itself.

A period of connecting and articulating follows in which the bird gradually "becomes" a *towhee*, even as that bird is a *sparrow*. It is during this period of articulation that the bird is "open" to our study. It is for a time an object of interest. (So also is any newly discovered species, new element, or new disease—for a time the new entity is "open" to us in a way in which sparrow, or oxygen, or nephritis is not—though it does not necessarily follow that everything is known about these latter.)

In the third stage, that of completed symbolic formulation, what does it mean to say that we know *what something is?* What the new bird is, even as the other is a sparrow?

3. The Symbol-Thing Complex

There occurs an interaction between symbol and thing (or rather my conception of the thing) toward the end that the latter becomes organized into a discrete tightly-knit *whole*. It is of the nature of symbolic formulation that it achieves completion and closure. There results a spurious fullness of knowledge in which the thing is regarded as having been completely disposed of through its formulation by symbol. The end-product is a tight complex in which symbol and conception interpenetrate and mutually reinforce each other to the exclusion of new data. This system is characteristically closed so that when the thing in question is experienced anew, it is simply referred to this system, by which act of reference the thing is considered to be taken care of.

Thus the sparrow. Once the new bird is identified as a sparrow, that is, in a sense, the end of the bird. The singular living creature is completely swallowed up in the symbol-conception complex. A particular trait of the bird, its bill, its mode of flight, tends no longer to be available to us; we are deprived of a direct gaze at it because the creature has been claimed, parts and whole, by the symbol-conception complex. The bird-watcher shrugs: "It's just a field sparrow"—and that is the end of it.

The paradox that that which is best known is in a sense least known is of little moment in the case of the sparrow. It is of far greater moment—and interest—in the case of other projects of identification, for example, in medical diagnosis. A disease entity, once it has been isolated by its particular medical genius and once the period of "openness" and novelty is past (a period when the profession eagerly contributes every sort of data to its proper formulation and for a while the journals are full of it), assumes inevitably a dense and spurious reification. Thus when a patient is examined and certain signs and symptoms noticed, an extraordinary shift of attention occurs. The patient "has," we will say, Tay-Sachs Disease. At first, he himself is examined minutely, then when the diagnosis is made, by a kind of irresistible suction, one's attention is pulled from him to the entity, *Tay-Sachs Disease*. It is thenceforward only with the greatest difficulty that one can see the patient as a fellow human being to whom something is happening; rather is he seen as someone who is participating in, or even captured by, *something else*. He has, in a sense, disappeared into his own disease. Characteristically, he becomes known throughout the hospital as a "case of Tay-Sachs Disease."

He is the great physician who is able to see his patient both essentially and existentially—as one "having" a disease which may be expected to follow a certain course within broad limits, but also as one to whom something is happening, a unique action that is in no way influenced by a textbook entity but is determined solely by the here-and-now interaction of patient and disease agent. As a great French physician put it: "There is no such thing as diseases, only men who have them."

Stuart Chase (1938) said of Ogden and Richards's triangle: "There is great activity on the left side of the triangle—from reference to symbol and back to reference again" (98). We would further specify the nature of this activity. It is not a linear action and reaction, as a behaviorist semiotic would require, but rather an organic union in which symbol and "reference" are united in a *whole:* the symbol-conception complex.

The upshot is that this dense, almost impenetrable, reification is global—everything in the word as experienced tends so to be rendered: not only "democracy," "spirit," "fascism," whose referents are in question, but "sparrow," "William," "grape," whose referents are perfectly definite. In most discussions of the symbol, there is generally exempted, as a great area of non-symbolic activity, the direct observation of things and the judgment of existing material things. This is highly questionable. Our naïve-realistic view to the contrary notwithstanding, one never sees the familiar thing for quite what it is. That oak, that chair, I *construe* as being something through an intentional identification which constitutes recognition. And in so doing I inevitably give it the impress of my construction, a kind of discreteness, wholeness, autonomy, which operates not only as a means of knowing but also as a means of concealment. That familiar objects tend to be encrusted by a symbolic simulacrum is dramatically attested by the experience of *rediscovering* a common thing—as Prince Andrey in *War and Peace* rediscovered clouds as he lay wounded on the field of Austerlitz. (See below.)

4. The Thingification of All Reality

As the result of the rendering of all experience through symbol-conception complexes, there tends to be bestowed upon everything, not only a spurious discreteness but a spurious similarity. We come to dwell in a kind of gallery of things in which literally *everything* has been ordered to the same genus, symbol-thing. Through a process somewhat like the composing of a newspaper page in which all events, no matter how diverse, are shaped by the same generic die—headline-and-story—the world too tends to become ordered as Alice's catalogue of items: shoes and ships and sealing wax. Besides cabbages and kings, there are also: Abraham Lincoln, Saturday night, being, proportional representation, want, Einstein's theory, the Presbyterian Church, Maggie and Jiggs, Bonny Scotland, bee-keeping, triangle, neurosis, height, to be or not to be, Buick, Genesis, force, button, having.*

These are the simulacra of Marcel, the dense clots which impede rather than facilitate thought. The very means by which we know are the same means by which we fall prey to ignorance. Two remedies have suggested themselves to the existentialists: avoiding the tired old husks of words altogether and making new words (Heidegger) or, by a deliberate effort, breaking through the simulacra and recovering the meaning of old words like "being" and "having" (Marcel). In any case,

* The game Twenty Questions is made possible because everything in the world and even some things that do not exist are given the same stamp of thingness and put in the same museum of things.

no formula will serve to correct an inescapable condition of human knowing. The only remedy of passivity and stasis is activity and freedom.

5. Meaning Formation without Reference

If it is true that familiar objects, qualities, actions, tend to become organized in closed systems, a common sensible which is ever more tightly organized under the auspices of the symbol—if this occurs in the case of the things we know first-hand—*what are the principles of organization when no common sensible is available*, when the referent is at some distance, either by being complex, physically remote, abstract, or nonexistent? Is it possible to approach by degrees a pure *a priori* of symbolic formation?

If we compare the following terms, we will see at once the difference between the order of logic and the order of figuration: logically, each pair (except the last) belongs to the same class, a classification which holds good regardless of the point of reference; figuratively, however, a pair may belong to quite different categories, a difference which depends entirely on the point of reference.

grass
veldt

buttermilk
breadfruit

Georgia
Egypt

Alice McGruder (if I know an Alice McGruder)
George Washington

oxygen
phlogiston

"Grass," "buttermilk," "Alice McGruder" are symbols which have been formulated by a common sensible extracted first-hand. "Egyptian," "veldt," "George Washington" are also tightly configured symbols—but configured by what? "Egyptian," we will immediately perceive to be a closely-knit gestalt comprising familiar second-hand elements: there enters into it a certain archaic hair style, a geography-book drawing of a tomb figure in silhouette, encyclopedia photographs of pyramids and sphinx, a Hollywood version of Cleopatra and Nile, and so on. "George Washington" is inevitably configured by Trumbull's portrait, crossing-the-Delaware, school-room odor, a pageantry-action of cutting down cherry tree, etc. "Veldt" is perhaps given substance by two associated complexes, "felt" and "velvet"—the point is, one has, *despite oneself*, a totally formed conception of the "veldt," so that upon seeing it for the first time, one is bound to be surprised: "So *that* is what the veldt is!" (not a felt-and-velvet field). "Breadfruit" I must necessarily conceive as a remarkable edible with a plumlike skin and a cornbread interior. If, however, I go to Pago Pago, the two complexes "bread" and "fruit" will gradually be submerged by the one symbol "breadfruit" which in turn will be informed by *what breadfruit actually is.*

A principle of operation begins to be clear. The symbolic formulation will, in lieu of a first-hand referent, *make use of whatever adventitial elements are at hand.* The formulative suction is absolutely indiscriminate and unscrupulous. The conception articulated by the symbol "George Washington" is formed not by an inner quality of the person (as in "Alice McGruder"), *but by the media through which the person is transmitted!*—the odor of book, two-dimensional pictures, etc. It is the irony of the passively received education that what will be apprehended is not the thing which is taught but the paraphernalia of teaching. The vehicle transmits not its passenger but only itself. It is not the poetry of Shakespeare which is committed to memory, but a certain-kind-of-print-on-a-certain-texture-of-paper-all-pervaded-by-the-personality-of-Miss-Hawkins. A day will perhaps come when modern theories of education will be judged extraordinarily naïve in their assumption that education can be transmitted by a technique and an apparatus and that the child distinguishes as does his teacher between technique and content. The likelihood is rather that the reverse takes place: that it is the technique and apparatus which is transmitted and not the content.

In the absence of first-hand referential material, the symbolic construction will make use of anything else that is available. There is no such thing as symbolic ignorance. Everything is, by hook or crook, formulated and totally formulated. Nor is the total absence of a referent a deterrent to formulation. "Phlogiston," the "humours," formulate a something-to-do-with-fire or blood, in terms of which the Western world thought for a thousand years (and perhaps also "force," "energy"?). It becomes such a solid quasi-entity that our thinking about fire is quite literally inconceivable without it—and it takes the rarest kind of genius and the fiercest of efforts to dispossess it.

The powerful concealing effect of symbolic formulation by adventitial elements is dramatically illustrated by the concealment of even the iconic symbol. The crucifix, for example: It is all but impossible for the Westerner, believer or unbeliever, to see it simply as what it represents, a dying man hanging from a piece of wood. A child can see it plainly (at first); a saint can see it; the ordinary believer can occasionally catch a glimpse of it. But by and large, it is irresistibly configured by the immediately experienced data associated with a certain referential point of view: popery-monkery-fetish or schoolroom-holy pictures-Sister-Anthony-rosary. In either case, the extraordinary consequence is that even the patent iconic symbol becomes all but invisible under the simulacrum of passive formulation. A man hanging from a piece of wood is seen as everything but what he actually is—in this sense the passive believer shares the same disability as the unbeliever—a pious simulacrum can be quite as impenetrable as a hostile one. One remembers Chesterton's remark that a Mongolian peasant is more open to Christianity than the Westerner who inherits his religion as a piece of cultural furniture.

In contrast to and as a remedy for the passive mode of figuration, there can occur a discovery of the existential object *through* the medium of the symbol. By means of an optional and an effortful activity, the simulacrum can be penetrated and the referent restored to the realm of the existential object in all its inexhaustibility. If I read a good biography of Washington, the source of my suddenly aroused interest is my discovery of him as a fellow human being subject to all the frailties and glories of the human condition so that his achievements appear extraordinary. Before, they had not: Crossing-the-Delaware had been taken to occur in a magic-pageantry mode; now it is seen to have occurred in the mode of a free action subject to all the perils of my own free actions. So with the saint and the symbol of the God-man. It is a paradox that insofar as the religious symbol is allowed to slip away into the zone of the "religious"—a dissociated realm of activity where only "religious" things happen—it loses its meaning for us.

The passive historical transmission is of its nature self-defeating. The past must be constantly recaptured. St. Francis, the man, tends to vanish, unless we reach for him, inside an attractive lay figure, a piece of garden statuary, who performed quaint miracles and had a way with birds.

6. The Recovery of Being from the Simulacrum

There begins to be delimited two ways of knowing—in both of which figuration is indispensable but distinguishable accordingly as passive figuration is allowed domination or as it is employed as a means of knowing, subserved to a free effortful activity. The "authentic" moment is the intersubjective celebration of the object as what it is, and is exemplified both by the aboriginal discovery of the object (Helen Keller and the water), but also by its belated recovery from its own simulacrum. There are the memorable moments when, under special circumstances (usually that of ordeal), a man is vouchsafed a fresh glimpse of the common thing. A sparrow, for example, which during the whole of one's life was simply referred to the symbol-thing system, which in turn claimed it and disposed of it, can, in a kind of revelation, be seen for what it really is. To the sick man, the exile, the prisoner, the contemplative, living his solitary life month after month, the sparrow nesting at his window is apt to become all at once a source of inexhaustible wonder. As he gazes at the little creature, his eyes seem to penetrate layer after layer of symbolic guise until there begins to be revealed—what? Prince Andrey, lying wounded on the field of Austerlitz, is suddenly lost in wonder at something he had seen all his life and yet never seen: the clouds drifting across the sky. The man who is recovering from a near-fatal heart attack suddenly sees his own hand, turns it this way and that, astonished by its perfection and intricacy. It is characteristic of these "glimpses," moreover, that they are always attended by a restoration of comradeship with others. The intersubjectivity of the original meaning-structure is recovered. The source of wonder entails by its very nature a need to be shared.

7. The Deterioration of Intersubjectivity and the Outsider "I"

In contrast to this aboriginal or belated mode of cognition, in the description of which we find ourselves resorting over and over again to the expressions "intersubjectivity," "discovery," "openness," "wonder," "authentic," "celebration," "activity," etc., we can delineate a cognitive relation which is perhaps best regarded as the term of deterioration of the former. With it we characteristically associate "boredom," "closedness," "simulacrum," "passivity," etc. The limit of decay of the I-Thou-Thing communion is the everyday Ego-Object relation which is so vividly set forth in the existentialists' descriptions of the "inauthentic" mode of existence. In this dichotomy, there is the world: a gallery of dense entities, in which everything, person and object alike, receives the same generic stamp of solid thingness—*with one huge exception*. Everything is something, but *what am I?* By an ironic twist, the formulative process which, left to itself, will divide and dispose of the whole world as a sort of wax-works of symbolic forms, *cannot dispose of itself!* That which symbolizes remains at the center of things as a gaping hole among forms: the aching wound of self (Marcel), the Nought (Sartre). In what can only be described as a fall, a falling prey to (Heidegger's *Verfallen*), I, who in my most authentic relation to the world, am a co-celebrant of being, become a despairing specter, a that-which-does-not-know-what-it-is, an emptiness amid a world of replete entities. It is the peculiar trait of one's self, that if it tries to grasp its own existence as a *what* in the same way as it succeeds in grasping other "things," it will inevitably fall prey to impersonations. One tries in the inauthentic mode of existence to "be" something else. *It may be of my essence*, as Marcel (1951b) puts it, *to be able to be not what I am* (13). The motto for the plight of the self surrounded by a gallery of dense symbol-thing entities is: this is water, that is a chair, you are Ralph, but *what am I?* Sartre's dichotomy of being, the being-for-itself, the Nought, the *passion inutile*, and the Being-in-itself, the sodden passivity of things, is thus not really an ontology but a masterly analysis of a term of deterioration.

CHAPTER IV

MAGIC COGNITION II: THE LAW OF PARTICIPATION

If it is possible to single out the symbol function as that which, empirically speaking, most patently sets man apart from the rest of the animals, it is also possible to delineate two distinctively human ways of knowing, in each of which the symbol plays an integral role and which are themselves distinguishable according to the degree pure symbolic constructions dominate the life of the mind or as they serve as instruments of the reason. Failure to recognize the all-pervasive, all-construing life of the symbolic imagination must necessarily lead to an equivocal view of man in which he is conceived from two entirely different and even mutually exclusive points of view—as object man and subject man, as organism adapting to an environment and as symbol-mongerer dealing in propositions. At one moment, as we view man as the object of an empirical science, we conceive him as a biological unit, equipped with highly-organized neurological equipment, to be sure, but reacting according to the universal canons of adaption and instrumentality. But in the next breath we are just as apt—especially if we are scientists, mathematicians, logicians—to be speaking to each other in terms of highly abstract formulae which bear a truth-falsehood relation to the world. We regard data-man as *animal adaptabile*, but we ourselves, knower-man, are *animal rationale.* Moreover, as logicians, whether positivist or scholastic, we tend to think of the discursive function to the exclusion or denigration of all else—of man as a sort of angelic calculator whose proper task, the spinning out of symbols into propositions and formulae, is performed *in vacuo* with little or no relation to the manifold life of figuration, of poetry and dreams. It is extremely hard to give man his middle place. Even the semioticist, who in his pragmatics makes sure to put him with the animals, elevates him to the angels in his semantics. This narrow view of man, which allows only one kind of knowledge, the discursive knowledge of propositions, not only overlooks the non-discursive but "true" knowledge of the art form, but misses the whole mysterious realm of "false" knowing to which man falls prey in pure symbolic constructions (Langer 1951, 63-83).

1. Two Modes of Thought: Logic Sign and Magic Sign

This division into two distinct modes of knowing we would take to correspond roughly with what Maritain (1948b) calls the two regimes of the life of the mind, "logic sign" and "magic sign"—the first embracing, not merely the discursive use of the symbol but "the whole luminous and regular life of the intellect," imagination fused with and regulated by reason; the other, the nocturnal and magic cognition of dreams, of childhood, of the primitive:

> In giving to the word "logic" a very broad and rather infrequent usage, but a usage which seems to me justified, I describe sign as a "logical sign," or a sign in the sphere of the Logos, when it is located in a certain functional status, wherein it is a sign *for the intelligence* (speculative or practical) taken as the *dominant factor* of the psychic regime or the regime of culture.... I describe sign as a "magical sign," or as a sign in the sphere of the Dream, when it is located in another functional status, wherein it is a sign *for the imagination* taken as a supreme arbiter or *dominant factor* of all psychic life or of all the life of culture. Whether the sign in itself be sensory or intelligential, it is then definitely addressed to the powers of the imagination; in the last analysis, it relates to a psychic regime immersed in the living ocean of the imagination. (227)

Or, as expressed in the language of the symbol function as we have so far determined it: one, magic cognition, is a falling prey to the *a prioris* of pure symbolic syntheses which occur inescapably and tend toward the total construction of the world as experienced; the other, a taking of action, by which the simulacra are penetrated and the inexhaustible thing restored to the living bond of existential knowledge.

2. Human Folly and Empirical Science

The acid test of any empirical theory of man is its applicability to primitive culture, that incredible efflorescence of rite and superstition which has so scandalized the psychogeneticist with his entirely understandable desire to fit man and his symbols into a plausible evolutionary schema. How can one possibly account for the manifold cruel practices, the mutilations of puberty rites, the human sacrifices, by a theoretical schema which has as its rationale a successful adaptation to the environment—whether this be conceived as a simple working in practice or as some more refined instrumentality, such as a conferring of "social solidarity"? If there is a pragmatic goal, why could it not be better served by some less patently unbiological practice than that of the Khouds of India who regularly kill female children before their name day because their souls are believed to go to a special generative reservoir from which they may return as boys? Here, as in so many cases, belief seems to militate against good biological practice. And do we solve our difficulties or simply postpone them by adding another "need" to the roster, as Mrs. Langer does, the "need of symbolization"? It is no wonder that the naturalist anthropologist often ends by throwing up his hands at man and his follies and convicting him of stupidity.

Primitive culture has proved to be no less a stumbling block for those attempts to "explain" primitive mentality by the logical categories of the Western mind. British animists, for example, supposed that the primitive, confronted with a mysterious phenomenon that he could not otherwise account for, posited a spirit world as a kind of reasonable inference. "Spirits are personified causes," according to E. B. Tylor. It was the great contribution of Professor Levy-Brühl to have shown that this kind of theorizing is based on the uncritical assumption that the primitive mind is responsive to the same exigencies of rational explanation as ours.* Whereas, the fact of the matter is, an unbiased study will show that at least in certain areas of cognition, the primitive mind "perceive[s] nothing in the same way as we do" (Levy-Brühl 1926, 43). When the North American Indian "regards his name, not as a mere label, but as a distinct part of his personality, just as much as are his eyes or his teeth, and believes that injury will result as surely from the malicious handling of his name as from a wound inflicted on any part of his physical organism" (Mooney quoted in Levy-Brühl 1926, 50), when in China, mourners about a coffin stand back a few steps when the lid is closed so that their shadows will not be imprisoned in the coffin (Groot cited in Levy-Brühl 1926, 54)—this manner of conceiving the world and causation can only arise from categories of thought fundamentally different from our own.

3. The Law of Participation

Levy-Brühl (1926) induces a general principle in all these mystic conceptions—"collective representations," as he calls them—of totemistic tribes. The one element never missing is mystic *participation* between one thing and another. His "Law of Participation" declares that things *"can be, though in a way incomprehensible to us, both themselves and something other than themselves* [emphasis added]" (76). The logical laws of identity and contradiction, the one and the many, the same and another, do not hold (77).

For example, the Bororo, a tribe in Northern Brazil, declare that they are parakeets. They do not mean by this that their aboriginal ancestors were parakeets or that after death they themselves will become parakeets. The "Bororos," says Von den Steinen, who would not believe it at first but finally had to give in to their explicit affir-

* I am aware that Levy-Brühl greatly modified his theory of the "prelogical mentality" before his death. So also do I modify it, in the belief that his observations have great value when salvaged from the doctrinaire evolutionary stages within which he placed them.

mations, "give one rigidly to understand that they are araras [parakeets] *at the present time*" (quoted in Levy-Brühl 1926, 77). The point is that under a law of participation inconceivable to us, a primitive can believe that he is a man and a parakeet at one and the same time. Professor Levy-Brühl cites hundreds of examples to support his thesis of a fundamentally different law of cognition.

Levy-Brühl's anthropology is, to a point at least, a good example of a *Verstehen* approach in which an attempt is made to understand cultural traits in the terms in which they are conceived by their practitioners rather than projecting our own frame of reference onto our data. Thus Frazer would explain the custom of placing a gold coin in the mouth of the dead by searching for a quasi-rational motive: it must be done so that the dead may buy food in the next life, etc.; whereas Levy-Brühl is able to grasp that the primitive conceives a connection between the coin and the man that is outside our rational categories: the dead man *participates* in the durability of the gold (76).

4. Symbol as Key to Levy-Brühl's Law

We shall be concerned in this chapter with two questions. First, what is the relation, if any, between Levy-Brühl's "Law of Participation," which he formulated purely on the basis of an empirical survey of primitive life and the *a priori* "laws" of pure symbolic construction, which can be arrived at not by ethnology but epistemologically through a phenomenological analysis of the symbolic mode of knowing? The second question is corollary to the first. Is not Levy-Brühl's characterization of magic cognition as "prelogical" mentality premature and doctrinaire, implying as it does a genetic *stage* through which the race is presumed to have passed for once and for all? As Malinowski (1954) points out, it is a preconception—and an extremely hard one to get rid of—"that 'origins' must be very crude" (23), that savage is the same thing as primitive, that is, early. To the cultural evolutionist or the Comtean positivist, it simply goes without saying that such cultural traits as magic, totemism, polygamy, polytheism, animism, etc., are "early" forms, of which monotheism, monogamy, metaphysics, poetry, are taken to be the late refined versions (or the rudimentary deposits). If one is committed in advance to a doctrine of cultural evolution from totemistic superstition to the more refined superstition of Christianity it becomes impossible to take account of evidence to the contrary—the work, for example, of Schmidt and Koppers (Koppers 1952) which shows that monotheism and monogamy are universal in most primitive societies and totemism relatively late.*

If it should turn out, however, that so-called "prelogical" mentality is an expression of one of the two regimes of the mind, not a genetic *stage* but an abiding *alternative* of the human way of knowing, we should expect two conditions to obtain. First, it should be possible to discover in primitive man—if he is as truly "man" as modern man—evidences of the operation of the same higher mode of knowing that also characterizes our best efforts: that of "logic-fused-with-imagination." Second, it should also be possible to discern in modern

* Professor Koppers (1952) relates the following anecdote about Baron Andrian Werberg, President of the Vienna Anthropological Society and also a strong cultural evolutionist:

> After reading Professor Schmidt's work on the Pygmy races, which appeared in 1910, he came to his friend Leopold von Schroeder in a state of consternation. I happened to be studying Sanskrit under Professor Schroeder and he told me the story. Andrian Werberg kept wringing his hands and asking how Father Schmidt, whom he highly esteemed, could come to write such a book. If there were truth in the ethnologist's conclusions about regulated matrimonial relations and an ethical faith in a Supreme Being among these relatively oldest representatives of the human race, then all the modern scientific theories about the mental and spiritual evolution of mankind would not have a leg to stand on. 'It can't be true!' he kept repeating, when Professor Schroeder (who was by the way a Protestant) pointed out that even this question would need to be calmly and carefully examined and that Schmidt's conclusions could not simply be ignored, because they were, as far as he could see, amply supported by facts. (178-9)

man an area of magic cognition, not necessarily in the form of material remnants, but as an alternative mode of conceiving the world under the same formal conditions that determine magic cognition in the primitive, those of passivity and remotion. Is magic cognition a stage in evolutionary time schema, or is it an alternative orientation to the world to which in ignorance, in magic, in dreams—in Biblical language: in idolatry—one falls prey?

One or two examples will suffice to illustrate the features of a typical "mystic participation," both its bizarreness—it is on the face of it totally foreign to anything in our experience—but also, what is not so apparent, its fundamental relation to symbolic identification (Part II, Chapter II).

The Arunta tribe in Australia uses certain fetish objects, *nurtunjas* and *churingas*, wooden poles and oblong stones, to represent other objects. "A *nurtunja* (sacred pole), is symbolic of one, and only one, thing, though, as far as its appearance and structure are concerned, it may be precisely similar to a *nurtunja* which means something totally different. Suppose, for example... a large *churinga* or a *nurtunja* represented a gum-tree, then, in the mind of the native it becomes so closely associated with that object that it cannot possibly mean anything else; and if a precisely similar *churinga* or *nurtunja* were wanted an hour afterwards to represent, say an emu, then a *new one must be made* [emphasis added]" (Spencer and Gillen quoted in Levy-Brühl 1926, 116-17).[*] And in respect of certain geometrical designs: "The

[*] A good example of the fatal subject object split comes to mind. *LIFE Magazine* (1955, December 12) in a single issue published two articles: one, purporting to show the early beginnings of religion with fetish worship (*nurtunjas*, etc.) and suggesting a gradual evolutionary ascent to Christianity; the other, an article about the current need to revitalize our Christian faith. The editors apparently saw nothing unusual in adopting a doctrinaire ethnology which guts religion and calling in the next breath for a return to religion. Again we recognize the mythist's motto: it may not be true, but for God's sake believe it. But perhaps the editors of *LIFE* are righter than they know; this is indeed life in the U.S.A.: evolutionary religion, return to Christianity, with a naked woman in between.

origin of these geometric drawings is quite unknown, and their meaning, if they have one, is a purely conventional one. Thus, for example, a spiral or series of concentric circles incised on the face of one particular *churinga* will signify a gum-tree, and a precisely similar design on another *churinga* will indicate a frog" (Spencer and Gillen quoted in Levy-Brühl 1926, 117).

In these examples, what strikes one immediately is that the primitive sees each of these rather indifferent objects, a pole, a stone, a geometrical design, *as something else*, and sees it as such so steadfastly that he is surprised at the white man's obtuseness when the latter only sees the pole or the stone. Moreover, if a particular *churinga* represents a gum-tree, it cannot represent a frog: a new one, identical in every respect must be made.

The two cardinal traits of symbolic transformation are immediately recognizable: one, it is a condition of symbolization that the symbol must be univocally *unlike* the thing; two, the symbol is itself totally transformed by that which is symbolized so that the original structure of the symbol is quite lost to view—the native no longer sees the spiral; he sees a frog. The tentative hypothesis is inescapable: Is it possible that the strange phenomenon common to most totemistic cultures which Levy-Brühl and other writers characterize by such names as "mystic participation," "mystic abstraction," "symbiosis," "close association with," and so on, is a manifestation of the same basic function which undergirds all human knowing and especially the linguistic symbol? A manifestation which is mainly distinguished by its wild proliferation uncontrolled by the saving corrective of reason and experience? Levy-Brühl (1926) cites this primitive identification of one thing with another as one of the salient differences between "prelogical" and modern cognition—and on the face of it, he would appear to be right. The Bororos's insistence that they are parakeets is foreign to anything in our experience. But what he fails to realize is the universal occurrence of symbolic transformation not only in primitive man but in modern man, that here too, one "thing" is identified with another. He lays it down as a qualitative difference that in modern man, the symbol bears a resemblance to the thing, whereas with primitive man it bears only an arbitrary relation (117). The fact is, however, that symbolization by *like* is, even with modern man, a marginal and unproductive form of symbolization. (See Part II, Chapter II.) The true symbol, i.e., that which lends itself to an intentional transformation, is the unlike-but-analogous symbol. We may be incredulous at the Aruntas' assertion that this *churinga* is a frog, but we make no objection to the ostensive definition *that is a stick*.

If we prescind momentarily from the striking differences and compare the "mystic participation" with various linguistic transformations of one and the same symbol, fundamental similarities will become evident. With the Aruntas, we can say, three similar visual symbols, three spirals, can represent three different things, a frog, a gum-tree, and an emu—so much so that the three spirals are differentially transformed and are no longer recognizable as three spirals, alike in every respect. In the case of our linguistic symbol, *stick*, three sounds which are alike in every respect, *stick stick stick* are differentially transformed so that each comes to articulate within itself an entirely different sensory configuration: inserting-a-point, applying-something-sticky, dry-brittle-twig (Part II, Chapter II). So thoroughly are these vocables transfigured that a slight effort of insight is required to see them as the same sound, as what the symbol is in itself prior to transformation.

The differences between our linguistic identification and the primitive's "participation" are, of course, obvious—and it is mainly a difference of insight into the intentionality of the symbol. Where the Bororo would insist that he really is a parakeet and the Arunta that his *nurtunja* really is a frog, the Westerner would protest with equal vehemence that the word "stick" is only a label for something already known. (And perhaps both would be wrong: the primitive in a logical sense in his failure to pay sufficient attention to the law of identity; the Westerner in an epistemological sense, in his failure to apprehend the cognitive role of the symbol.) It must be pointed out, however, that perhaps Levy-Brühl overstates his case—that the primitive's identification of one thing with another is not as univocal as he pretends. Even the Bororo, who insists he is a parakeet, would not presumably try to fly or to mate with another parakeet. The Huichol Indians in Mexico maintain emphatically that deer is *hikuli* (a sacred plant), *hikuli* is corn, corn is a plume (Lumholtz cited in Levy-Brühl 1926, 122). But as Oliver Leroy writes, "The logic of a Huichol would be deficient only on the day when he would prepare a wheat porridge while he thought he was making a stag stew" (quoted in Maritain 1948b, 238n).

There should be no confusion between magic symbol and Christian sacrament, because generically they are two different things: one, an assertion of an identity which does not exist; the other, a sign effecting the change which it signifies. To the primitive, magic symbol serves to meet a pressing conceptional need, the need at any cost to construe the world and himself. To him, the assertion of identity, *I am a parakeet*, *fire is a plume*, are cognitively more tolerable than the awful unformulability of self and the awful mystery of fire. It is a natural recourse of the mind before an otherwise intolerable situation. But the sacred words, *This is my Body* (which is not an assertion of identity between two different things but a sign effecting a change), is a hard saying before which, in the natural order, the mind staggers and turns away. To the symbolific function, the sacraments of Christ appear not as cognitive food for magic appetite, but as a stumbling block and a contradiction. It is precisely because Baptism and The Eucharist did not offer themselves as symbolic allurements to Nicodemus and a great number of His (Christ's) followers that the former asked, how such things could come to be, and the latter turned away and "went back to their old ways" (see John 3:1-6:67, Knox translation).

Moreover, the Eucharist does not, as Maritain (1948b) points out, assert the identity between two things. "The sacred words... operate (as an instrumental cause) a change (transubstantiation). Far from resting upon an identity between the sign and the signified, the sacrament of the Eucharist adds to the relationship of the sign to signified that of cause to effect and implies the intervention of the First

Cause producing the most radical change of which we can conceive, a change which affects being in so far as it is *being*" (226).

5. Magic Causality

The other major expression of the "Law of Participation" besides the "mystic participations," these remarkable identifications of one thing with another, is the construing of a mystical connection or magic causality between one thing and another. In the most diverse parts of the world, Australia, East Africa, the Dakotas, there are not only characteristic ways of conceiving *what* things are but also *how* they are related to each other. Here one encounters perhaps the most universal of all the traits of magic cognition, that of the ubiquitous mystic force, variously called "*mana*," "*makosie*," "*wakan*," "*orenda*," "*taboo*," etc. No end of confusion has resulted, according to Levy-Brühl (1926), from the proclivity of the Western observer, whether he be of Christian or animist persuasion, to read into this primitive conception the Western dichotomy of natural-supernatural, and to interpret "*mana*" as God or at least as a kind of transcendent power to whom he can appeal for assistance. Nothing could be more alien to the conception of "*mana*." It is above all a *natural force*, immanent in all things. In the performance of the rain *intichiumas*, there is no notion of appealing to a supernatural being. According to the Dakotas, all life is *wakan*. It is Levy-Brühl who stresses as the outstanding characteristic of the totemistic cultures of Australia and South America the utter absence of any idea of the supernatural (134-135).

Everything is *mana*, but it is the mysterious rhythms of nature, the ebb and flow of life, with which this all-pervasive force is most characteristically associated. The coming of the seasons, the rains, the heavens, what lies beyond the horizon, life and death, puberty and marriage—these are the things in the conception of which the primitive has recourse in his mystical force, *mana*. It is the enigmatic, the uncertain, the dangerous, the remote, the mysterious, to which is irresistibly imputed this magic power. The causal principle is *post hoc, ergo propter hoc*. If, instead of the two-masted trading schooner which regularly passes the island, a three-masted vessel appears, it immediately becomes invested with an air of mystery and incalculable potency. Anything can happen. A missionary has the bad luck to unpack a strange-looking black mackintosh just before a prolonged drought. The connection is inescapable. Mackintosh causes drought.

6. Primitive Magic and Primitive Truth

It is not necessary to adduce more evidence of the peculiar traits of magic cognition in primitive societies. The striking ways in which they differ from our own way of conceiving the world are rather well-known and are in fact more likely to be emphasized than not. The question which is germane to our discussion, and the question which Malinowski asks, is rather: Is the primitive's worldview entirely "mystical" as Levy-Brühl implies, or does he have another way of construing the world akin to our own rational view, based on experience guided by reason? Drawing upon his own extensive work among the Papuo-Melanesian tribes of Eastern New Guinea and the surrounding archipelagoes, who are reputed to be especially magic-ridden, Malinowski (1954) delineates a special area of thought and activity in which empirical knowledge and reason rule supreme. It is in the pursuit of the homely arts that the primitive thinks and acts as effectively as the Westerner—agriculture, house-building, lagoon-fishing, homely technics, where he displays a shrewd knowledge of soil conditions, botany, skill with tools, and so on (26). He may indeed plant a magic stone to teach the yam and the yaro to grow big, but he would not dream of neglecting his practical farming. The areas in which he falls prey to magic are, on the other hand, precisely those encounters with events beyond the zone of his everyday knowledge and control—life and death, the seasons, the coming of day and night, the stars and the sun, remote places, the origins of plants and animals—in a word, the manifestations of *nature*. The two zones might be characterized as follows: the world of the familiar thing, existing in a familiar milieu of causal relations, identity, predictable change, and susceptible of control by a familiar pattern of tool-using, manipulation, and so on—

and the world of the remote, the autonomous, the mysterious, in which, by the very fact of their remotion, things are open to mystic participations and magic causes (29).

7. Magic Cognition Is Not a Primitive but a Perennial Mode

May we not then agree with Malinowski, Leroy, and Maritain, that what Levy-Brühl has so brilliantly formulated is not so much a "prelogical stage" of cognition as a perennial mode or regime of knowing which occurs under certain conditions—i.e., passivity, remotion—but which never entirely displaces, even in the most magic-ridden tribe, a proper existential mode of knowing things as they really are, discerning causes, predicting effects, and employing technics?

Where are we to look for "magic cognition" in Western civilization? Shall we look for certain material traits which are held for *a priori* reasons to be the evolutionary remnants of "collective representations"? It is characteristic of the "religious presuppositions" of materialist anthropologists that all cultural phenomena, including religion, are lumped together under an instrumental schema; theoretical continuity must be established at any cost, so that atomic functions, organic needs, and cultural traits can be deciphered by the same code (Dawson 1954, 131). Thus Levy-Brühl does not find it inconsistent to emphasize in the first part of his book the total absence of the transcendent in the immanent symbolic constructions of totemistic tribes and in the last chapter to dispose of transcendent religion as a residue of "prelogical mentality." Or shall we rather look for the traits of magic or pure symbolic construction in modern life and the formal conditions under which they might be expected to occur?

8. Technics as the Magic Mode in Modern Life: The Reversal

We have seen that it is possible to delineate in primitive life two formal modes of orientation to the world. One is a true, a properly human, awareness of the world, an awareness achieved through the active employment of reason and imagination. Another is a magic view of reality, a passive falling prey to the mysterious under the mode of pure symbolic constructions. The material content of the two regimes of the mind is found in primitive life to comprise, in the first case, the real knowledge and employment of rude *technics*; in the second case, the magic knowledge of events of *nature*. In modern life, we are aware at once of a curious reversal. Where, in modern life, is to be found the mysterious, the remote, the autonomous? Hardly in nature. To the apartment dweller in New York, nature is a trivial affair, a patch of sky between buildings, a few wilted trees, a few bedraggled zoo animals. To the suburbanite, nature is a backdrop to be manipulated like stage scenery. A landscape "architect" and a bulldozer can transform nature as easily as a decorator can transform a house. Modern man, whether by a fortunate enlightenment or by a tragic alienation, sees nothing mysterious or wonderful about natural events. Nature has been explained. The planets revolve, cells divide, organisms flourish and perish. *The mystery and remotion and complexity to which the mass man in a technical society falls prey is to be found nowhere else than in the world of technics which he has created, or rather which others have created for him, and which he as a consumer enjoys passively.* The great question that both Ortega and Marcel put is this: What happens to a man who buys an automobile toward which he has contributed nothing and about whose workings he has not the slightest curiosity? For the strange fact is that he does not primarily buy the car as a means of getting about from place to place, but in order to *have* the car. He becomes subject to a dialectic of fashion in which his old car, though it runs well enough, has somehow been emptied out; the new car constitutes itself by virtue of its new style as an overwhelming something to which he falls prey. If he can only have the new car, his own nothingness (which has invaded his old car) will surely be informed. The proper conjuration of technical man is not Tiger! Tiger! but Jaguar! Jaguar!

Levy-Brühl's mistake was twofold. He discovered the symbolic mode of conception that, without the correctives of reason, results in mytho-magic modes of thought. He was mistaken first, as Malinowski has shown, in overlooking the considerable areas in primitive thought which are anything but magical. But he was also mistaken in seeing magic cognition as a *material* moment in an evolutionary ascent from "prelogical" cognition to the rational scientific thought of the Western world. Modern anthropologists have grave objections to Levy-Brühl's and Comte's "natural laws" of linear cultural evolution. There is such a thing as cultural progress but, as David Bidney (1953) said, it comes about not as an inevitable process but as a result of human effort and rational selection (126). Magic cognition is not a prelogical "stage" which evolution puts behind us once and for all. It is rather a perennial pitfall. Equally gratuitous and doctrinaire is Levy-Brühl's identification of monotheism, Christianity, as a material "remnant" of mythical thought. In the first place, we must not forget that Christianity was and is a "hard saying" to the primitive man, who, like the countrymen of Jesus, is all too likely to shake his head and "return to his old ways," e.g., his mythical ways. In the second half of the twentieth century we have a clearer view of the myth-minded man than did Levy-Brühl and Comte. Is he the practicing Christian and Jew, or is he the mass man of our culture? Who is more likely to fall prey to the myths of the state, the magic of technics? Levy-Brühl's error lies in his level of abstraction. He recognized instances of mytho-magic thought correctly, but he mistook its hallmark. His criterion of magic cognition was *material content:* thoughts about religion are mythic; thoughts about science are rational. At the next level of abstraction it is seen that it is not the content of conception which determines its magic or true character, but its *mode.* Unless we realize this, we shall never be able to understand our own times. The mythic mode of thought is the same today as 4000 years ago. But its content, in many cases, is reversed. The modern analogue of the Arunta tribesman is not the Christian Communicant; it is the passive consumer of technics who in his selflessness and anonymity is easy prey for magic and fetishism in his consumer goods and tyranny in his government.

9. The Law of Participation in a Technical Society

In order to illustrate the analogue of magic cognition and participation in modern life, it will perhaps be useful again to consider examples which, in linguistic form, are quite similar in logical structure but entirely different in their configuration. The great difference, as we have seen (Part II, Chapter III), is that whereas the logical structure of a sentence is the same regardless of point of view, its figurative structure will depend on the referential position of the knower as he conceives it. Does the action or identification occur in the zone of the really, the existentially known, or does it occur in the milieu of the pure symbolic construction?

Let us consider the following examples under their attendant conditions:

Condition: that I am a carpenter.

Propositions: I (a) John Smith is a carpenter.
(b) Paul Jones is a doctor.
II (a) Carpenters repair houses.
(b) Doctors treat patients.

As logical symbols, the terms of both propositions under (I) bear the same logical relation to each other. The propositions are examples of the same logical form and might be expressed symbolically as an *A*; individual *a* is-a-member-of class *A*.

But they are totally different figuratively.

To a carpenter, the proposition, *John Smith is a carpenter*, means that John Smith is a man like myself who does carpentry as I do, a familiar business entailing familiar tools and operations. It is a statement of confraternity in a common world, a world of which one has real existential knowledge, an exquisite balance of figuration and reason, that fusion of qualities and forms with measuring and predicting which constitutes human knowing in the best sense.

But the proposition, *Paul Jones is a doctor*, means something quite different—that is, its immediately taken meaning, effortlessly received, is quite different. It means not that Paul Jones, a man like myself, belongs to a certain group of men who have learned to perform certain operations, different from carpentry, but belonging to the same human mode of doing and making and subject to the same natural laws—it means rather that Paul Jones *is* something else. He, a man like myself, has participated in another identity. (This is not the place to consider the role of magic in medicine, both the good and the bad of it: that it is only on the condition that my boyhood friend, the man like me, does *change* and *become* a doctor, that I will allow him to treat me.)

When a child says *I am a cowboy*, he does not mean that I am riding and roping and that as a consequence of my activities, I belong to a certain class of performers. He means what he says: I *am* a cowboy. He is transformed first, he participates in another identity, and he does cowboy things as a result of his transformation.

Proposition I (b) expressed (or can express) the relation of magic participation, in which the non-doctor falls prey to the magic potency of a technic—that is, he allows medical technics to constitute itself as a zone of reality which obeys laws entirely foreign to his experience.

Propositions II (a) and (b), also logically alike, are different figuratively.

Carpenters repair houses means that men like myself perform certain familiar operations on familiar structures. The operations take place in a human milieu and according to familiar kinetic and sensory configurations: feeling, judging, lifting, hitting, measuring, prizing, pushing, fitting, etc. There is predicated the whole intricate, yet natural, interplay of human knowing and doing.

10. Magic Causality Today

Doctors treat patients, however, means to me, a carpenter, or is apt to mean, that certain transfigured individuals perform certain mysterious operations on people like me to whom something mysterious has occurred. The verb "treat" contains within itself all the paraphernalia and magic gesture which "science" holds for the layman (but not only science: lawyers *practice* law, *try* cases, Hemingway *publishes* a book, sailors *trim* tackle, kings *rule* states, George Washington *crossed-the-Delaware*—are all propositions which the layman, that is, anyone who is at some remotion from the action, almost inevitably takes to occur magically). Even though I, as an educated carpenter, might protest that I am well aware that medical and surgical treatment obeys universally valid scientific laws—my knowledge is apt to be only a kind of acquiescence to a schoolroom or a Sunday supplement science. I am not likely to mean that I really believe that surgery takes place in the same human milieu of cutting and fitting and pushing as my carpentry (as the surgeon knows it does). No. Despite, or perhaps because of, my education, I am more likely to conceive that the doctor does certain "medical" and "surgical" things as a result of his having become a doctor and through the mediation, not of real causes, but of magic immanentism.

Even the educated layman, who has "had" chemistry and physics in college, is under the temptation to conceive that scientific research takes place immanently. One decides to "become" a nuclear physicist; having become a nuclear physicist, one is envisioned as surrounding himself with the appropriate apparatus, one adopts a suitable mien, then "performs" experiments which more or less occur of themselves. The extent to which any vocation is viewed magically is gauged by its popularity in the movies. For acting is a participation in another identity by assuming its accidental characteristics. A revealing example of magic gesture is related of Whistler's students. On one occasion before giving a painting lesson, he had been busy etching, when after each cutting he would blow away wood shavings. While demonstrating brush painting, by force of habit he went on blowing after each stroke. Subsequently most of the class were observed doing the same thing, blowing on the paint after each stroke.

It remains to be determined to what degree popular scientism is a respect for and interest in the real achievements of science and to what degree a seduction by that mysterious entity "Science." Perhaps the major task of a real scientific education is to disabuse the student of his expectations of participation and magic and to restore "Science," the autonomous and the immanent, to science of real knowing and doing. Thc difference between the sophomore in science and the genuine research man is that one conceives the whole of reality as a closed field under the strict governance of known "laws" and is therefore impatient of second looks—or of any looks—at what is actually the case, while the other, who may have spent his entire life in one tiny department of one science is aware, if he is aware of nothing else, of the openness and inexhaustibility of his field: it is not just the infinite richness of the reality before him which binds him to his laboratory for life by a bond of delight beside which all else seems shoddy, but—and this no matter what his overt allegiance to a particular epistemology—the inescapable fact that his mind and the reality before him are mutually ordained to an endless knowing and being known. The science student is characteristically offended when he first encounters a genuine scientist. For the latter is apt to be both more human than the student and less sure of himself. But worst of all, he manifests a certain lack of reliance, amounting to contempt, for technical devices and the general accoutrements of the laboratory which are so dear to the student. The true botanist sees the flower; the sophomore sees only the botanical diagram.

11. Three Traits of Magic Cognition

At least three traits of magic cognition may be discerned in the process of simulacrum formation and magic participation. By magic cognition I mean the effortless *a priori* synthesis of pure symbolic transformations dissociated from either experiential or abstract knowing. Pure symbolic knowledge, the knowledge of dreams, of magic, of idolatry, is neither apprehension nor comprehension, knowledge of nor knowledge about. Here is surely to be found, rather than in ideational thought—Maritain's logic-fused-with-imagination—the true domicile of the *a priori* category and the archetype.

(a) *Totality of conception.* The figurative world, whether it be that of the bushman or the logical positivist, is totally articulated. There are no gaps in the figurative horizon and hence no passive awareness of ignorance. It is a condition of the symbolic transformation that everything be transformed. The popular misconception is that ignorance should be manifest. We imagine that the Melanesian islander must wonder what lies beyond the seas. But he already "knows" what lies beyond. He cannot not know. He has a total conception—he could not have any other kind—supplied in part by his meager experiential and inferential knowledge, but largely by magic cognition. By the very nature of conceiving, there can be no areas that are not totally formulated. The traveler has, despite himself, a total conception of Canada, and if he has never been there, it is apt to be conceived in terms of a large pink place transected by lines.

(b) *Law of participation.* This principle, far from being a peculiar trait of prelogical mentality, is the very essence of the symbolic transformation itself—as it operates without the saving correctives of reason and experience.

In modern life, as in primitive life, magic cognition manifests itself under the analogous conditions of lapse of experiential and discursive knowing.

Thus the sentences,

> When I, a young Bororo, grow up, I shall become a parakeet.
>
> When I, a young American, grow up, I shall become a nuclear physicist.

while they may be logically different (one is nonsense, the other is not necessarily), are figuratively alike. For in each case, there is the expectation that the self will participate in and be informed by another identity.

(c) *Magic gesture.* The magic operation, whether in primitive or in modern mentality, occurs under analogous conditions of remotion and suggestibility.

The sentence

> Roentegenologists treat patients by giving them doses of x-rays.

is liable to be conceived in the same figurative mode as

> Hunters tire their prey by dropping hot coals in their footprints (Levy-Brühl 1926, 235).

The point is that the "magic" is not regarded as such by either the modern or the primitive layman. In one case the layman would protest that he knows that the activities of the roentgenologist are subject to universally valid "laws," or at least is willing to believe that they are, and to this extent perhaps he has the advantage of the islander, who, however, would be equally outraged by the charge of superstition or even of religious faith, since to him the principle of *mana* or *wakan* is eminently natural in its operation. But the real question is: in what terms does the mass man conceive the operation of a "scientific law"? Does he not inevitably conceive the gamma rays of the cathode tube to act on the tissue by a kind of magic gesture? Whereas the research man—who is truly interested—is precisely concerned to discover those intermediate steps by which the action is possible, in other words, to restore the action of the gamma ray to the same milieu of intelligibility as the action of the carpenter who drives a nail into a board. The layman, that is, anyone outside a particular technical specialty, is peculiarly prone to conceive the operations, not according to his own canons of intelligibility, but magically—as the association of one symbol-thing complex with another in an *a priori* category of magic causality.

Magic cognition, as opposed to abstract or experiential thought, postulates an immanent and autonomous activity. The motto is, *A* causes *B*, not through the mediation of secondary causes, but directly and of itself. All operations in dreams, in childish syntheses, in the passive consumer's conception of technics, occur in the purely symbolic rather than the existential mode. Thus, when I dream of a doctor curing patients, a dog having puppies, a manufacturer making Chevrolets, Event *B* follows upon Event *A*, not through any succession of circumstances which I recognize as valid for my experience, but immanently: the manufacturer makes a manufacturing-pass-with-a-tool over the raw metal and there emerges a Chevrolet. The source of my interest (and surprise) in visiting the Chevrolet assembly line would be the discovery that with all the technics, Chevrolets are still made in the same milieu of prizing, shaping, fitting, as my carpentry. My reaction will invariably be: so that is how a fender is made! (Not the way I thought it was made—magically.)

I have tried in the last two chapters to do three things: (1) to delineate the essential features of *pure* symbolic knowing, as it can be arrived at through an examination of one's figuration of linguistic symbols and sentences; (2) to examine some of the more obvious traits of primitive cognition for what light the "*a priori* categories of pure symbolic knowing" may throw upon them; (3) having established a rough conception of the formal conditions under which "magic cognition" occurs in primitive society, to turn again to modern life in order to determine whether or not under analogous conditions, magic cognition may not also occur.

Different though the wildest symbolic identification of a totemistic tribe may seem to be from our sober ostensive definition, *this is a lupin*, they would appear to share at least one fundamental trait. It is a cognitive condition of both kinds of identification that one thing is transformed into another and that the original symbol is in a sense lost to sight. The symbolic transformation occurs in both cases; however, the matter of the transformation is different and the insight into the intentionality of the transformation is different. In one case, a *word* (sound) is intentionally transformed into a *thing;* however, in the primitive, a *thing* (*nurtunja*) is transformed into a *thing*. (In a sense, our transformation of the sound "glass" into the thing glass is even more astonishing than the Aruntas' transformation of the *nurtunja* into an emu, for it is a trans-sensory transformation.)

It occurs to one that the primitive's tendency to construe his world by means of bizarre symbolic participations is not a peculiar trait of "prelogical mentality," but is rather the uncontrolled proliferation of a cognitive function that is the very condition of any sort of human knowing at all.

In the light of the categories of pure symbolic synthesis—which might be called an anatomy of error—an obvious hypothesis suggests itself to account for two stubborn facts: one, that magic, totemism, fetish, "mystic participation" in general, take extraordinarily similar forms in the most diverse parts of the world; two, that these are apparently "late," degenerate forms, because what invariably characterizes the most primitive of all societies is a relatively pure monotheism, monogamy, exogamy, etc. It is well-known, as Professor Koppers (1952) points out, that cultural evolutionists will posit crude beginnings in social, ethical, and religious phenomena, purely out of consideration for doctrinaire belief and without a "scrap of confirmatory evidence" (2). Yet how can one account for the striking similarity of these later degenerative forms? Levy-Brühl has provided the clue. There is a "law" of magic cognition, and once we extract it from its context of a "prelogical stage," we see its significance at once. For it is not, as we have seen, a more primitive form of cognition, either culturally, in the case of human societies, or genetically, in the case of the individual. (See Part II, Chapter III.) Rather it is the regime of the pure symbolic synthesis to which one *falls prey* in lieu of the full appropriation of man's full estate. But the great discovery with which Levy-Brühl must be credited, despite its theoretical distortion, is that even error is lawful. Its relevance for Jung's archetype is equally clear. The occurrence of the same archetype in diverse times and places is evidence, not of a "collective psyche," but of the natural proclivities of pure symbolic synthesis: the magic *a prioris*.

But perhaps the most fertile consequence of the recognition of symbolic knowing as it constitutes itself, either as an alternative mode of knowing or as an indispensable instrument of existential knowing, will be the illumination and grounding of the existentialists' conception of man as faced with a *choice*. Neither the purely biological nor the purely rational view of man can make provision for the existentialist (and Christian) dichotomy of authentic/inauthentic, freedom/falling-prey-to, wonder/boredom, and so on. If man is ordained to being in all its inexhaustibility, its causal implications, its degrees of perfections, it is precisely the price of this gift that he can fall prey to idolatry and magic—which, after all, is the only thing that is really dull.

To summarize: it is possible in the study of primitive culture to induce a general law of magic cognition. This is that man most characteristically conceives the world magically when the area of knowledge consists of the remote, ill-understood, enigmatic, etc., and most characteristically conceives the world shrewdly and scientifically when the area of knowledge consists of the homely and familiar. Magic cognition takes place in general whenever symbolic processes operate without the corrective of referential matter. When this *formal* law is applied to modern man, it suggests a *material* reversal. Whereas phenomena of nature comprised the mysterious and technics comprised the familiar in primitive life, in modern life nature becomes a pedestrian affair, and it is technics which takes on the aspect of the mysterious and to which modern man most characteristically falls prey.

PART III

SYMBOL AND EXISTENCE

CHAPTER I

SYMBOL, CONSCIOUSNESS, AND INTERSUBJECTIVITY

Consciousness seems incurably ambiguous as a subject of inquiry. It lends itself equally well to two different approaches that not only appear to have nothing in common but even seem to be mutually exclusive. First, it would seem proper to treat consciousness as a phenomenon, some thing or relation in the world, like any other phenomenon, some thing or relation in the world, and make it an object of scientific inquiry. Like any other event—a solar eclipse, urine secretion, nuclear fusion, substernal pain—consciousness can surely be studied by the objective-empirical method, a method which takes its origin from the inexpugnable belief, as Whitehead (1950) put it, that phenomena can be explained, that is, "correlated with [their] antecedents in a perfectly definite manner, exemplifying general principles" (18). There would appear to be no good reason to exempt consciousness from such an inquiry. We all know there is such a thing as consciousness, even if we have trouble defining it; it is a phenomenon that happens to an organism and that therefore falls within the province of a science of organisms.

Yet there is something about consciousness that sets it apart from all other phenomena, something in virtue of which it would seem to be entitled to a privileged status, a status anterior to the method and corpus of empirical science. Consciousness is that by which I know anything at all, including scientific data. Therefore everything in the world is relative to my consciousness—except my consciousness itself. Consciousness can be regarded therefore as a realm of absolute priority (Gurwitsch 1955, 307). A truly radical science, in this view, would not be content to study consciousness (or anything else) as a phenomenon that was assumed to be happening in a spatio-temporal world and that was believed, by an "inexpugnable faith," to be correlated with other phenomena. Natural science entails, from this point of view, too many presuppositions. A presuppositionless science would study consciousness itself, this absolutely privileged realm of being, study it moreover not from the perspective of an explanatory psychology that seeks to derive it from antecedent events in a spatio-temporal world, but by a phenomenology that confines itself to the description of the acts and structures of consciousness.

The first approach to consciousness is the explanatory-psychological and is perhaps best exemplified by the work of the American social behaviorist, George H. Mead. The second, of course, is the descriptive method of Husserl's transcendental phenomenology.

Confronted by two such disciplines, which go their separate ways with complete assurance, laying hold of the same subject with techniques that contribute nothing, one to the other, which show no signs of converging—as electromagnetic theory converges with atomic theory—one sooner or later begins to wonder if something has not been overlooked. Without presuming to offer a critique either of Mead or Husserl, I would like to explore this stubborn divergence in respect of their basic methodological assumptions about consciousness and in the light of a relatively new insight: man's symbolic orientation in the world. It is an insight, which neither man, in my opinion, was sufficiently aware of and which opens, I further believe, new vistas toward the reconciling of the psychological and phenomenological methods.

Unless we are standing astride an incurable dichotomy of subject-science and object-science, with phenomenologists of consciousness on one side and psychologists of meaning on the other, somewhere along the way a sign has been misread. Moreover, the same sign must have been misread twice: once as reading to the left, once as reading to the right. That is to say: if we investigate the habitual difficulties of the phenomenologist in his treatment of consciousness and the habitual difficulties of the objective-empiricist, we should find valuable clues and coordinates for charting the original oversight.

Each approach to consciousness seems to present unimpeachable credentials. Natural science, to be sure, is based on a *faith* in a lawful reality in which things can be correlated with their antecedents—yet it is a faith which is amply justified by past performance. But if one wishes to be sure, why not push back the starting point of our science one last notch and begin at a point anterior to existential belief? Instead of accepting the world as existing as a spatio-temporal reality, why not regard this attitude itself and this appearance itself—the world appearing to exist as a spatio-temporal reality—as subject-matter of science? In this case, all experience is viewed from the apparently invulnerable position of a pure consciousness examining its own intentional acts. Thus phenomenology, not contenting itself with faith, however warranted, makes a methodological try for certitude.

I have chosen the work of Husserl and Mead as exemplars of the subject-science and object-science of consciousness because it seems to me that each man stands at or near the end of a road, the same two roads Descartes charted for us in his great bifurcation of reality. It is impossible for me to conceive a more radically positive science than Mead's social behaviorism, for he concerns himself only with the physico-causal relations which obtain among his data, and yet he does not shrink (as did Watson) from the "datum" of consciousness. As for Husserl, of course, it is his avowed purpose in the phenomenological reduction to found for once and for all a presuppositionless science of consciousness.

I think it will be possible to show (1) that the characteristic difficulty that the transcendental phenomenology of consciousness encounters, as Husserl himself was acutely aware, is intersubjectivity, the problem of other selves; (2) that the chief oversight of an explanatory psychology of consciousness is a presupposing of this same intersubjectivity;[*] and (3) that positive psychology in its allegiance to

[*] As Schütz (1954) has pointed out, "Intersubjectivity is simply presupposed as the unclarified foundation of the social sciences" (265). What account can the social behaviorist give of the process by which he writes a paper and a colleague understands it?

the *sign*-response as the basic schema of psychogenesis has failed or refused to grasp the peculiar function of the *symbol* in the origin of mind and consciousness. I would like finally to suggest that an empirical analysis of the symbol-relation may provide a fresh avenue of approach to both intersubjectivity and consciousness, that in fact intersubjectivity and consciousness are intimately bound up with man's symbolic orientation in the world.

This particular approach to the problem of consciousness implies, I am frank to confess, a prejudice in favor of a broad empirical method. Such a method, it seems to me, has one great advantage to recommend it: it tends in the end to be self-corrective. To give one example: if the sign-response should turn out to be inadequate as a theoretical basis for the understanding of meaning and mind, then it is possible within the method to consider another approach, say, the symbolic orientation. In transcendental phenomenology, however, everything is staked on a single methodological cast at the very outset. If the original reduction, the famous *epoché*, is faulty, then no amount of phenomenological analysis thereafter will restore the defect.

1. Husserl's Consciousness: A Privileged Realm

Husserl perceived, as did Descartes, that one's natural attitude about the reality of the world is open to methodological doubt. That is to say, its nonexistence is thinkable, and what Husserl was interested in was an apodictic starting point, the denial of which is unthinkable. Here enters the *epoché*. The natural standpoint is not eliminated or even doubted, as was the case with Descartes—it is simply disqualified, put out of action, bracketed (Husserl 1952, 108). I do not even change my conviction that the natural world is really there. The thesis is simply suspended (*aufgehoben*).

This novel procedure seems justifiable in the light of the stated objective—a radical presuppositionless science. For the empirical sciences are not without presuppositions, presuppositions, moreover, that cannot be validated within the principles of empiricism. The animating principle of empiricism, that "of the grounding of all facts in experience, is not," Husserl (1952) declares, "itself open to empirical insight" (93). The empirical sciences depend for their validity upon an original positing of a real world, a spatio-temporal world subject to causal conditions within which the scientific objects and their laws are exemplified (Collins 1952, 32). Whitehead (1953) has called attention to the strange contradiction between the faith of empirical science in an order to be discovered and the skepticism of scientific-empiricist philosophers (6). It is perhaps just as well that scientists have not paid much attention to their philosophers.

In the *epoché*, therefore, I disconnect not only the natural reality but also the theoretical attitude toward it. "*I disconnect them* all, *I make absolutely no use of their standards, I do not appropriate a single one of the propositions that enter into their systems, even though their evidential value is perfect, I take none of them, no one of them serves me for a foundation*" (Husserl 1952, 111).

Then what survives the phenomenological reduction? Only one thing. The *cogito*-consciousness itself. Husserl sees his contribution as a correction of Descartes's oversight; instead of using the indubitable *cogito* as a jumping-off point, Husserl turns about and fixes upon the *cogito* itself as the field of a radical science, *the* radical science. "*Consciousness in itself has a being of its own which in its absolute uniqueness of nature remains unaffected by the phenomenological disconnexion.* It therefore remains over as a '*phenomenological residuum*', as a region of Being which is in principle unique, and can become in fact the field of a new science—the science of Phenomenology" (Husserl 1952, 113).

It is hard to resist the force of Husserl's method. For does not everything in the world exist as it is relative to my consciousness?

> We have to recognize that relativity to consciousness is not only an actual quality of our world, but, from eidetic necessity, the quality of every conceivable world. We may, in a free fancy, vary our actual world, and transmute it to any other which we can imagine, but we are obliged with the world to vary ourselves also,

> and ourselves we cannot vary except within the limits prescribed to us by the nature of subjectivity. (Husserl 1929, 701)

Everything I know is an object intended by my consciousness, and my knowing is intrinsically an intending of the object as having certain determinations.

Transcendental consciousness is disclosed therefore as a realm of absolute priority and as such does not fall under the purview of the natural sciences. Husserl (1952) does not deny that consciousness may be studied empirically-psychologically like anything else, but that does not detract from its transcendental priority (164):

> But the transcendental subjectivity, which for want of language we can only call again, "I myself," "we ourselves," cannot be found under the attitude of psychological or natural science, being no part at all of the objective world, but that subjective conscious life itself, wherein the world and all its content is made for "us," for "me." We that are, indeed, men, spiritual and bodily, existing in the world, are, therefore, "appearances" unto ourselves, parcel of what "we" have constituted, pieces of the significance "we" have made. The "I" and "we," which we apprehend, presuppose a hidden "I" and the "we" to whom they are "present." (Husserl 1929, 701)

The purified transcendental consciousness is anterior to all physico-causal systems. It:

> must be reckoned as *a self-contained system of Being*, as a system of *Absolute Being*, into which nothing can penetrate, and from which nothing can escape; which has no spatio-temporal exterior, and can be inside no spatio-temporal system; which cannot experience causality from anything nor exert causality upon anything, it being presupposed that causality bears the normal sense of natural causality as a relation of dependence between realities.
>
> On the other side, the whole *spatio-temporal world*, to which man and the human Ego claim to belong as subordinate singular realities, is *according to its own meaning mere intentional Being*, a Being, therefore, which has the merely secondary, relative sense of a Being *for* a consciousness. It is a Being which consciousness in its own experiences (*Erfahrungen*) posits, and is, in principle,

> intuitable and determinable only as the element common to the... motivated appearance-manifolds, but *over and beyond* this, is just nothing at all. (Husserl 1952, 153)

It is absurd to try to establish a causality between "objective" physical being and "subjective Being" because "causality... belongs in principle [only] to the... constituted intentional world" (Husserl 1952, 162). The positing of a mythical bond between consciousness and physical reality no doubt accounts for the futility of organismic explanations of consciousness which by the nature of things can only achieve some sort of parallelism.

The question arises then, if the transcendental consciousness is, of its very nature, exempted from the traditional empirical inquiry, what sort of knowledge can be had of it (Gurwitsch 1955, 309)? The answer is that the pure Ego is itself indescribable and can only be known through its intentional acts:

> The "being directed towards", "the being busied with", "adopting an attitude", "undergoing or suffering from", has this *of necessity* wrapped in its very essence, that it is just something "from the Ego", or in the reverse direction "to the Ego"; and this Ego is the *pure* Ego, and no reduction can get any grip on it.... [But] the experiencing Ego is still nothing that might be taken *for itself* and made into an object of inquiry on its *own* account. Apart from its "ways of being related" or "ways of behaving", it is completely empty of essential components, it has no content that could be unravelled, it is in and for itself indescribable: pure Ego and nothing further. (Husserl 1952, 233)

It is the act of intending (*noesis*) and that which is intended (*noema*) which are the proper subjects of the eidetic science of transcendental subjectivity.

As Gurwitsch (1955) has observed, phenomenological investigations must be carried out in a *strictly descriptive orientation*, since after the performance of the phenomenological reduction, we are left only with "things" and "objects" meant and intended which accordingly have to be *taken as they are meant and intended* (309; Husserl 1952, 118). A positive psychological approach, on the other hand, is an *explanatory* enterprise in which consciousness is treated as an event which takes place in an organism.

It becomes evident that consciousness, insofar as it is knowable, is an act. "I perform an act of consciousness" (Husserl 1952, 118). Moreover, it is the intentional character of the act that is manifest. "It is intentionality which characterizes *consciousness* in the pregnant sense of the term, and justifies us in describing the whole stream of experience as at once a stream of consciousness and the unity of *one* consciousness" (Husserl 1952, 242). Consciousness is noematic intentionality in general.

Unquestionably the greatest difficulty encountered by Husserl in his radical transcendental idealism is, as Collins (1952) has pointed out, "that of escaping from solipsism or isolation within the self alone" (33). That this is so, is attested by Husserl's strenuous efforts to give an account of intersubjectivity in the later *Cartesian Meditations* and by the many assurances on this score in the *Britannica* article and in the preface to the English edition of the *Ideen*. The attempts to allow for a real community of selves appear to take two forms—indeed, given the original rigor of the transcendal reduction, they can only take two forms. One, the other selves are, along with everything else, simply constituted by the Ego-subject (Husserl 1950, section 41); or two, the other selves somehow survive the reduction and become co-transcendal:

> "I, the transcendental, absolute I, as I am in my own life of transcendental consciousness; but besides myself, the fellow-subjects who in this life of mine reveal themselves as co-transcendental, within the transcendental society of 'Ourselves', which simultaneously reveals itself." It is thus within the intersubjectivity, which in the phenomenological reduction has reached empirical givenness on a transcendental level, and is thus itself transcendental, that the real (*reale*) world is constituted as "objective", as being there for everyone. (Husserl 1952, 21-22)

Transcendental subjectivity thus becomes transcendental intersubjectivity.

Husserl's predicament is obvious. If intersubjectivity is to be provided for within the strictures of the original method, other selves must be taken as simply intended objects enjoying a status no different from any other intended object, in which case only a pseudo-intersubjectivity results. No real account is given of that special meeting of minds in virtue of which Husserl can deliver a lecture or write a paper on this very subject and someone else can take what he means. On the other hand, if the community of "Ourselves" is to survive the transcendental reduction, this can be managed only by a serious compromise of the original *cogito*. For the whole enterprise of transcendental phenomenology is grounded on methodological doubt, and it is hard to see how, on the basis of this method, other selves can be given a certificate of indubitability which is withheld even from the empirical sciences. The entire force of the transcendental reduction is generated by the absolute certainty of my own consciousness as compared with anything else. If there is such a thing as transcendental intersubjectivity, there is no provision for it in the Cartesian method.

It seems to be a case of something being excluded by method and reinstated by empirical necessity. Another great transcendentalist was franker about the problem. Kant (1929) declared that it was a "scandal of philosophy" that so far the problem of our knowledge of other minds, and in connection therewith, of the intersubjectivity of our experience of the natural as well as the socio-cultural world, has not found a satisfactory solution and that, until rather recent times, this problem has even escaped the attention of philosophers (34). If it was a scandal in Kant's day, it is no less a scandal today.

Sartre (1957) observes that the reality of the Other, you, is so unmistakable that it survives even the phenomenological reduction. The greatest resistance to the solipsistic argument is "based on the fact that the Other is given to me as a concrete evident presence which I can in no way derive from myself and which can in no way be placed in doubt nor made the object of a phenomenological reduction or of any other epoché" (271).

But the admission of the existence of the Other and of a certain knowledge of him brings serious difficulties to one committed to a self-sufficient phenomenology. In a long section of *Being and Nothingness* Sartre gives a close analysis of the difficulties that the three "H"s—Hegel, Husserl, and Heidegger—have encountered in trying to do justice to the existence of others. Once the Kantian revolution is accepted, it appeared that the only chance of escaping solipsism was to "seize at the very heart of the consciousness a fundamental, transcending connection with the Other which would be constitutive of each consciousness in its very upsurge" (233). The task is, however, a desperate one. Husserl, he considers to have advanced only slightly beyond the Kantian *a priori* constitution of the Other: Husserl's Other is not a real existent but a kind of supplemental category which would allow a world to be constituted (234).

It was Hegel's brilliant intuition in *Phenomenology of Mind* to see that my consciousness depends on the Other for its very existence. Sartre writes: "The problem of the Other should not be posited [according to Hegel] in terms of the *cogito*; on the contrary, the existence of the Other makes the *cogito* possible as the abstract moment when the self is apprehended as an object" (236). By a dialectical movement, the I and the Other, the famous master-slave relation which so profoundly influenced Marx, is derived from self-consciousness in general. Sartre, following Kierkegaard, observes that Hegel's "I-am-I" has nothing in common with concrete consciousness. The being of self-consciousness cannot be defined in terms of knowledge: my consciousness was there before it was known. "No logical nor epistemological optimism can cover the scandal of the plurality of consciousnesses" (244).

Heidegger attempted to solve the problem within the ontological structure of the *Dasein*. The existential trait of *Mitsein*, being-with, is an essential part of the constitution of the existing self. But what has this ontological derivation got to do with the concrete empirical encounter of Pierre and Annie? Nor does Heidegger escape the spectre of solipsism. As Sartre points out, if I am the being by which there are others, then there are no real others (248). "It [my being-with] does not constitute the slightest proof of the Other's existence, not the slightest bridge between me and the Other" (249).

Sartre's own solution appears contradictory. First, he declares that the Other's existence is indubitable. I do not constitute the Other: I encounter him (250). I encounter him in his look. Who is the Other? It is he who is looking at me. At first the Other is only an object to me, a man like other objects, trees, ink-pots, in the world. I, consciousness-for-itself, look upon him, an object. But when he looks at me, the situation is reversed. He becomes a subject and I become an object for him. We may not doubt the existence of the Other. But if he is not an object, then what is he? He is the one who is looking at me, the transcendence which is not mine. The Other resists any *epoché* (271). On the other hand, Sartre makes it clear that the other self must remain forever outside my experience. If the problem of the existence of other creatures on Mars is at the present time a matter of pure conjecture and must await the proper instruments of observation, the "structure of the Other is on principle such that no new experiment will ever be able to be conceived, that no new theory will come to validate or invalidate the hypothesis of his existence, that no instrument will come to reveal new facts inspiring me to affirm or to reject this hypothesis" (251). Then how shall I proceed with regard to this inscrutable Other? I simply affirm him (251). And why are there Others? They just are. "So it is" (301). Sartre's solution of the problem of others reminds one of the Categorical Imperative.

One wonders if Sartre's difficulties do not arise from a collision of method and empirical insight. There is, on the one hand, the phenomenology of the look which is a brilliant disclosure, at an empirical level, of the unique status of the Other. This insight would appear to be valid apart from theoretical considerations—one immediately senses that Sartre is right in declaring that the Other is grasped as a subject rather than as an object. But there is, on the other hand, his commitment to a self-sufficient phenomenology, a commitment which one cannot really allow for other acts of existence nor draw inferences therefrom.

2. Mead's Consciousness: A Social Response

There has always been something of a fool's errand about the objective-empirical approach to consciousness. Such "explanations" are liable to be either perfunctory, undertaken with little enthusiasm, or, as in the case of Watsonian behaviorism, missing altogether—as though there were the prescience at the very outset that the nature of the subject was such as to place it beyond the reach of the scientific method. Symposia on positivism and naturalism characteristically omit the word "consciousness" from their indices.

Physiology and psychology have sought for explanations of processes within the organism and of interactions between organism and environment toward thc end that these processes shall stand in continuity with physico-chemical reactions. Continuity does not necessarily imply reducibility. In both sciences there have been certain areas which have been notably accessible to the explanatory approach. For example, in urine secretion the glomerular filtrate is a simple function of blood pressure and plasma osmotic pressure and is expressible as a mathematical function, $a = f(b)(c)$. And in psychology, animal behavior is understandable, up to a point, in terms of the neurophysiology of the stimulus-response arc. Higher organic activities resist such explanations and for reasons other than those of complexity, as witness the breakdown of the constancy hypothesis in perception. Before the fact of consciousness, positive psychology, including Gestalt theory, is almost altogether silent. What conceivable connection can a functional formulation have with the peculiar and ineluctable fact that I am conscious of this chair? By the very nature of things, it does not seem possible to get hold of consciousness by the objective-empirical method (Sellars 1949, 98). The term of a materialistic approach to consciousness seems to be some such nominal characterization as Sellars's: "Why may not a neural event 'contain' consciousness as a qualitative dimension of its existential content?" (99).

Yet the abiding faith that animates the empirical enterprise is that nothing experienced need be surrendered to a transcendental realm, a realm exempt from empirical inquiry. Is it possible that some of the difficulties encountered by an objective-empirical approach to consciousness stem from a doctrinaire narrowing of the empirical method—a method which Hocking (1954) refers to as a "broad heterodox empiricism" (449)?

Certainly one of the most notable attempts to give an objective-empirical rendering of mind and consciousness is that of the social behaviorist, George H. Mead. It was Mead's great virtue to have met the problem head on, and it was his great insight that consciousness is not a private endowment, a trait of the individual organism, but is intimately bound up with the social process. Fully alive to the accountability of psychological theory for any and all psychological realities, and alive therefore to the radically unscientific character of Watson's denial of consciousness—"for the existence of such of mind or consciousness, in some sense or other, must be admitted"—Mead (1952) undertook not "to *reduce* mind or consciousness to purely behavioristic terms... [but] to *explain* it in these terms" (10). It was his conviction that the only alternative to a behavioristic "explanation" was the relinquishing of consciousness to the domain of the "transcendental," as a kind of spiritual stuff superadded to the organism. The substance of his argument consists, as a consequence, of a transposition of the stimulus-response schema to the societal level in the expectation that with sufficient refinement it would yield the necessary entities of mind, awareness, language, etc. In Morris's (1952) view, he succeeded: "mind and the self are, without remainder, generated in a social process" (xv).

Mead (1952) perceived at the outset the futility of trying to derive mind from individual organismic processes:

> It is absurd to look at the mind simply from the standpoint of the individual human organism; for, although it has its focus there, it is essentially a social phenomenon; even its biological functions are primarily social. The subjective experience of the individual must be brought into relation with the natural, socio-biological activities of the brain in order to render an acceptable account of mind possible at all; and this can be done only if the social nature of mind is recognized. The meagerness of individual experience in isolation from the processes of social experience—in isolation

> from its social environment—should, moreover, be apparent. We must regard mind, then, as arising and developing within the social process, within the empirical matrix of social interactions. (133)

How does the mind arise from the social matrix? By means of language. "Out of language emerges the field of mind" (133).

Since it is a fact that the word "means" the same thing to speaker and hearer—a situation quite different from the ordinary biological stimulus—the problem, as Mead sees it, is to derive a set of conditions under which a stimulus can evolve the same response from the organism which emits it as it does from the organism which receives it, "to get this relationship between the idea and the symbol itself into the conversation of gestures" (54).

The clue is to be found in the uniqueness of the vocal gesture. It is the only stimulus which is generated and received by the same organism: I can't see the expression of my face but I can hear the sound of my voice.

In an ordinary "conversation of gestures," such as a dog fight, there is a sequential alternation of stimulus and response:

> The act of each dog becomes a stimulus to the other dog for his response. There is then a relationship between these two; and as the act is responded to by the other dog, it, in turn, undergoes change. The very fact that the dog is ready to attack another becomes a stimulus to the other dog to change his own position or his own attitude. He has no sooner done this than the change of attitude in the second dog in turn causes the first dog to change his attitude. We have here a conversation of gestures. They are not, however, gestures in the sense that they are significant. We do not assume that the dog says to himself, "If the animal comes from this direction, he is going to spring at my throat and I will turn in such a way." What does take place is an actual change in his own position due to the direction of the approach of the other dog. (42-43)

How does a gesture become "significant"? A vocal gesture becomes a "significant symbol" when "the individual responds to his own stimulus in the same way as other people respond" (67). The task then is to derive the "significant symbol" from the classical stimulus-response schema: to explain, in other words, how it is that whereas the lion's roar does not "mean" the same thing to the roarer as it does to the hearer—since presumably the lion is not frightened by his own roar—a word or a sentence does mean the same thing to you, the speaker, as it does to me, the hearer. Mead accomplishes this by his well-known concept of role-taking. "There is no particular faculty of imitation in the sense that the sound or the sight of another's response is itself a stimulus to carry out the same reaction" (68), but there is a possibility of role-taking which can lead to imitation. Thus when a sparrow and canary are left together, it will turn out that there are certain notes that are common to both; in the conversation of gestures between them, the canary's note *A* will arouse response *B* from the sparrow. But if the sparrow also has note *A*, it will respond in the same way to its own stimulus:

> Such are the situations in which the sparrow does take the role of the canary in so far as there are certain notes to which it tends to react just as the canary does. There is a double weight, so to speak, upon this particular note or series of notes. It is in such a fashion that we can understand the learning by the sparrow of the canary's song. One has to assume a like tendency in the two forms if one is going to get any mechanism for imitation at all. (63)

Mead lays great stress on the general mechanism of role-taking:

> because it is of very fundamental importance in the development of what we call self-consciousness and the appearance of the self. We are, especially through the use of the vocal gestures, continually arousing in ourselves those responses which we call out in other persons, so that we are taking the attitudes of the other persons into our own conduct. The critical importance of language in the development of human experience lies in this fact that the stimulus is one that can react upon the speaking individual as it reacts upon the other. (69)

In the integrity of his vision, Mead could not fail to be offended by any theory that either tacitly presupposed consciousness or relinquished it to the sphere of the autonomous, the separate substance.

Admitting the difficulties attending a behavioristic rendering, he calls attention to the much greater difficulties of either denying consciousness or of supposing that consciousness simply makes its appearance and runs parallel in some way or other to the anatomical nervous state. He insists that:

> it is possible to take the behavioristic view of the world without being troubled or tripped up by the conception of consciousness; there are certainly no more serious difficulties involved in such a view as has been proposed than there are in a conception of consciousness as a something that arises at a certain point in the history of physical forms and runs parallel in some way with specific nervous states. Try to state that conception in a form applicable to the work of the psychologist and you find yourself in all sorts of difficulties that are far greater than those in the conceptions of emergence and relativity. If you are willing to approach the world from the standpoint of these conceptions, then you can approach psychology from the behaviorist's point of view. (333-4)

In having recourse to the "philosophical concepts," as he calls them, of emergence and relativity, Mead attempts to supply an empirical grounding. Thus "consciousness, in the widest sense, is not simply an emergent at a certain point, but a set of characters that is dependent upon the relationship of a thing to an organism" (329). In a narrower sense, consciousness as a "particular sort of intelligence that we ascribe to the human animal, so-called 'rational intelligence,'.... [can be brought] back to a certain type of *conduct*, the type of conduct in which the individual puts himself in the attitude of the whole group to which he belongs" (334). Through language he can do this, and consciousness or rationality "can be stated in terms of such behavior if we recognize that the gesture can affect the individual as it affects others so as to call out the response which belongs to the other" (335). *Consciousness is "the response of an organism to its own responses* [emphasis added]" (Mead 1932, 78).

I do not pretend to have given the substance of Mead's argument, but only to have indicated the general quarter from which he approaches the subject. There are explications of role-taking, the process of reflection, social organization, and so on, which probably could not be summarized without doing them a serious injustice. But perhaps it would not be unfair to say that most of this material is a further ramification and refinement of the stimulus-response mechanism—as indeed it is Mead's intention that it should be—toward the end of deriving therefrom the molar entities of mind and self. Consciousness is always defined in terms of an interaction, a response, a type of conduct. I will also pass over certain difficulties which Mead himself seems to be aware of. He is obliged, for example, by the exigencies of his theory to say that when I ask you to bring the visitor a chair, I must also arouse in myself a tendency to get up and fetch the chair—a palpable confusion of signal function and symbol or denotative function. And perhaps a falling prey to the same error he discovers in Wundt: a tendency to posit self in deriving self, a saying, in effect, that in order to become an "I," I must take the role of another.

What is at issue is of much graver import. The old embarrassing question remains: What, after all, has any schema of stimulus-response events got to do with the ineluctable fact that I am aware of this chair? Mead's formulae are at their best objective correlates running a course parallel to something from which they are separated by an abyss. And what is accomplished by terming consciousness an "emergent" from the social matrix, beyond the assigning of a verbal characterization? How does it fructify our thinking on the subject? Have we in truth come one inch from the old theories of parallelism? When we read such statements as "Consciousness as such refers to both the organism and environment and cannot be located simply in either" (Mead 1952, 332), in what way shall we take them as empirically meaningful? How does it rectify our everyday notion of consciousness as a private and autonomous awareness? How is it operationally meaningful? The fact remains, when all is said and done, consciousness is not, and we all know it is not, "a type of conduct" or a "response," and it simply does not help to say that it is.

Although Mead criticized the reductive procedure of the strict behaviorist, he retained the general conviction that psychic events are susceptible of causal-sequential explanation. When he says that mind is derivable from the social matrix, he is quite explicit in specifying the social matrix as an *interaction* between organisms. Mead's enterprise is essentially, then, an effort, albeit a heroic one, to extract consciousness, a selective intentional act, from the causal relation of signification. It must have seemed imperative to him, as it does to most psychogeneticists, for reasons of continuity to retain the function of animal signification as the basis of human meaning. The act of symbolization is *pari-passu* seen as a refinement of the sign-response. As a matter of fact, Mead (1952) did perceive the uniqueness of the symbol and its prime role in the origin of consciousness, but was barred from an exploitation of the insight by his article of faith that a departure from the stimulus-response mechanism is a departure from science. Thus, he admitted, that symbols are not mere stimuli but

> stand for the meanings of those things or objects which have meanings; they are given portions of experience which point to, indicate, or represent other portions of experience.... The symbol is thus more than a mere substitute stimulus—more than a mere stimulus for a conditioned response or reflex. For the conditioned reflex—the response to a mere substitute stimulus—does not or need not involve consciousness; whereas *the response to a symbol does and must involve consciousness* [emphasis added]. Conditioned reflexes plus consciousness of the attitudes and meanings they involve are what constitute language. (122)

Here is a tantalizing glimpse. For the first time we have an inkling that the symbol with its peculiar representative or denotative function plays an indispensable role in consciousness. But instead of exploring this new relation of denotation for what light it might shed on consciousness, Mead hurries back to the old treadmill and tries to fit symbol and consciousness into sign-response. What have the relations "stand for," "represent," got to do with the standard significatory relations "lead to," "call out," "indicate"?

In Mead, despite every effort to get hold of it, consciousness remains incorrigibly related to social interaction as a plus.

3. Symbol and Intersubjectivity

It would perhaps not be too gross a simplification to observe that the phenomenologist, having ruled out intersubjectivity in his reduction, has the greatest difficulty in reinstating it thereafter; and that the behaviorist simply takes intersubjectivity for granted, writes papers about physico-causal responses which he expects his colleagues to understand (and not merely to respond to). It is one thing to be aware, as the phenomenologists are aware, that a fundamental connection with the Other must be seized, in Sartre's (1957) words, "at the very heart of the consciousness" (233). Whether such a connection can be allowed by the method of the phenomenological reduction is something else again. If something is missing in both cases, it would seem that the better chance for recovering it lies with the empirical method, for reasons which have been stated: that the latter method tends on the whole to be self-corrective. I confess to the prejudice that the posture of Western science, the realistic assumption that we are real knowers confronting a lawful reality about which something can be known and concerning which one knower can communicate to another, will be more fruitful of results than a methodological pronunciamento at the very outset. For this reason I shall be chiefly concerned with the general approach of George H. Mead.

The most conspicuous divergence in Husserl's and Mead's approach to consciousness, aside from the methodological differences, is the opting of the one for the individual Cartesian character of consciousness and of the other for its intrinsically social character. Let us suppose for the moment that Mead (1952) is right—that we may study consciousness empirically as arising from the social matrix, that "it is absurd to look at the mind simply from the standpoint of the individual human organism" (133). Let us admit, moreover, that he—along with many others—is probably right in focusing upon language as the key to the mysteries of mind and consciousness. Is it possible that Mead fell short of his goal precisely because of his failure, or refusal, to recognize the unique character of that strange "sign" that the human animal has discovered—the symbol? Mead, along with most other American theorists has felt obliged to construe the symbol as a sort of sign and symbolic meaning as a refinement of the sign-response (for example Morris 1946, 25). Mead quite frankly declared that once you abandon the social or biological response, there is no alternative but "transcendentalism," by which he apparently meant not Kant's legislating consciousness but the notion of mind as a sort of spiritual stuff, added ghostwise to the physical organism.

What would happen if we pursued the route of exploration indicated by Mead himself in his inkling that the symbol meaning-relation lies at the very heart of consciousness?

One must sooner or later become aware, as Susanne Langer (1951) has said, that the interpretation of symbol as a kind of sign that "announces" ideas, calls forth responses, "strikes a strained and unnatural note, which is usually a fair warning that the attempted interpretation misses the most important feature in its material" (51). What is missed? It is the obvious but nonetheless extraordinary relation of denotation. A symbol above all denotes something.

Now there is nothing new in this. Semioticians take due notice of the relation of denotation in semantics, which is that dimension of semiotic that has to do with the *rules* by which a symbol is said to denote an object (Morris 1955, 84). What concerns us, however, is what one is to make of this relation of denotation from an objective-empirical point of view, rather than a logical one, as something that is actually taking place in the "data" before us, as assuredly it does take place. To put the problem concretely: Given the "phenomenon" in which the normal child or the blind deaf-mute Helen discovers that this stuff "is" water, what we wish to know (and what Mead wished to know) is not the "semantic rule" by which Helen and Miss Sullivan agree to call the stuff "water"—this is a convention not an explanation—what we wish to know is *what happens?* Something very real has happened when the sign is suddenly discovered to "mean," denote, something. What is it? Semioticians dodge the issue by parceling out the biological sign-function to "behavioristics" and symbolic denotation to "semantics" (and the relation of one symbol to another to "syntax"). Mead's objective was to bring all entities, mind, consciousness, sign, symbol, under the single gaze of the empirical method. If there is such a thing as denotation, naming, and if it does assuredly take place in the public realm we are studying, then what exactly does take place, and what is its relevance for the phenomena of intersubjectivity and consciousness? How does it illumine these realities, which, as we have seen, no refinement of signification seems to get hold of?

I only wish to call attention, without pretending to have determined their precise role in the act of consciousness, to two characteristics of the symbol meaning-relation, *as they are empirically ascertainable*, which distinguish it from the sign-relation and which have the utmost relevance for the topics under consideration.

The first is a unique relation between the "organisms" involved in the symbolic meaning-structure, a relation that can only come about through a radical change in the relations that obtain in the sign-response. Signification is essentially and irreducibly a triadic meaning-relation; whereas symbolization is essentially and irreducibly a tetradic relation (Percy 1957, 240).* The three terms of the sign-response are related physico-causally. The schema, sign—organism—significatum, has so persistently recommended itself as the ground of meaning, human and sub-human, because it deals with physical structures and with causal† relations and energy exchanges between these structures. Thus, no matter whether we are considering a solitary polar bear responding to the sound of splitting ice, or a bee responding to the honey-dance of another bee, or a human responding to the cry of "Fire!" in a crowded theater, each case is understandable as a sequential stimulus-response action acquired or inherited according to the exigencies of biological adaptation: sign → sound waves (or light waves) → sensory end-organ → afferent nerve impulse → cortical pattern → efferent nerve impulse → motor (or

* Editors' note: Percy later evolved his thinking on the irreducibility of tetradic relations. (See Percy's *The Message in the Bottle* 1975, 167.)

† I use the word "causal" without prejudice, to mean whatever the reader would have it mean. It does not matter for the argument whether it is read as efficient causality or as a probability function.

glandular) activity with reference toward (or away from) significatum. Whether we are trying to understand the behavior of a solitary organism in an inorganic environment (polar bear) or a society of organisms (bee hive), the behavior in each case may be understood as a response of single organisms to environments. In one case the organism is responding to an inorganic environment (splitting ice), in the other case to an organic environment (other bees). The central concept in both cases is that of an organism-in-an-environment.

The symbol relation is radically and generically different. It is a tetradic relation in which the presence of the *two* organisms is not merely required as an irreducible minimum but in which the two are co-related in an unprecedented fashion. Denotation, the act of naming, of its very nature requires the *two*, Namer and Hearer (Percy 1957, 232-3). My calling this thing a chair is simply another way of saying that it "is" a chair for you and me. It takes two to make a semantical "rule." It is inconceivable that a human being raised apart from other humans should ever discover symbolization. For there is no way I can know this "is" a chair unless you tell me so. But not only is the presence of the two a genetic requirement of symbolization—as the presence of two is a genetic requirement of biological fertilization—it is its *enduring condition.* Even Robinson Crusoe writing in his journal after twenty years on his island is performing a through-and-through social act. Every symbolic formulation, whether it be language, art, or even thought, implies a real or an ideal *someone else* for whom the symbol is intended as meaningful. *Denotation is an exercise in intersubjectivity* (Percy 1956, 525). The two are no longer related as organisms in a nexus of interaction but as an I and a Thou, co-conceivers and co-celebrants of the object under the auspices of a common symbol.

It is a fool's errand to attempt to derive intersubjectivity by theorizing about physico-causal interactions among data. As Schütz (1954) has pointed out, such theorizing must presuppose intersubjectivity as its unclarified foundation (261, 265). Physico-causal theory is formed entirely *within* the intersubjective milieu and cannot of its very nature transcend it. A physical function, $a = f(b)$, is a saying of one scientist to another, an I to a Thou, about quantifiable relations among the data before them. If we wish to study the knowers themselves, the I-Thou relation, we must speak some other language, perhaps an ontological one rather than a physico-causal one. Cross-reference Marcel's (1951b) "intersubjective nexus":

> It is a metaphysic of *we are* as opposed to a metaphysic of *I think*.... But it is apparent by definition that what I may call the intersubjective nexus cannot be given to me, since I am myself in some way involved in it. It may not perhaps be inaccurate to say that this nexus is in fact the necessary condition for anything being given to me.... Without doubt the intersubjective nexus cannot be in any way asserted: it can only be acknowledged.... the affirmation should possess a special character, that of being the root of every expressible affirmation. *I should readily* agree that it is the mysterious root of language [emphasis added]. (10-12)

Symbolization can only occur by a radical shift in the elements of the old meaning-structure of sign-organism-significatum. I do not know whether it is more proper or fruitful to speak of this new state of affairs as an "emergent" or as a mode of being, but in any case there has come into existence a relation that transcends the physico-causal relations obtaining among data. This relation is intersubjectivity. It is a reality which can no longer be understood in the instrumental terms of biological adaptation. The "organisms" implicated are no longer oriented pragmatically toward their environment but ontologically as its co-knowers and co-celebrants. Intersubjectivity may not be construed as an interaction. It requires instead a suitable phenomenology that takes due notice of its most characteristic property, a polarity of authenticity-inauthenticity. Here a normative terminology is unavoidable. One must recognize the authentic I-Thou relation and the deteriorated I-It of Buber. Symbolization bridges the gap between the behavioristics of Mead and the existentialia of Marcel.

4. Symbol and Consciousness

The selective and intentional character of consciousness has been stressed by empiricist and phenomenologist alike. The conscious act is always intentional; one is never simply conscious but conscious of this or that. Consciousness, in fact, is defined by the phenomenologist as noematic intentionality in general. But quite as essential to the act of consciousness is its symbolic character. Every conscious perception is of the nature of a recognition, which is to say that the object is recognized as "being" what it is. To amend the phenomenologist, it is not enough to say that one is conscious *of* something; one is also conscious of something *as* something. There is a difference between the sensory apprehension of a form and the grasping of it under its symbolic vehicle. "We should need to distinguish between the intuition of a sensory appearance, which alone is given, and the denotative selection of a thing-object which is believed in and characterized" (Sellars quoted in Chisholm 1954, 36). (Sellars used "denote" more or less interchangeably with "perceive" and "intend.") As I gaze about the room, I am aware of a series of almost effortless acts of *matching:* seeing an object and knowing it for what it is. If my eyes fall upon an unfamiliar something, I am immediately aware that one term of the match is missing; I ask what it is. Marcel has observed that when I see an unfamiliar flower and ask what it is, I am more satisfied to be given a name than a scientific classification, even though the name may mean nothing to me. Is this the residue of name-magic, or is it the need of a something of comparable ontological weight (the sensuous symbol) to lay alongside the object in order that the latter be known? It is the *pairing* in the act of perception which must not be overlooked. It is a relation, moreover, which goes far beyond the attaching of a label to something already known—as the semanticists suggest. Rather is it the pairing or formulation itself, as Cassirer has pointed out, which comprises the act of knowing. Cassirer stands at the opposite pole from the semanticists. So far from it being a case of a thing being known and a label later attached by a semantical "rule," it is the symbolic formulation, which is itself the act of knowing. The "real" object tends to vanish into Kant's noumenon. Each conscious recognition may be regarded as an approximation, a cast of one thing toward another toward the end of a fit. Thus, if I see an object at some distance and do not quite recognize it, I may see it, actually see it, as a succession of different things, each rejected by the criterion of fit as I come closer, until one is positively certified. A patch of sunlight in a field I may actually see as a rabbit—a seeing which goes much further than the guess that it may be a rabbit; no, the perceptual gestalt is actually construed, stamped by the essence of rabbitness; I could have sworn it was a rabbit. On coming closer, the sunlight pattern changes enough so that the rabbit-cast is disallowed. It vanishes and I make another cast; it is a paper bag, etc. Is not symbolization, the pairing of sensuous symbol with an impression, a kind of judgment and abstraction? In even its most primitive form, a pointing at and a naming, it is a saying that is "one of these." It is an abstraction, however, which is a far cry from the conventional notion of concept-formation by which two given representations are combined. We must, as Cassirer (1953b) says, take a step further back. This will take us to Lotze's "first universal," the primitive abstraction by which impressions are raised to symbolizations (281).

Awareness is not only intentional in character; it is also symbolic. The phenomenologist tells only half the story. I am not only conscious *of* something; I am conscious of it *as* being what it is. If there is a wisdom in the etymologies, the word "consciousness" is surely a case of it, for "consciousness," one suddenly realizes, means a *knowing-with!* In truth it could not be otherwise. The act of consciousness is the intending of the object as being what it is for both of us. The most notable element of Helen Keller's discovery that this liquid "is" water was the sudden heightening of consciousness. She describes all previous experience as something less than conscious; she speaks of thinking before the great event then adds, "if a wordless sensation can be called a thought" (Keller 1928, 25).

It does not of course solve the problem of consciousness to say that it is an exercise in intersubjectivity. I only wish to suggest that the conviction of the phenomenologists that intersubjectivity must somehow be constituted at the very heart of consciousness, a consummation devoutly to be desired but evidently not forthcoming under the phenomenological method, is confirmed by the empirical method, a method which takes account of natural existents, organisms and sensuous symbols and objects to be known, and real relations in the world. Consciousness and intersubjectivity are seen to be inextricably co-related; they are in fact aspects of the same new orientation in the world, the symbolic orientation.

This empirical insight into the intersubjective nature of consciousness does, however, suggest an important corrective for the transcendental reduction. Is the phenomenologists' stronghold of the absolute priority of the individual consciousness so invulnerable after all? Is there in fact such a thing as the "purified transcendental consciousness" (Husserl 1952), or is it a chimera from the very outset? Is it an abstraction masquerading as an empirical reality? If my every act of consciousness, not only genetically speaking, my first act of consciousness, but each succeeding act, is a through-and-through social participation, then it is a contradiction in terms to speak of an aboriginal ego-consciousness. There may be such a thing as an ego-consciousness, but far from being the apodictic takeoff point of a presuppositionless science, it would appear to correspond to Buber's term of deterioration, the decay of the I-Thou relation into the objectivization of the I-It.

Sartre's even more radical revision of transcendental consciousness falls equally short of the mark. Declaring that the Cartesian *cogito* is insufficiently radical, that it is a derived condition of consciousness in which consciousness intends itself as an object, Sartre probes back to the "Pre-reflective *cogito*." This fundamental reality is a non-posited, non-objectified, pre-reflective consciousness. But is there such a thing? Or is it not the very nature of the search that the most radical back-tracking into consciousness cannot carry us beyond what Marcel calls the "intelligible milieu" by which he means the prime and irreducible character of intersubjectivity?

Mead's major thesis was that the individual transcendental consciousness is a myth, that mind and consciousness are indefeasibly social realities. This thesis, it seems to me, is not borne out by Mead's physico-causal theorizing, by behavioristics, but is dramatically confirmed as soon as the true character of the symbolic orientation is recognized.

Sartre would amend the Cartesian and Husserlian formula for the originary act of consciousness

> I am conscious of this chair

to read

> There is consciousness of this chair

both of which presuppose the individual consciousness as the ultimate reality. An empirical study of the emergence of symbolization from the biological elements of signification suggests the following revision of Sartre:

> This "is" a chair for you and me

which co-celebration of the chair as being what it is under the auspices of the symbol, is itself the very constituent act of consciousness (Percy 1956, 526).

CHAPTER II

SEMIOTIC AND THE PROBLEM OF KNOWLEDGE

A student of current philosophies of science must sooner or later become aware of a curious state of affairs. If he is accustomed to the discipline and unity of a particular science, he may reasonably expect that a philosophy of science will in turn confer a larger unity on the elements of the scientific enterprise, not merely the various data of the sciences but also the conclusions and the activities of the scientists themselves. This is not, however, what he will find. What he is more apt to encounter in the various symposia and encyclopediae of unified science is an inveterate division of subject matters. Some may be written entirely in one language, some entirely in the other; some may be a mixture of both, but neither seems to have much to do with the other. The two approaches are: (1) the nomothetic method with which he is familiar, arising from the "inexpugnable belief," as Whitehead (1953) put it, "that every detailed occurrence can be correlated with its antecedents in a perfectly definite manner exemplifying general principles" (18); (2) the quite different program which Russell (1914), after completing the *Principia Mathematica*, staked out for philosophy as its sole concern: the logical analysis of empirical propositions established by perception and science.

Take the most ambitious and interesting example of a "meta-science," semiotic, the science of signs. It is interesting because, unlike pure symbolic logic, it tries to unite logical analysis with the explanatory enterprise of science, and because, whatever its shortcomings, it has at least hit upon the fruitful notion of man as the sign-using animal. Here too one encounters the same division of subject matters with no visible means of getting from one to the other, despite the many assurances that semiotic confers unity. If one expected a larger epistemological unity in which the relation of logical analysis to the scientific explanation of natural events is to be made clear, he will be disappointed. He will get logical analysis, and he will get scientific theorizing, but he will not learn what one has to do with the other. "Languages are developed and used by living beings operating in a world of objects, and show the influence of both the users and the objects. If, as symbolic logic maintains, there are linguistic forms whose validity is not dependent upon nonlinguistic objects, then their validity must be dependent upon the rules of the language in question" (Morris 1955, 67). Characteristically, semioticists do not find it remarkable that sign-using animals should have developed symbolic logic "whose validity is not dependent on nonlinguistic objects." It is therefore not worth investigating how this could have come about, but only necessary to note that it has and to define this unusual activity as the "syntactical dimension" of semiosis.

There are studies on the biology of sign-function, and here one recognizes a basic continuity with the manifold of natural phenomena. When one speaks of animal *A* responding to buzzer *B* by salivation in expectation of food *F*, one is speaking a language familiar to psychologist, physiologist, and physicist alike, the language of spatio-temporal events that lend themselves to causal hypothesis. Stimulus and response events occur among natural existents and are mediated by physical structures and a causal nexus that is recognized as valid for organic and inorganic matter. Nor should one be confused by the encyclopedists' disavowals of determinism in favor of the probability approach, which is supposed to resolve the nomothetic-ideographic dichotomy of object-science and history (Brunswik 1952, 696). For, as becomes abundantly clear, the laws of probability are relied upon as quite as heavily as strict causality (Friend and Feibleman 1937, 180). As Nagel (1953) insists, although laws connecting micro-states may be statistical in character, that does not mean that laws connecting macro-states are not strictly deterministic (437).

Thus, whatever the limitations of a biological science of signs in man and animals, one readily recognizes its validity as far as it goes; for example, the methodological negation of mental entities and the inability to take account of Gestalt qualities (Klubertanz 1951, 70).

But then one suddenly finds oneself in the charged atmosphere of the Polish semanticists with their scoldings at the human *abuse* of signs. At one moment, one is studying sign behavior as a natural science in which "interpreters" behave according to lawful empirical regularities, and in the next, as a quasi-ethical science in which "interpreters" disobey semantical rules and in general behave stupidly and perversely. There will also be articles dealing exclusively with syntactical rules in logic and mathematics, with the arbitrary formation of calculi, with the principles of logical implication. Or one may read statements by the same semioticist that (1) "the basic terms of semiotic are all formulable in terms applicable to behavior as it occurs in an environment" (Morris 1946, 19), and (2) semiotic can be presented as a deductive system with undefined terms and primitive sentences which allow the deduction of other sentences as theorems (Morris 1955, 86).

The fact is that a man engaged in the business of building a logical calculus is doing a very different sort of thing from an animal (or man) responding to a sign, and it is a difference which is not conjured away by ignoring it or by leaping nimbly from *res extensa* to *res cogitans* as though there were no epistemological abyss in between. I cannot say it as well as Professor Crockett (1954): "I do not know whether one should try to describe the universe or whether one should play games in which marks are arranged according to certain rules; but I do know that one should decide which of these vastly different kinds of activities one is engaged in and inform the reader accordingly" (91).

It is not my intention to make a case against either of the two major components of semiotic, symbolic logic and behavioristics—the shortcomings of each are well known by now. Rather it is my hope to show that a true semiotic, far from being the *coup de grâce* of metaphysics, may prove of immense value in as much as it validates and illumines a classical metaphysical relation, *and this is at an empirical level.*

I think it will be possible to show (1) that the "unified science of semiotic" is a spurious unity conferred by a deliberate equivocation of the word "sign" to designate two generically different meaning-situations (the sign-relation and the symbol-relation); and (2) that a purely "semiotical" analysis of symbolization will shed light on two metaphysical relations. The first, the cognitive relation of identity by which a concept, a "formal sign," comes to contain within itself *in alio esse* the thing signified; the second, the relation of intersubjectivity, one of the favorite themes of modern existentialists. It may well turn out that the semioticist has good reason to ignore the symbol-relation in view of his dictum that sign analysis replaces metaphysics since an impartial analysis of symbolization can only bring one face-to-face with that very thing which the semioticist has set out at any cost to avoid: a metaphysical issue.

Let us not be too hasty in surrendering the symbol to the symbolic logician, nor, as is sometimes done, to the mythist. It is possible that a free empirical inquiry into the symbol-function, that is, an inquiry undertaken without the dogmatic limitations of positivism, may provide fresh access to a philosophy of being.

1. Syntax and Science

Semiotic, the science of signs, is an attempt to bring together into the formal unity of a single science three separate disciplines: (1) the semantical rules by which symbols are applied to their designata, (2) the logical analysis of the relations of symbols as they appear in sentences, (3) the natural science of behavioristics (to use Neurath's terminology), in which organisms are studied in their relation to the environment as it is mediated by signs. It was soon discovered, as Sellars (1949) points out, that the limitation of scientific empiricism to logical syntax is suicidal, and so the semantical and biological study of signs was added under the guidance of C. W. Morris (94). According to Morris (1955), these three disciplines may be regarded as three "dimensions" of the same science: the semantical dimension of semiosis, the syntactical dimension, and the pragmatic dimension. "It will be convenient to have special terms to designate certain of the relations of signs to signs, to objects, and to interpreters. '*Implicates*' will be restricted to *Dsyn.*, '*designates*' and '*denotes*' to *Dsem* and '*expresses*' to *Dp*. The word 'table' implicates (but does not designate) 'furniture with a horizontal top on which things may be placed,' denotes the objects to which it is applicable, and expresses its interpreter" (84-85). Note the ambiguity of the term "expresses its interpreter." "Implicates," "designates," and "denotes," are purely semantical syntactical terms with no biological analogue. But what are we to take "expresses" to mean? Is it to be taken in the biological sense of a sign "announcing" its significatum to its interpreter, or in the symbolic sense of "expressing a meaning"?

This division is held to be analogous to the division of biology into anatomy, ecology, and physiology (Morris 1955, 121). A symbolic logician, a semanticist, and a behaviorist are said to be emphasizing different aspects of the same science. Physiology requires anatomy and ecology requires both; all three conform admirably to the biologist's conception of organism as a system reacting to its environment according to its needs of maintaining its internal milieu and reproducing itself. Physiology is complemented by anatomy; one flows into the other without a hitch. But how does syntactical analysis flow into behavioristics? One may make syntactical analysis of the sentences written down by a behaviorist, or one may study the knee jerks of a symbolic logician, but in what larger scheme may the two be brought into some kind of order? We find symposia written from either point of view, from the physicalist's who starts with matter and its interactions and tries to derive mind therefrom (such as, for example, *Philosophy for the Future: The Quest of Modern Materialism* (Sellars et al. 1949)) or from the purely logical, which conceives the task as the syntactical investigation of the language of science. Far from the one flowing naturally into the other, the fact is that one has very little use for the other. It takes an encyclopedist to bring them together.

It is well known that logical empiricism is without a theory of knowledge since it restricts itself to an abstract theory of the logic of language (Cornforth 1949, 518). It is equally well known—and perhaps one is a consequence of the other—that the history of logical empiricism is the history of wide fluctuations on the mind-body axis (Feigl 1953). Examples of the extremes are the solipsism of Mach, Wittgenstein, and the early Carnap of *Der Logische Aufbau;* and the physicalism of the American behaviorists and the later Carnap. But even in the more modern attempts at unity, one is aware of the tendency to construe the field exclusively from the logical or the physicalist point of view—and indeed, how can it be otherwise when the problem of knowing is ruled out of court? A semioticist can easily take the position that the only genuine problem, as Carnap claimed, was one of logical analysis, i.e., the question of the formal relations between the concepts that describe the data of first-person experience, the concepts of physics, and those of behaviorist psychology (Feigl 1953, 615). Or one can begin at the other end with the causal relations between signs and interpreters and derive mind and consciousness with never a thought for syntactical analysis. (See, for example, Mead 1952.) Anatomy is indispensable to physiology, but syntax can get along very well without neurology. Neither symbolic logicians nor behaviorists are constrained to make contact with each other, and it is perhaps proper that they do not. But it is the semioticists who have brought them willy-nilly together to form the new organon. It is not unreasonable, therefore, to expect that this meta-science will provide a larger order. Perhaps, then, it is the semanticists who fill the gap. For semantics professes to deal with both the words of the logicians and the natural objects of the scientist.

We are destined to disappointment. Semantics, it turns out, abstracts from the user of language and analyzes only the expressions and their designata (Carnap 1948, 9). Like syntax, it operates from the logical pole in that it is chiefly concerned with formation of "rules" for the application of symbols to things (Morris 1955, 101). Korzybski (1952), we discover, is not interested in how it is that words get applied to things, in the extraordinary act of naming, but only in our perverse tendency to use words incorrectly, and in making a "structural differential" so that one may use words with the full knowledge of the level of abstraction to which they apply (386). Or if we turn to Tarski's (1944) classic paper on the semantic conception of truth with high hopes that at last we have come to the heart of the matter, we will find as the thesis of the article the following criterion of "material adequacy": "*X is true if, and only if, p is true*" (357), which when interpreted yields: "'*Snow is white' is true if, and only if, snow is white*" (343). I do not wish to deny the usefulness of Tarski's criterion within the limits he has set; I only wish to point out that Tarski by his own emphatic asseveration is not concerned with the problem of knowing. For example, in answer to the charge that his "snow is white" sentence seems to imply a naïve realism when it lays down the condition "if and only if snow is white," Tarski (1944) writes: "The semantic definition of truth implies nothing regarding the conditions under which a sentence like (1): *snow is white* can be asserted. It implies only that, whenever we assert or reject this sentence, we must be ready to assert or reject the correlated sentence (2): *the sentence 'snow is white' is true.* Thus, we may accept the semantic conception of truth without giving up any epistemological attitude we may have had; we may remain naïve realists, critical realists or idealists, empiricists or metaphysicians—whatever we were before. The semantic conception is completely neutral toward all these issues" (361-2).

If, in order to bring the twain together by the semiotic method, we strain forward to the farthest limits of behaviorism and backwards to the earliest takeoff point of semantics, we will find that the gap between them is narrow but exceedingly deep. Logical syntax begins *with* the "protocol statement," the simplest naming sentence; and semantics is exclusively concerned with its rules of designation. In regard to the logical syntax of the language of science, Carnap writes, "'Science is a system of statements based on direct experience and controlled by experimental verification.... Verification is based on *protocol statements.*' Protocol statements are 'statements needing no justification and serving as the foundations for all the remaining statements of science'" (quoted in Cornforth 1949, 510).

Behavioristics, even taken at its own estimation, brings us to a point considerably short of the relation of denotation and the protocol sentence. It deals with the sign behavior of animals and man according to the method of natural science: that of discerning empirical regularities and later attributing them to a causal function $a = f(b)$. An organism's response to a stimulus is resolvable into a sequential series of commotions mediated by structures, beginning with an air vibration and ending with an efferent nerve discharge into a glandular end organ. Nor does the Gestaltist, for that matter, take us an inch closer to the mysterious act of naming. By his concept of field forces and perceptual wholes, he can make sense of molar phenomena which escape the behaviorist. He can arrive at certain traits of configuration that apply alike to chickens and humans. (See for example the Jastrow illusion in Koffka [1935, 32].) But neither the behaviorist nor the gestaltist has anything to say, indeed does not wish to have anything to say, about the naming act. The very methodology of an object-science precludes its consideration of an object-sentence as such, perhaps for no other reason than that the object-science takes place within the very intersubjective nexus which language implies.

An object-science of behavior can only make sense of language by trying to derive it from some refinement of sign-response. As Susanne Langer (1951) has pointed out, when the naming act is construed in these terms, when the situation in which you give something a name, and it is the same for you as it is for me, when this peculiar relation of denotation is construed in terms of stimulus-response, one has the feeling that it leaves out the most important thing of all. What is left out, what an object-science cannot get hold of by an intrinsic limitation of method is nothing less than the relation of denotation—"**a name, above all, *denotes* something** [bold, emphasis added]" (51). If you say "James" to a dog whose master bears that name, the dog will interpret the sound as a sign and *look* for James. Say it to a person who knows someone called thus, and he will ask, "What about James?" That simple question is forever beyond the dog; signification is the only meaning a name can have for him (51).

The upshot is, even if we go no farther than Mrs. Langer, who is otherwise in sympathy with the positivism of the semioticists, that semiotic symbol analysis and the science of sign-behavior are brought willy-nilly together into a unity that has no other justification than that both have something to do with "sign." No larger sanction can be forthcoming because of the dictum that sign analysis replaces metaphysics. To say to a semioticist that he is confusing the logical with the real is unacceptable because of the "metaphysical" presuppositions involved. One might nevertheless expect that within the limits of the semiotical method, some attempt might be made to achieve the continuity so highly prized by semioticists since the time of Peirce. Continuity "is the absence of ultimate parts in that which is divisible" (Peirce 1935, 118). It is "nothing but perfect generality of a law of relationship" (117). Failing this continuity, one can't help wondering whether to do so, to explore the gap between pragmatics and symbol analysis, will not run squarely into an "extra-semiotical" relation—not as a "metaphysical presupposition" nor a "naïve realism" but as an issue that is precisely arrived at by the semiotical method itself.

2. Sign and Symbol

Semiosis uses as its basic frame of reference the meaning triad of Charles Peirce (1955, 99):

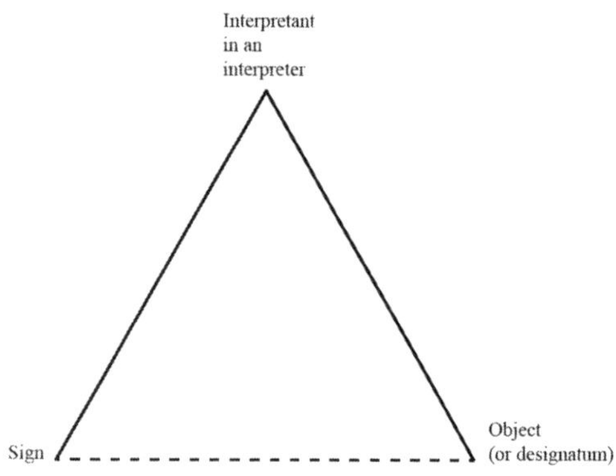

Its three components are sign, interpretant, and object. The "interpretant" in man is equivalent to "thought" or "idea" or, in modern semiotical usage, to "taking-account-of-something" (Morris 1955, 82). The interpretant therefore implies an organism in which the interpretant occurs, the interpreter. The virtue of the triadic conception of the meaning relation is that it is conformable with the biological notion of stimulus-response, in which the sign is equivalent to a stimulus, the conditioned response to the interpretant, and the designatum to the object of the response.

The triad can be looked at in either its biological (pragmatical) or its logical dimension. That is to say, it can be conceived either as a causal relation obtaining between natural existents and mediated by neural structures, sound waves, etc.; or it can be viewed syntactically-semantically. Thus, in the biological dimension, the buzzer (sign) has no direct relation to the object (food) whereas in the semantical dimension the word (sign) has the direct relation of designation with the object, precisely in so far as it is specified by a semantical rule to designate the object. Syntactics has to do with the logical relation which one sign bears to another.

The semioticists, however, when they speak of the meaning-relation as it is taken to occur among natural existents whether human or subhuman, and regardless of whether they are speaking of the pragmatical or semantical dimension, always assume that it is a causal sequential event. (I use the word "causal" unprejudicially to mean whatever the reader would take it to mean in the context. It does not matter for the argument whether one interprets this cause as efficient causality or as a probability function.) These semioticists are careful to use *response* instead of conception or thought or idea: "terms gain relations among themselves according to the relations of the responses of which the sign vehicles are a part, and these modes of usage are the pragmatical background of the formation and transformation rules" (Morris 1955, 95). Even in Ogden and Richards's (1953) variation of Peirce's triad in which the terms symbol and thought (or reference) and referent are used, it is stated that "between a thought and a symbol causal relations hold" (10).

We may therefore express the basic semiotic relation in terms of the simple biological triad:

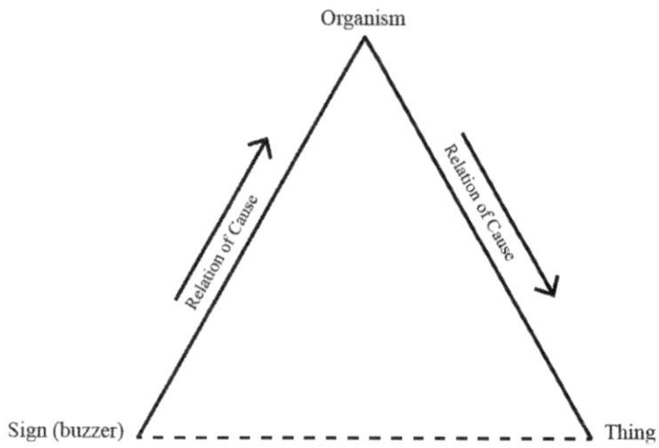

Between the sign and organism, organism and object, "real," causal relations hold (Ogden and Richards 1953, 12). The line between sign and object is dotted because no real relation holds, but only an imputed relation, the semantical relation of designation. A major doctrine of the semanticists is that most of the difficulties which thought encounters come about through the imputation of a real relation where only a semantical one exists (Ogden and Richards 1953, 12; Chase 1938; Korzybski 1952).

One knows at once what Ogden and Richards mean by "real" even though latter day semioticists would avoid the term. Signification occurs as a material happening among natural existents, from the sound of the buzzer to an electro-colloidal change in the dog's brain to glandular secretion. There is, however, no such "real" relation between sign and object. It is irrelevant that in the case of thunder announcing rain, the thunder happens to have a real connection with the rain-process. The same relation of signification could be made to take place in a deaf organism by using a blue light to announce rain. Thus, to use St. Augustine's nomenclature, whether the sign is natural or conventional, the mode of response is the same.

Two considerations arise in connection with the semiotical theory of meaning. The first is simply this: If the semioticists insist on giving a biological account of the meaning-relation as it is taken to occur among natural existents (human organisms, words, things), what account are they prepared to give in these terms of the imputed and logical relations which occur in semantics and syntax? If the semantical relation between sign and designatum is not "real," then what is its status? Is its status settled by the nominal device of calling it an "imputed" relation? Is it simply "wrong" as one might gather from the semanticists? The answer is not forthcoming. One simply speaks in one breath of concepts as "responses" and in the next of the logical relations between concepts. This treatment is, as we have seen, ambiguous. It can either mean that the semantical-syntactical relation stands in so obvious a continuity with sign behavior that nothing more need be said about it. Or it may mean that of course it is "mental" and has nothing to do with sign behavior and that it goes without saying that the Cartesian dualism of *res extensa* and *res cogitans* prevails. At any rate, it is unsatisfactory to be required to shift attention without further ado from the great corpus of natural science to an "unreal but imputed" relation. It would not seem unreasonable to ask what one is to make of this queer relation in terms of a "unified science."

The second consideration, and one which on investigation leads to such unexpected consequences, has been raised, not by a hostile critic of semiotic, but by an erstwhile symbolic logician. There is something wrong, writes Susanne Langer (1951), about regarding the word-symbol as a sign and a conception as a response. Since the notion of meaning as signification in the narrow sense, as a response, "misses the most important feature in its material" (51), *what is this feature and what are its epistemological consequences?*[*]

---

[*] If we had hoped that Mrs. Langer would follow up the epistemological consequences of this most important insight into the non-causal character of symbolic meaning, we shall be disappointed. She drops it quickly, restates her allegiance to positivism and goes on to the esthetic symbol as the form of feeling. See Langer 1953.

What is this most important feature left out by a causal rendering of meaning? It is, of course, the relation of denotation as opposed to signification. To give something a name, at first sight the most commonplace of events, is in reality a most mysterious act, one which is quite unprecedented in animal behavior and imponderable in its consequences. The semioticists are obliged by method to render symbol as a kind of sign. Morris (1946) defines a symbol as a sign produced by its interpreter which acts as a substitute for some other sign with which it is synonymous (25). Thus, in a dog, hunger cramps can take the place of the buzzer in the control of the dog's behavior: "hunger cramps for instance might themselves come to be a sign (that is, a symbol) of food at the customary place" (25)!! Although we may sympathize with Morris's purpose not to disqualify "mind" but simply to advance semiotic as a science (28), the fact remains that this is an extraordinary use of the word "symbol"—certainly it has nothing to do with denotation. It is the relation of denotation, as Mrs. Langer points out, which has been completely overlooked. The question is this: Can denotation be derived by a refinement of behavioral reaction or is it something altogether different? Can any elaboration of response issue in naming? Why is it, we begin to wonder, the semioticists refuse to deal with symbolization, excepting only as it is governed by semantical rules?

That symbolization is radically and generically different from signification is confirmable in various ways. There is the sudden discovery of the symbol in the history of deaf-mutes, such as the well-known incident in which Helen Keller, who had understood the word water (spelled into her hand) but only as a sign to which she must respond by fetching the mug and drinking the water, awoke to the extraordinary circumstance that the word "water" meant, denoted, the substance water. The significance of her discovery that this "is" water may be judged from the fact that having discovered what water "was," she then wanted to know what everything else "was" (Keller 1928, 25). (See also the experiences of Marie Huertin, Lywine Lachance, and the well-authenticated account of Victor, the wild boy of Aveyron, who discovered the symbol *despite* every attempt of his positivist teacher to present it as a sign of a want (Langer 1951, 97).) There are the genetic studies of normal children, as, for example, the observation of Schachtel (1954), who speaks of the autonomous object interest of young children as being altogether different from the earlier need-gratification interest. "These considerations cast some doubt on the adequacy of Freud's theory of the origin and nature of thought.... According to Freud thought has only one ancestor, the attempt at hallucinatory need-satisfaction.... I believe that thought has two ancestors rather than one—namely, motivating needs *and* a distinctively human capacity, the relatively autonomous capacity for object interest" (318). Symbolization can be approached genetically, as the proper subject of empirical psychology; or it can be set forth phenomenologically, as a meaning-structure with certain irreducible terms and relations.

Let us first take notice of the gross elements of the symbol meaning-situation and later of the inter-relations that exist between them.

3. The Second Organism and the Relation of Intersubjectivity

What happens then when a sign becomes a symbol, when a sound, a vocable that had served as a stimulus in the causal nexus of organism-in-an-environment, is suddenly discovered to *mean* something in the sense of denoting it?

It will be recalled that the relation of signification is a triadic one of sign-organism-object. This schema holds true for any significatory meaning-situation. It is true of a dog responding to a buzzer by salivation; it is true of a polar bear responding to the sound of splitting ice; it is true of a man responding to a telephone bell; it is true of little Helen responding to the word "water" by fetching water. It is also true of a human responding to the shout "fire!" in a crowded theater. (See Mead (1952).) Here, characteristically, the semioticist confuses symbol and sign by citing human significatory responses as illustrative of human meaning in general. One may indeed respond to a word, and in this respect our understanding is similar to Helen's understanding of signs prior to her discovery of the symbol and is in fact generically the same as a dog's response to a spoken command. But it is an altogether different situation when a father tells his child that this "is" fire, and the child awakes to the fact that by this odd little sound "fire," his father means this leaping flame. The essential requirement of signification is that there be an organism in an environment capable of learning by effecting an electro-colloidal change in the central nervous system and as a consequence responding to a stimulus in a biologically adaptive fashion. It does not matter for the present purpose that some intelligent responses are acquired by conditioning and that others are congenital dispositions of the organism. The learned response of the dog to the buzzer and the innate response of the chick to the sight of grain are both explicable in physico-causal terms as an event in an electro-colloidal system. (See the "IRM," the Innate Response Mechanism in Bowlby (1953).)

It is important to realize that whereas signification often occurs between two or more organisms, it is not essential that it should and that generically the sort of response is the same whether one or more organisms are involved. The action of a dog in responding intelligently to the bark or feint of another dog—Mead's (1952) "conversation of gestures" (43)—is generically the same sort of meaning relation as that in which a solitary polar bear responds to the sound of splitting ice. It is the *environment* to which the organism responds in an unbiologically adaptive fashion, and the mode of response is the same whether the environment consists of other organisms or of inorganic nature.

Only a moment's reflection is needed to realize that the minimal requirement of symbolization is quite different. By the very nature of symbolic meaning, there must be *two* "organisms" in the meaning-relation, one who gives the name and one for whom the name becomes meaningful. The very essence of symbolization is an entering into a *mutuality* toward that which is symbolized. It is the very condition of my conceiving the object before me under the auspices of a symbol that you name it for me, or I name it for you. The act of symbolization requires another besides the Hearer; it requires a Namer. Without the presence of another, symbolization cannot conceivably occur because there is no one from whom the word can be received as meaningful.

When Robinson Crusoe writes in his diary after twenty years alone on the island, his action is nevertheless a social phenomenon. *The irreducible condition of every symbolic act is the rendering intelligible, that is to say, the formulation of an experience for a real or an implied someone else.*

The presence of two organisms is not merely a prior condition, a *sine qua non* of symbolization; it is rather its enduring condition, its indispensable climate. Any act of symbolization, a naming, a creating, perhaps even thought itself, implies another as a co-conceiver, a co-celebrant of the thing that is symbolized. If there is a natural wisdom in etymologies, perhaps this is a case of it—for "conceive," one suddenly realizes, means to "take with." Symbolization is an exercise in intersubjectivity.

A new and indefeasible relation has come into being between the two organisms by virtue of which they are related not merely as one organism responding to another, but as a Namer and a Hearer, an I and a Thou. Mead's two dogs quarrelling over a bone exist in a conversation of gesture, a sequential order of gesture and counter gesture. But a Namer and a Hearer of the name exist in a mutuality of understanding towards that which is symbolized. Here the terminology of an object-science falls short. One must use such words as mutuality or intersubjectivity, however unsatisfactory they may be. Whatever we choose to call it, the fact remains that there has occurred a sudden co-intending of the object under the auspices of the symbol, a relation which of its very nature cannot be construed in causal language.

Is it possible then that an unprejudiced semiotic may throw some light on the interpersonal relation, the I-Thou of Buber, the intersubjectivity of Marcel? As things stand now, the empirical mind can make very little of this entity "intersubjectivity" and the behaviorist nothing at all. Like other existential themes, it seems very much in the air. Yet an empirical approach to the genesis of symbolization is bound to reveal it as a very real, if mysterious, relation. Perhaps the contribution of a new semiosis will be that *inter*subjectivity is by no means a reducible, or an imaginary phenomenon, but is a very real and pervasive bond and one mediated by a sensible symbol and a sensible object that is symbolized. Hocking (1954) writes of intersubjectivity as a direct unmediated bond from which mind and language arise: "without the direct experiential knowledge of 'We are,' the very ideas of 'sign,' 'language,' 'other mind' itself, could not arise" (453). Yet one might wonder whether it is not the other way around—whether the relation "We are" does not arise through a mutual intending of the object through its symbol, the word that you give me and I can say too. It would perhaps be more characteristic of angelic intelligences to experience such an immediate intuitive knowledge rather than a knowledge mediated by sensible signs and objects.

We may therefore revise the sign triad as the symbol tetrad:

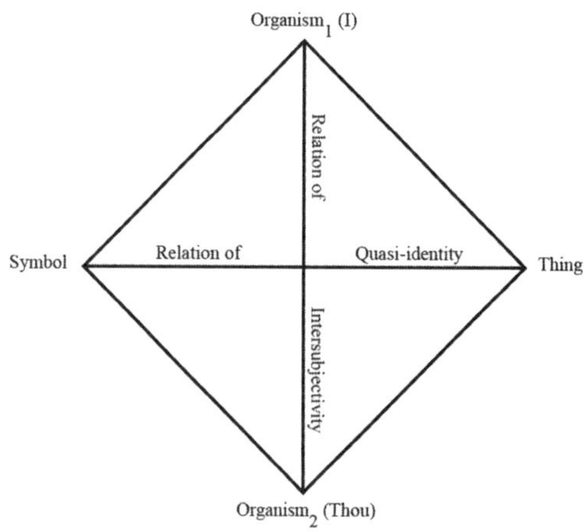

The "organisms" no longer exist exclusively in a causal nexus, but are united by a new and non-causal bond, the relation of intersubjectivity.

But a new relation has also arisen between the object and its symbol. What is the nature of the "imputed relation of identity"?

4. The Intentional Relation of Identity

Mead (1952) said that a vocal gesture (sign) becomes a symbol when the individual responds to his own stimulus in the same way as other people respond. Yet one cannot fail to realize that something is amiss in construing Helen's revelation that this "is" water as a response. And certainly it misses the peculiar representative function of language to declare that when I ask you to do something, I also arouse in myself the same tendency to do it (67).

What then is changed in the semiotic relation by Helen's inkling that this "is" water? Physically, the elements are the same as before. There is Helen, there is Miss Sullivan, there is the water flowing over one hand, and there is the word spelled out in the other. Yet something of very great moment has occurred. Not only does she have the sense of a revelation so that all at once the whole world is open to her, not only does she experience a very great happiness, a joy which is quite different from her previous need-satisfaction (compare Schachtel's "autonomous object interest" above), but immediately after discovering what the water "is," she must then know what everything else "is."

The critical question may now be raised. In discovering the peculiar denotative function of the symbol, has Helen only succeeded in opening Pandora's box of all our semantical ills of "identification," or has she hit upon the indispensable condition of our knowing anything at all, perhaps even of consciousness itself? (Compare her comment on pre-symbolic thought: "if a wordless sensation may be called a thought" (Keller 1928, 25).) Is her joy a "hallucinatory need-satisfaction," an atavism of primitive word-magic, or is it a purely cognitive joy oriented toward being and its validation through the symbol?

It comes down to the mysterious naming act, this "is" *water* (the word spelled out in her hand). Here, of course, is where the trouble starts. For clearly, as the semanticists never tire of telling us, the word is *not* water. You cannot eat the word "oyster," Chase (1938) assures us, but then not even the most superstitious totemistic tribesman would try. In regard to primitive identification, Olivier Leroy writes: "The logic of a Huichol [who mystically identifies stag with wheat] would be deficient only on the day when he would prepare a wheat porridge while he thought he was making a stag stew" (quoted in Maritain 1948b, 238). Yet in some sense, the symbol is identified with the thing, a sense, moreover, which is open to superstitious abuse. Yet the semanticists themselves are the best witnesses of the emergence of an extraordinary relation—which they deplore as the major calamity of the human race—the relation of an imputed identity between word and thing. Undoubtedly the semanticists have performed a service in calling attention to the human penchant for word-magic, for reifying meanings by simply applying words to them. Gabriel Marcel frequently speaks of the same tendency of "simulacrum" formation by which meanings become hardened and impenetrable to thought. Yet one wonders if it might not be more useful to investigate this imputed identity for what part it might play in human knowing, rather than simply deploring it—which is after all an odd pursuit for a "scientific empiricist."

To awake to the remarkable circumstance that something has a name is neither a response nor an imputed real identity. No one believes that the name is really the thing, nor does the sentence "this is water" mean this. Then what is the relation? It might clarify matters to eliminate the mysterious copula, leaving the sentence, "this: water." Or even more simply, eliminate the word "this," leaving a pointing at and a naming (in semiotic language, an indexical sign plus a symbol). In its essence the making and the receiving of the naming act consists in a coupling, an opposing of two real entities, the uttered name and the object. It is this pairing which is unique and unprecedented in the causal nexus of significatory meaning. But what is the nature of this pairing? The two terms, it is clear, are related in some sense of identification, yet not a real identity. To express it in modern semiotical language, the water is conceived through the vehicle of the symbol (compare Langer 1951, 49). In scholastic language, the symbol has the peculiar property of containing within itself *in alio esse*, in another mode of existence, that which is symbolized. As John of St. Thomas writes: "*Quid est illud in signato conjunctum signo, et praesens in signo praeter ipsum signum et entitatem ejus? Respondetur esse ipsummet signatum in alio esse*.... What may be that element of the signified that is joined to the sign and present in it as distinct from the sign itself? I answer: No other element than the very signified itself in another mode of existence" (quoted in Maritain 1948b, 220). Helen knows the water *through* and by means of the symbol.

The word is that by which the thing is conceived or known. It is, in scholastic language, an intention. The scholastics speak of concepts as "formal signs," intentions whose peculiar property it is, not to appear as an object, but to disappear before the object (Maritain 1948b, 222). But here we are not dealing with concepts or mental entities. We are dealing with natural existents, the object and the vocable, the sound which actually trembles in the air. It is this latter which is in some sense intentionally identified with the thing. Or rather the thing is intended by the symbol. Perhaps much of the confusion which has arisen about the "identification" of the symbol with its designatum could have been avoided by an appreciation of the phenomenological (and scholastic) notion of intentionality and by distinguishing real identity from the intentional relation of identity.

An interesting question arises in connection with the intentional function of the symbol: is it possible that the symbol is a primitive precursor of the concept or "formal sign" of the scholastics? The latter contains its object in an intentional mode of existence, *in alio esse. But so in an extraordinary fashion does the sensuous symbol!* In cases of false onomatopoeia, the symbol is transformed intentionally to imitate the thing symbolized (i.e., "crash," "glass," "limber," "furry," "slice," etc.). The word "glass" bears no resemblance to the thing glass. Yet it actually seems to transmit a quality of brittleness, glossiness, etc. The fact is that a symbolic transformation has occurred whereby the drab little vocable has been articulated by its meaning. "The natural sound element has been taken up into and practically disappears from our consciousness in its significant symbolic connotation. In other words, the natural sounds have been completely transmuted into conventional sound-symbols" (Wilson 1948, 220).

One can establish this transformation to his own satisfaction by a simple experiment. Repeat the word *glass* many times; all at once it will lose its symbolic guise, its "glassiness" and become the poor drab vocal that it really is. Yet it is from its original poverty that its high symbolic potentiality derives. It is for this reason, as Mrs. Langer says, that a vocable is very good symbolic material and a peach very poor.

The semanticists supply a valuable clue by their protestations. Confronted by a pencil, Korzybski (1952) says, it is absolutely false to say that this is a pencil: to say that it is can only lead to delusional states. Say whatever you like *about* the pencil, but do not say that it is a pencil. "Whatever you might *say* the object 'is', well it is not" (35). The pencil is itself unspeakable. True, but in so far as it remains unspeakable, that is, not validated by you and me through a symbol, it is also inconceivable. Clearly the semanticists are confusing an epistemological condition with a true identity.

How does it happen, Cassirer (1953b) asked, that "a finite and particular sensory content [can] be made into the vehicle of a general spiritual 'meaning'?" (93). And we know his answer. It is the Kantian variant that it is not reality which is known but the symbolic forms through which reality is conceived. Yet the empirical approach belies this. An empirical semiotic deals with natural existents and takes for granted a lawful reality about which something can be truly known. Even a strict behaviorist operates publicly in a community of other knowers and data to be known; he performs experiments on real data and publishes papers which he expects other scientists to understand. What account, after all, can Cassirer or any other idealist give of intersubjectivity? If it was, according to Kant, a "scandal of philosophy" in his day that no satisfactory solution could be found to the problem of intersubjectivity, is it any less a scandal now? But a broad semiotical approach can only bring one into the territory of epistemological realism. Since we do not know being directly, Wilhelmsen (1954) writes, we must sidle up to it, and at the symbol-object level, we can only do this by laying something of comparable ontological status alongside. "Existence is attained immediately in judgment; but judgments necessarily entail the use of phantasms, and, except in direct judgments of existing material things, the phantasms employed are symbolic. The philosopher must go through the phantasm to reach being" (40). Perhaps it would be truer, genetically speaking, to say that the primitive act of symbolization, occurring as it does prior to conception and phantasm, consists in the application, not of the phantasm, but of the sensuous symbol to the existing thing. A being is affirmed as being what it is through its denotation by symbol. Marcel (1951b) observes that when I ask the name of a strange flower, I am more satisfied to be given a nondescriptive name than a scientific classification. "But now we find the real paradox—the first unscientific answer [it is a lupin, it is an orchid], which consisted in giving the *name* [emphasis added] of the flower, although it had practically no rational basis, yet satisfied the demand in me which the interpretation by reduction tends... to frustrate" (13). Is it not possible that what I primarily want in asking *what* something is, is not an explanation but a validation and affirmation of the thing itself as it is—a validation which can only be accomplished by laying something else alongside the symbol?

We might therefore reverse Korzybski's dictum: It is *only* if you say what the object is that you can know anything about it at all.

The symbol meaning-relation may be defined as not merely the intentional but as a co-intentional relation of identity. The thing is intended through its symbol which you say and I can repeat, and it is only through this quasi-identification that it can be conceived at all. Thus it is, I believe, that an empirical and semiotical approach to meaning illumines and confirms in an unexpected manner the realist doctrine of the union of the knower and the thing known. The metaphysical implications of semiotic are clear enough: knowing is not a causal sequence but an immaterial union. It is a union, however, which is mediated through material entities, the symbol and its object. Nor is it a private phenomenon—rather is it an exercise in intersubjectivity in which the Thou serves as an indispensable colleague.

Both the relation of intersubjectivity and the intentional relation of identity are real yet immaterial bonds.

To render human cognition physico-causally can only end in the hopeless ambiguity of current semioticists who must speak in two tongues with no lexicon to translate: the language of the scientist who deals with signs as natural existents and the language of the formal logician who deals with the syntactical relations between signs.

The intentional relation of identity is not only the basic relation of logical forms, as Professor Veatch (1952) has pointed out; it is also the basic relation of symbolization. No wonder then that the symbolic logician has no use for it—for once the intentional character of knowing is recognized, "so far from being independent of metaphysics or first philosophy, [it] necessarily presupposes it" (18).

CHAPTER III

NAMING AND BEING

What is naming? Is it an event which we can study as we study other events in natural history, such as a solar eclipse, urine secretion, nuclear fusion, a stimulus-response sequence?

Let us take a concrete instance. A father tells his two-year old child that this is a ball. The child understands him, and whenever his father speaks the word, the child looks for the ball and runs to get it. But this is not naming. The child's understanding is not qualitatively different from the understanding that a dog has of the word "ball"; it can be construed in terms of response conditioning, sound waves, neural impulses, brain patterns, etc. It is in other words a sequence of happenings which takes place among material beings and is in this respect not utterly different from a solar eclipse, urine secretion, or nuclear fusion.

But one day the father utters the word "ball," and his son suddenly understands that his father does not mean: *run find the ball!* or *where is the ball?* but rather, this *is* a ball, that the word "ball" *means* this round thing.

Something has happened. We may quarrel about the good and bad of it, some saying with the Polish semanticists that what has happened is a major catastrophe for the human race, some saying with Helen Keller and Ernst Cassirer that what has happened is nothing less than the discovery of the world and the coming to oneself as a person. But beyond doubt something has happened. During the next few weeks, the child will hold the ball and speak its name a thousand times to anyone who will listen or to no one. In so doing he experiences a joy which has nothing to do with the biological need-satisfactions which have specified all previous joys. What then has happened? Is the child launched upon a delusional state that will plague him the rest of his life, or has he hit upon the secret of knowing what the world is and of becoming a person in the world?

Whatever has happened, it is a scandal to modern philosophers of meaning. The semioticists are determined that meaning shall be a response not utterly different from a solar eclipse or dog salivation. But having said this, they are left with the problem of accounting for man's often foolish behavior with symbols and of dealing with the offensive little sentence, *this is an oyster*, for clearly, as they never cease to tell us, this is not an oyster and a man can't eat the word "oyster." It is for this reason that so many semioticists are bad-tempered—for they are forced to be moralists and to scold man for his follies. One can easily imagine that astronomers would be bad-tempered too if, after discovering the laws of planetary motion, they discovered that solar eclipses refused to obey these laws and in general behaved perversely. But it would be a very poor astronomer who spent his time scolding the planets instead of trying to figure out why they behaved as they did.

Naming is a scandal to the behaviorist and semanticists because something unprecedented has taken place: naming is in fact different from a solar eclipse or a conditioned response. If one tries to explain naming as a sequential happening among material existents—as a sound calling forth a thought or referential activity—one misses the point, or as Mrs. Langer (1951) says, one leaves out the most essential feature of the material. A name does not call forth something; it names something.

But it does not help very much to say that a name names something. So it does, but in leaving it at that, in speaking of the relation of denotation, we only succeed in concealing rather than clarifying a most mysterious happening. What takes place when something is named? What is the meaning of the mysterious question: *What is that?* What is the meaning of the even more mysterious answer: *That is a ball?* Let us consider the situation immediately before and immediately after the act of naming. The elements are the same in each case. There are four elements, the father, the child, the ball, and the word "ball" which trembles in the air. What happens is clear enough when the child understands the word "ball" as a signal and looks for the ball. It is a sign-response sequence. (The situation is very similar, in fact, to Mead's (1952) "conversation of gestures" entailing two dogs, barks, and a bone.) But then it dawns upon the child that the mouthy little sound "ball" means the round thing. He holds the ball before him and utters the same sound, and now he too intends that this sound shall mean the ball. From this point forward we may no longer use the causal-sequential frame of reference, which had served so well for the understanding of every event in the universe from stellar phenomena to urine secretion; henceforward, we must find some other frame of reference. What has changed in the situation? The four elements are the same: the father, the child, the ball, the word "ball." And yet we know very well from the testimony of blind deaf-mutes as well as from the observation of normal maturation that not only has something new happened but that it is very likely the most portentous happening in the development of the person. Here we encounter a difficulty. Trying to penetrate the act of naming is like trying to get hold of the medium by which we get hold of everything else. As a consequence naming passes itself off as the most trivial of events: A thing is named and what of it? What could be more transparent? Where is the mystery?

We begin to appreciate the mystery when we realize that the act of denotation, naming, is generically without precedent in all of natural history. I mean this in the most radical way possible. One may reply with a shrug that so is urine secretion or a conditioned response without precedent in the universe. But considered in the broadest frame of reference, urine secretion and a conditioned response are the same sort of events as a stellar explosion or a nuclear fusion. There occurs an energy exchange mediated by structures, a sequential interaction which lends itself to formulation as a function of variables, $a = f(b)$. The state following a nuclear fusion is a function of the state before. The glomerular filtrate of urine is a function of blood pressure and the osmotic pressure of the plasma proteins. A dog's response to the signal "ball" is a function of the stimulus and the electro-colloidal state of the dog's brain. But when one names a thing or understands from another that a thing is so named, we may no longer understand this event as a causal function.

Something has happened rightly enough, but it is not an interaction. It is something utterly different. It is an affirmation. Naming, denotation, symbolization, may be defined as the affirmation of the thing as being what it is under the auspices of the symbol. When the child understands that by the word "ball" his father means the round thing, his understanding is of the nature of a yes-saying. Helen Keller's memorable revelation was the affirmation of the water as being what it is. But an affirmation requires two persons, the Namer and the Hearer. *This is water* means that this is water for you and me. Only a person may say yes, and he may say it only to another person. A dog may appear to say yes by acquiescing to a command, but its acquiescence is a reaction and not a yes-saying.

1. The New Orientation

By the sign, an organism is oriented to the world according to its needs of survival and reproduction. As J. G. Herder observed, an animal only takes notice of a thing that is either dangerous to it or beneficial. That which is neither dangerous nor beneficial is passed over. At the sounds of thunder, he will take cover; at the smell of flesh, he will salivate; but at the sight of a swallow in the sky, he will do nothing. But the child who learns that this is a ball will then wish to know what is this here and what is that over there. He will wish to know the name of the swallow in the sky even though the swallow is nothing to him biologically. The swallow is ignored by the tiger, but the child must know what the swallow "is." The scandal is, as Gabriel Marcel has said, that when I ask what is this strange flower, I am more satisfied to be given a name, even though the name may mean nothing, than to be given a scientific classification. If I see a strange bird and ask my bird-watcher friend what it is, and he tells me it is a blue-gray gnatcatcher, I am disappointed. I can't help thinking that he is telling me something *about* the bird—that its color is blue-gray and that it catches gnats—when what I really want to know is what it *is*. If he tells me it is a starling, I am satisfied. This is enough to make a semioticist lose his temper. He will tell me that I am only falling victim to primitive word-magic. There is something in what he says, as we shall see. Yet it is possible that there is another reason for my satisfaction. It has to do with the new orientation that has come about as the result of naming. This orientation is no longer biological; it is ontological. It has to do with a new need which is no longer an adaptive or a reproductive need but is the need to affirm the thing as being what it is for both of us. But how can this strange bird be affirmed? It can only be affirmed by a name. As Allen Tate (1952) has pointed out, it was a general belief in the West until the seventeenth century that human beings do not know things directly, as do the angels, but only through the medium of something else: the symbol. In order that the strange bird be known and affirmed, a *pairing* is the source of the scandal, for it occurs by the use of the copula "is" (260-61). This is monstrous when understood as a real identity, but the difficulty disappears when it is understood as an intentional relation of identity. Korzybski became angry when anyone picked up a pencil and said *this is a pencil*. Say anything at all *about* the pencil, he insisted, but never say it *is* a pencil. But unless you and I say it is a pencil, unless it *is* a pencil for both of us, we may not say anything about it at all.

Naming brings about a new orientation toward the world. Before naming, one is an organism responding to his environment; one is never more or less than what he is; he either flourishes or he does not flourish. A tiger is a tiger, no more or less, whether he is a sick tiger or a flourishing tiger: but as soon as one becomes a Namer or a Hearer of a name, one no longer coincides with what he is. Henceforward, he must exist either authentically or inauthentically. An organism exists in the biological scale flourishing/not-flourishing; a person exists in the normative scale authentic/inauthentic. The scales are not the same. A person may flourish biologically while at the same time living a desperately alienated and anonymous life, or a person may sicken biologically and at the same time live authentically. In the joy of naming, one lives authentically. No matter whether I name or hear the name of a strange bird, write or read a line of great poetry, form or understand a scientific hypothesis—I thereby exist authentically as a Namer or Hearer, an I or a Thou, in either case a co-celebrant of what-is. But when names no longer discover being but conceal it under the hardened symbol, when the world comes to be conceived as Alice's gallery of name-things—shoes and ships and sealing wax—then I am bored. I exist as a nought in the center of the picture-book world of the *en soi*. A tiger neither celebrates being nor is bored by it. Confronted by being which is neutral biologically, he goes to sleep. Since a person does not coincide with what he is, he may be either better or worse than a tiger.

2. Naming and Truth

An organism is oriented to the world according to its organismic needs, but a person is oriented to the world in the mode truth-untruth. It is a mistake to speak of truth-untruth in connection with an organism and a sign. A duck may make an error about a sign and mistake a hunter's call for a duck call. Yet, even if he is killed, until the very moment of his death, he never ceases to be what he always was, an organism responding to a sign according to a conditioned brain pattern. But for a person, the selfsame symbol that discovers being may be the means by which being is concealed and lost. The symbol "sparrow" at the beginning is the means by which a creature is known and affirmed and by which you and I become its co-celebrants. Later the same symbol "sparrow" may serve to conceal the creature until it finally becomes invisible. A sparrow becomes invisible in ordinary life because it disappears into its symbol. If one sees a movement in a tree and recognizes it and says it is only a sparrow, one is disposing of the creature through its symbolic formulation. The sparrow is no longer available to me. Being is elusive; it tends to escape, leaving only a simulacrum of symbol. Only under the condition of ordeal may I recover the sparrow. If I am lying wounded or in exile or in prison and a sparrow builds his nest at my window, then I may see the sparrow. This is why new names must be found for being, as

Heidegger thinks, or the old ones given new meaning, as Marcel thinks.

3. Naming and Anxiety

The fear of an organism is appropriate; it is no more or less than is warranted by the sign that arouses fear. The measure of the fear and the visceral and muscular response to the fear is specified by the character of the threat. But the anxiety that follows upon symbolization is ambiguous. The same anxiety may be destructive biologically—for it serves no biological function: one is afraid of nothing—and at the same time be a summons to an authentic existence. It is for this reason that a physician and a metaphysician take opposite views of anxiety—Freud looking upon anxiety as a symptom of a disorder to be gotten rid of, Kierkegaard looking upon anxiety as the discovery of the possibility of becoming a self.

Anxiety may simply occur when something is encountered that can neither be ignored or named. Thus anxiety may vary all the way from a slight unease to terror before the uncanny. A strange bird causes me some slight unrest until it is named. But the appearance of a three-masted trading schooner in place of the usual two-masted one may provoke terror among Melanesian islanders. In the everyday world, one is under the strongest compulsion to construe things one way or another—even things that are in fact unknown tend to be construed as things which are already known. Once Helen knew what the water was, she had to know what everything else was. After this total construction of the world, it is only when something is radically different and resists the strongest symbolic casts in its direction that one experiences the uncanny. (The word, "uncanny," after all, means that which is not yet known or symbolized.)

By the same token, anxiety may also occur when one discovers that of all the things in the world, oneself is the only being that cannot be symbolized. Everything else in the world tends to become ever more densely formulated by its name: this is a "chair," that is a "ball," you are "Robert," we have "democracy" and "freedom." But I myself escape every such attempt at formulation. A person who looks at a group picture looks for himself first: everyone else in the picture looks more or less as he knew they would—they are what they are—but he does not know what he is, and so he looks to see, and when he finds himself, he always experiences a slight pang: so that is who I am! But this formulation is ephemeral, and he will do the same thing with the next group picture. The being of the Namer slips through the fingers of naming. If he tries to construe himself in the same mode by which he construes the rest of the world, he must necessarily construe himself as nothing, as Sartre's characters do. But this is not to say that I am nothing; this is only to say that I am that which I cannot name. I am rather a person, a Namer and a Hearer of names. Nor are you formulable under the auspices of a symbol. If I do conceive you as a something in the world rather than as a co-celebrant of the world, I fall from the I-Thou to the I-It. Yet I am not able to dispose of you as finally as I dispose of shoes and ships and sealing wax. There remains your stare which may not be symbolized. If I am determined to dispose of you by formulation, I had better not look at you.

4. Naming and Being

Naming, in even its most primitive form, is a kind of judgment. It is also a kind of primitive abstraction. It is an affirming of a thing to be one of a sort of things. But this sort is not usually what is meant by a concept. It is far less abstract—I take it to be roughly equivalent to Lotze's "first universal" (quoted in Cassirer 1953b, 281-84). This primitive abstraction contains the anlage both of scientific abstraction and of poetical naming. When a tribesman utters a single word which means the-sun-shining-through-a-hole-in-the-clouds-in-a-certain-way, he is combining the offices of poet and scientist. His fellow tribesmen know what he means. We have no word for it because we have long since analyzed the situation into its component elements. But we need to have a word for it, and it is the office of the poet to give us a word. If the poet is good and names something which we secretly and privately know but have not named, we rejoice at the naming and say *Yes! I know what you mean!* Once again we are co-celebrants of being. This joy is as cognitive and as ontological as the joy of a hypothesis. It is a perversion of art to look upon science as the true naming and knowing and upon art as a traffic in emotions. Both science and art discover and neither may patronize the other.

> Daffodils,
>
> That come before the swallow dares, and take
>
> The winds of March with beauty.

This is a naming and a knowing and a truth-saying at least as important as a botanical classification.

If we must speak of a "need" in connection with human behavior, let us speak of it as Heidegger (1949) does: "The need is: to preserve the truth of Being no matter what may happen to man and everything that 'is'. Freed from all constraint, because born of the abyss of freedom, this sacrifice is the expense of our human being for the preservation of the truth of Being in respect of what-is. In sacrifice there is expressed that hidden *thanking* which alone does homage to the grace wherewith Being has endowed the nature of man, in order that he may take over in his relationship to being the guardianship of Being" (389).

PART IV

SYMBOL AND ART

In Mississippi, the coin record players, which are manufactured by Seeburg, are commonly known to Negroes as seabirds.

* * *

During the Korean War, one way of saying that someone had been killed was to say that he had bought the farm.

* * *

I remember hunting as a boy in South Alabama with my father and brother and a Negro guide. At the edge of some woods we saw a wonderful bird. He flew as straight and swift as an arrow, then all of a sudden folded his wings and dropped like a stone into the woods. I asked what the bird was. The guide said it was a Blue Dollar Hawk. Later my father told me the Negroes had got it wrong: it was really a Blue Darter Hawk. I can still remember my disappointment at the correction. What was so impressive about the bird was its dazzling speed and the effect of alternation of its wings, as if it were flying by a kind of oaring motion.

***

As a small boy of six or seven walking the streets of Cambridge I used often to pass little dead-end streets, each with its signpost which at its top read, say, Trowbridge Place or Irving Terrace, and underneath in letters of a different color and on a separate board, the following mysterious legend: Private Way Dangerous Passing. The legend meant of course merely that the City of Cambridge, since it neither built nor maintained the roadbed of this place or this terrace, would not be responsible for injury to life or property sustained through its use. But to me it meant something else. It meant that there was in passing across its mouth a clear and present danger which might, and especially at dusk, suddenly leap out and overcome me. Thus, to say the least of it, I had the regular experience of that heightened, that excited sense of being which we find in poetry, whenever I passed one of those signs.

~R. P. Blackmur, *Language as Gesture*

***

Misreadings of poetry, as every reader must have found, often give examples of this plausibility of the opposite term. I had at one time a great admiration for that line of Rupert Brooke's about

The keen
Impassioned beauty of a great machine,

a daring but successful image, it seemed to me, for that contrast between the appearance of effort and the appearance of certainty, between forces greater than human and control divine in its foreknowledge, which is what excites one about engines; they have the calm of *beauty* without its complacence, the strength of *passion* without its disorder. So it was a shock to me when I looked at one of the quotations of the line one is always seeing about, and found that the beauty was *unpassioned*, because *machines*, as all good nature-poets know, have no hearts. I still think that a prosaic and intellectually shoddy adjective, but it is no doubt more intelligible than my emendation, and sketches the same group of feelings.

~William Empson, *Seven Types of Ambiguity*

* * *

The fourth day of this, my second experiment, I succeeded to the utmost of my wishes [in teaching Victor language]; I heard Victor pronounce distinctly, in a manner, it must be confessed, rather harsh, the word *lait*, which he repeated almost incessantly; it was the first time that an articulate sound had escaped his lips, and of course I did not hear it without the most lively satisfaction. I nevertheless made afterwards an observation, which deduced very much from the advantage which it was reasonable to expect from the first instance of success. It was not till the moments, when, despairing of a happy result, I actually poured the milk into the cup which he presented to me, the word *lait* escaped him again, with evident demonstrations of joy; and it was not till after I poured it out a second time, by way of reward, that he repeated the expression. It is evident from hence, that the result of the experiment was far from accomplishing my intentions; *the word pronounced, instead of being the sign of a want, it appeared, from the time in which it was articulated, to be merely an exclamation of joy* [emphasis added].

~Dr. Itard, quoted in Langer, *Philosophy in a New Key*

* * *

… and the delighted spirit
To bathe in fiery floods, or to reside
In thrilling region of thick-ribbed ice;
To be imprison'd in the viewless winds,
And blown with restless violence round about
The pendent world.

~Shakespeare, *Measure for Measure*

* * *

Daffodils,
That come before the swallow dares, and take
The winds of March with beauty.
~Shakespeare, *The Winter's Tale*

* * *

A veiled sunlight lit up faintly the grey sheet of water where the river was embayed. In the distance along the course of the slowflowing Liffey slender masts flecked the sky and, more distant still, the dim fabric of the city lay prone in haze. Like a scene on some vague arras, old as man's weariness, the image of the seventh city of Christendom was visible to him across the timeless air, no older nor more weary nor less patient of subjection than in the days of the thingmote.

Disheartened, he raised his eyes towards the slow-drifting clouds, dappled and seaborne. They were voyaging across the deserts of the sky, a host of nomads on the march, voyaging high over Ireland, westward bound. The Europe they had come from lay out there beyond the Irish sea, Europe of strange tongues and valleyed and woodbegirt and citadelled and of entrenched and marshalled races. He heard a confused music within him as of memories and names which he was almost conscious of but could not capture even for an instant; then the music seemed to recede, to recede, to recede...

~James Joyce, *A Portrait of the Artist as a Young Man*

* * *

Glory be to God for dappled things—
For skies of couple-color as a brinded cow;
For rose-moles all in stipple upon trout that swim;
Fresh-firecoal chestnut-falls; finches' wings;

Landscape plotted and pieced—fold, fallow, and plough;
And all trades, their gear and tackle and trim.
All things counter, original, spare, strange;
Whatever is fickle, freckled (who knows how?)
With swift, slow; sweet, sour; adazzle, dim;
He fathers forth whose beauty is past change:
Praise him.
~Gerard Manley Hopkins, "Pied Beauty"

* * *

CHAPTER I

METAPHOR AS MISTAKE

Ten of the examples given above are mistakes, misnamings, misunderstandings, or misrememberings. But they are mistakes which, in each case, have resulted in an authentic poetic experience—what Blackmur (1952) calls "that heightened, that excited sense of being" (4)—an experience, moreover, that was notably absent before the mistake was made. I have included the eleventh, the Korean War expression "he bought the farm," not because it is a mistake but because I had made a mistake in including it. The expression had struck me as a most mysterious one, peculiarly potent in its laconic treatment of death as a business transaction. But then a kind Korean veteran told me that it may be laconic all right, but he didn't see anything mysterious about it: the farm the G.I. was talking about was six feet of ground. This is probably obvious enough, but I have preserved this example of my own density as instructive in what follows.

It might be useful to look into the workings of these accidental stumblings into poetic meaning because they exhibit in a striking fashion that particular feature of metaphor which has most troubled philosophers: that it is "wrong," and further, that its beauty often seems proportionate to its degree of wrongness or outlandishness. Not that the single linguistic metaphor represents the highest moment of the poetic imagination; it probably does not. Dante, as Allen Tate (1952) reminds us, uses very few linguistic metaphors.

The "greatest thing by far," which Aristotle (*Poetics* Part XXII) had in mind when he spoke of the mastery of metaphor as a sign of genius, may well have been the sort of prolonged analogy which Dante did use, in which the action takes place among the common things of concrete experience and yet yields an analogy—by nothing so crude as an allegorization wherein one thing is designated as "standing for" another but by the very density and thingness of the action.

As Tate puts it: "Nature offers the symbolic poet clearly denotable objects in depth and in the round, which yield the analogies to the higher syntheses" (262). Yet the fact remains that the linguistic metaphor is, for better or worse, more peculiarly accessible to the modern mind. It may indeed be a distinctive expression of modern sensibility. It has the added advantage from my point of view of offering a concentrated field for investigation—here something very big happens in a very small place.

Metaphor has scandalized philosophers, including both scholastics and modern semioticists, because it seems to be wrong: it asserts of one thing that it is something else. And it is wrongest when it is most beautiful: it is those very figures of Shakespeare which eighteenth century critics undertook to "correct" because they had so obviously gotten off the track logically and were sometimes even contradictory. It is just these figures that we now treasure most.

This element of outlandishness has resulted in philosophers' washing their hands of beauty and literary men being glad that they have—in other words, in a divorce of beauty and ontology, with unhappy consequences to both. The difficulty has been that inquiries into the nature of metaphor have tended to be either literary or philosophical with neither side having much use for the other. The subject is divided into its formal and material aspects: philosophers trying to arrive at the nature of metaphor by abstracting from all metaphors, beautiful and commonplace; critics paying attention to the particular devices by which a poet brings off his effects. Beauty, the importance attached to beauty, marks the parting of the ways. The philosopher attends to the formal structure of metaphor, asking such general questions as:

What is the relation between metaphor and myth?

Is metaphor an analogy of proper or improper proportionality?

and in considering his thesis is notably insensitive to its beauties. In fact, the examples he chooses to dissect are almost invariably models of dreariness, such as smiling meadow, leg of a table, John is a fox, etc. One can't help wondering if Aristotle's (*Poetics* Part XXI) famous examples of "a cup as the shield of Dionysius" or "a shield as the cup of Ares" didn't sound like typical philosopher's metaphors to contemporary poets. Literary men, on the other hand, once having caught sight of the beauty of metaphor, once having experienced what Barfield (1952) called "that old authentic thrill, which is so strong that it binds some men to their libraries for a lifetime" (171), are constrained to deal with beauty alone, with the particular devices which evoke the beautiful, and let the rest go. If the theorist is insensitive to the beauty of metaphor, the critic is insensitive to its ontology. To the question, *why is this beautiful?* he will usually give a material answer, pointing to this or that effect that the poet has made use of. He is unsympathetic—and not without cause—to attempts to get ahold of art by some larger schema, such as a philosophy of being—feeling in his bones that when the cold hand of theory reaches for beauty, it will succeed in grabbing everything except the beautiful.

Being neither critic nor philosopher, I feel free to venture into the no man's land between the two and to deal with those very metaphors which scandalize the philosopher because they are "wrong" and scandalize the critic because they are accidental. Philosophers don't think much of metaphor to begin with, and critics can hardly have much use for folk metaphors, those cases where one stumbles into beauty without deserving it or working for it. Is it possible to get a line on metaphor, to figure out by a kind of lay empiricism what is going on in those poetic metaphors and folk metaphors where the wrongness most patently coincides with the beauty?

1. The Mysterious Efficacy of the "Wrong" Metaphor

When the Mississippi Negro calls the Seeburg record player a "seabird," it is not enough to say that he is making a mistake. It is also not enough to say that he is making a colorful and poetic contribution to language. It is less than useless to say that in calling a machine a bird he is regressing into totemism, etc. And it is not even accurate to say that he knows what the thing is and then gives it a picturesque if far-fetched name. In some fashion or other, he conceives the machine under the symbol "seabird," a fashion, moreover, in regard to which we must be very wary in applying the words "right" or "wrong," "poetic" or "discursive," etc. Certainly the machine is not a seabird, and no one imagines that it is, whatever the semanticists may say. Yet we may make a long cast and guess that in conceiving it as a *seabird*, the Namer conceives it with richer overtones of meaning, and in some sense neither literal nor figurative, even as being more truly what it is, than under its barbarous title: Seeburg automatic coin record player. There is a danger at this point in my being misunderstood as trying to strike a blow for the poetic against the technical, feeling against science, and on the usual aesthetic grounds. But my intention is quite the reverse. I mean to call attention to the rather remarkable fact that in conceiving the machine under the "wrong" symbol "seabird," we somehow know it better, conceive it in a more plenary fashion, have more immediate access to it, than under its descriptive title. The sooner we get rid of the old quarrel of artistic vs. prosaic as constituting the grounds of our preference, the sooner we shall be able to understand what is going on. Given these old alternatives, I'll take the prosaic any day—but what is going on here is of far greater moment. The moments and elements of this meaning-situation are more easily grasped in the examples of the boy seeing the strange bird in Alabama. The first notable moment occurred when he saw the bird. What struck him at once was the extremely distinctive character of the bird's flight—its very great speed, the effect of alternation of the wings, the sudden plummeting into the woods. This so distinctive and incommunicable something (the word that occurs to one is Hopkins's "inscape") the boy perceived perfectly. It is this very uniqueness that Hopkins (1937) specifies in inscape: "the unspeakable stress of pitch, distinctiveness, and selving" (309).

2. The Pre-Symbolic Tension

The next moment is, for our purposes, the most remarkable of all, because it can receive no explanation in the conventional sign theory of meaning. The boy, having perfectly perceived the flight of the hawk, now suffers a sort of disability, a tension, even a sense of imminence! He puts the peculiar question, *what is that bird?* and puts it importunately. He is really anxious to know. But to know what? What sort of answer does he hope to hear? What in fact is the meaning of his extraordinary question? Why does he want an answer at all? He has already apprehended the hawk in the most vivid, most plenary way—a sight he will never forget as long as he lives. What more will he know by having the bird named? (No more, say the semioticists, and he deceives himself if he imagines that he does.)

We have come already to the heart of the question, and a very large question it is. For the situation of the boy in Alabama is very much the same sort of thing as what Cassirer (1946) calls the "mythico-religious Urphenomenon." Cassirer, following Usener and Spieth, emphasized the situation in which the primitive comes face to face with something which is both entirely new to him and strikingly distinctive, so distinctive that it might be said to have a *presence*—an oddly shaped termite mound, a particular body of water, a particular abandoned road. It is in the two ways in which this tensional encounter is resolved that the Urphenomenon is said to beget metaphor and myth. The Tro or momentary god is born of the sense of unformulated presence of the thing; the metaphor arises from the symbolic act in which the emotional cry of the beholder becomes the vehicle by which the thing is conceived, the name of the thing. "In the vocables of speech and in primitive mythic configurations, the same inner process finds its consummation: they are both resolutions of an inner tension, the representation of subjective impulses and excitations in definite objective forms and figures" (88).

One recognizes the situation in one's own experience, that is, the metaphorical part of it. Everyone has a Blue Dollar Hawk in his childhood, especially if he grew up in the South or West where place names are so prone to poetic corruption. Chaisson Falls, named properly after its discoverer, becomes Chasin' Falls. Scapegoat Mountain, named after some Indian tale, becomes Scrapegoat Mountain—mythic wheels within wheels. And wonderfully: Purgatoire River becomes Picket Wire River. A boy grows up in the shadow of a great purple range called Music Mountain after some forgotten episode—perhaps the pioneers' first hoedown after they came through the pass. But this is not how the boy conceives it. When the late afternoon sun strikes the great pile in a certain light, the ridges turn gold, the crevasses are cast into a thundering blue shadow, then it is that he imagines that the wind comes soughing down the gorges with a deep organ note. The name, mysterious to him, tends to validate some equally mysterious inscape of the mountain.

3. An Instrumental or Ontological Need?

So far so good. But the question on which everything depends and which is too often assumed to be settled without ever having been asked is this: Given this situation and its two characteristics upon which all agree, the peculiar presence or distinctiveness of the object beheld and the peculiar need of the beholder—is this "need" and its satisfaction instrumental or ontological? That is to say: it is the function of metaphor merely to diminish tension or to discover being. Does it fit into the general scheme of need-satisfactions?—and here it doesn't matter much whether we are talking about the ordinary pragmatic view or Cassirer's symbolic form. Both operate in an instrumental mode: one, that of biological adaptation; the other, according to the necessities of the mythic consciousness. Neither provides for a real knowing, a truth-saying about what a being is. Or is it of such a nature that at least two sorts or realities must be allowed: one, the distinctive something beheld; two, the beholder (actually *two* beholders, one who gives the symbol and one who receives the symbol as meaningful, the Namer and Hearer) whose special, if imperfect, gift it is to know and affirm this something for what it actually is? The question can't be bracketed, for the two paths lead in opposite directions, and everything one says henceforth on the subject must be understood from one or the other perspective. In this primitive encounter, which is at the basis of man's cognitive orientation in the world, either we are trafficking in psychological satisfactions, or we are dealing with that unique joy which marks man's ordainment to being and the knowing of it.

4. The Authority of the Namer and the Ontological Pairing

We come back to the "right" and "wrong" of Blue Dollar Hawk and Blue Darter Hawk. Is it proper to ask if the boy's delight at the "wrong" name is a psychological or ontological delight? And if the wrong name is cognitive, how is it cognitive? At any rate, we know that the hawk is named for the boy, and he has what he wants. His mind, which had really suffered a sort of hunger (an ontological hunger?), now has something to feast on. The bird is, he is told, a Blue Dollar Hawk. Two conditions, it will be noticed, must be met if the naming is to succeed. There must be an authority behind it—if the boy's brother had made up the name on the spur of the moment, it wouldn't have worked. Naming is more than a matter of a semantic "rule." But apparently there must also be—and here is the scandal—an element of obscurity about the name. The boy can't help but be disappointed by the logical modifier, Blue Darter Hawk—he feels that although he has asked what the bird *is*, his father has only told him what it *does*. If we will prescind for a moment from premature judgments about the "prelogical" or magic character of the boy's preference, and also forego the next question, *why is it called a Blue Dollar Hawk?* which the boy may or may not have put but probably did not because he knew there was no logical answer the guide could give—or if the guide does give an answer, it would be its very far-fetchedness which would satisfy: "They calls him that because of the way he balls hisself up and rolls." The function of the answer will become clearer. It is connected with the circumstance that the mysterious name, Blue Dollar Hawk, is both the "right" name—for it has been given in good faith by a Namer who should know and carries an *ipso facto* authority—and a "wrong" name—for it is not applicable as a logical modifier as Blue Darter is immediately and univocally applicable. Blue Dollar is not applicable as a modifier at all, for it refers to a *something else* besides the bird, a something that occupies the same ontological status as the bird. Blue Darter tells us something about the bird, what it does, what its color is; Blue Dollar tells, or the boy hopes it will tell, what the bird *is. For this ontological pairing, or, if you prefer, "error" of identification of word and thing, is the only possible way in which the apprehended nature of the bird, its inscape, can be validated as being what it is.* This inscape is, after all, otherwise ineffable. I can describe it, make crude approximations by such words as darting, oaring, speed, dive, etc., but none of these will suffice to affirm this so distinctive something which I have seen. This is why, as Marcel has observed, that when I ask what something is, I am more satisfied to be given a name even if the name means nothing to me (especially if?), than to be given a scientific classification. Percy Bysshe Shelley, in his "A Defense of Poetry," said that poetry pointed out "the before unapprehended relations of things." Wouldn't it be closer to the case to say that poetry validates that which had already been privately apprehended but had gone unformulated for both of us?

5. Symbol Affirms Being in Two Ways: What It Is and That It Is

Without getting over one's head with the larger question of truth, one might still guess that it is extraordinarily rash of the positivist to limit truth to the logical approximation—to say that we cannot know what things are but only how they hang together. The copy theory gives no account of the *what* we are saying *how* about. As to the what: since we are not angels, it is true that we cannot know what it is intuitively and as it is in itself. The modern semioticist is scandalized by the metaphor, *flesh is grass* (Isaiah 40:6), but he is also scandalized by the naming sentence, *this is flesh*. As Professor Veatch (1952) has pointed out, he is confusing an instrument of knowing with what is known

(18). The word "flesh" is not this solid flesh, and this solid flesh is not grass. But unless we name it "flesh," we shall not know it at all, and unless we call flesh "grass," we shall not know how it is with flesh. The semioticist leaves unexplained the act of knowing. He imagines naively that I know what this is and then give it a label, whereas the truth is, as Cassirer has shown so impressively, that I cannot know anything at all unless I symbolize it. We can only *conceive* being, sidle up to it, by laying something else alongside. We approach the thing not directly but by pairing, by apposing symbol and thing. Is it not premature to say with the mythist that when the primitive calls the lightning serpentine, he conceives it as a snake and is logically wrong? Both truth and error may be served here, error in so far as the lightning is held to participate magically in snakeness, truth in so far as the conception *snake* may allow the privately apprehended inscape of the lightning to be formulated. I would have a horror of finding myself allied with those who in the name of instrumentality or inner warmth or whatnot would so attenuate and corrupt truth that it meant nothing. But an analysis of the symbol relation reveals aspects of truth that go far beyond the notion of structural similarity of which the symbolic logicians speak. Two other traits of the thing are discovered and affirmed: one, that it *is;* two, that it is *something*.

Everything depends on this distinction between the thing privately apprehended and the thing apprehended and validated for you and me by naming. But is it proper to make such a distinction? Is there any difference, no difference, or the greatest possible difference between that which I privately apprehend and that which I apprehend and you validate by naming in such a way that I am justified in hoping that you "mean" that very ineffable thing?

6. Metaphor neither Right nor Wrong but Analogous

For at the basis of the beautiful metaphor—which one begins to see as neither logically "right" or "wrong" but analogous—at the basis of that heightened sensibility of the poetic experience, there is always the hope that this secret apprehension of my own, which I cannot call knowing because I do not even know that I know it, has a chance of being validated by what you have said.

There must be a space between name and thing, for otherwise the private apprehension is straitened and oppressed. What is required is that the thing be both sanctioned and yet allowed freedom to be what it is. Heidegger (1949) said that the essence of truth is freedom, letting a thing be what it is. The essence of metaphorical truth and the almost impossible task of the poet is, it seems to me, to name unmistakably and yet to name by such a gentle analogy that the thing beheld by both of us may be truly formulated for what it is.

7. Blackmur's Gesture

Blackmur's and Empson's examples are better mistakes than mine. The street sign in Cambridge, "Private Way Dangerous Passing," misunderstood, allowed the exciting possibility that it was one's own secret forebodings about the little dead-end streets that was meant. But for all of Blackmur's unsurpassed analysis of this mysterious property of language, I think it unfortunate that he has chosen to call it "gesture," in view of the semioticist's use of the word to denote a term in a stimulus-response sequence (i.e., Mead's "conversation of gesture")—because this is exactly what it is not. It is a figurational and symbolic import in that sense which is farthest removed from gestural intercourse (such as the feint and parry of Mead's two boxers). It is, in fact, only when the gesture, word, or thing is endowed with symbolic meaning, that is, united with a significance other than itself, that it takes on the properties which Blackmur attributes to it.

8. Empson's Ambiguity

In Empson's (1947) examples, the beauty of the line depends on an actual misreading of what the poet wrote or on a corruption of the spelling. In the former case the poetic instincts of the reader are better than the poet's. What is important is that the reader's "mistake" has rescued the poet's figure from the logical and univocal similarity, which the poet, despite his best efforts, could not escape and placed at a mysterious and efficacious distance. The remembering of Brooke's "unpassioned machine" as "impassioned machine" is a good example of this (205). Another is a line of Thomas Nashe, which may or may not have been a mistake. What matters for our purpose is that it could have been.

> Beauty is but a flower
> Which wrinkles will devour.
> Brightness falls from the air.

There is a "cynical theory," Empson writes, that Nashe "wrote or meant 'hair'" ("Brightness falls from the hair"), which is appropriate to the context, adequate poetically but less beautiful. Why? I defer to Professor Empson's analysis and venture only one comment. It may be true, as he says, that the very pre-Raphaelite vagueness of the line allows the discovery of something quite definite (46). In the presence of the lovely but obscure metaphor, I exist in the mode of hope, hope that the poet may mean such and such, and joy at any further evidence that he does. What Nashe's line may have stumbled upon (if it is a mistake) is a perfectly definite but fugitive something—an inscape familiar to one and yet an inscape in bondage because I have never formulated it and it has never been formulated for me. Could the poet be referring to that particular time and that particular phenomenon of clear summer evenings when the upper air holds the last trembling light of day: one final moment of a soft diffused brilliance, then everything falls into dusk?

But Empson's most entertaining mistake is:

> Queenlily June with a rose in her hair
> Moves to her prime with a langorous air.

For what saves the verse from mediocrity is the misreading of queenlily as Queen Lily, where the poet had intended the rather dreary adverb of queenly! Again I defer to Professor Empsons's *material* analysis of what gives the misread line its peculiar charm. The question I would raise, in regard to this and many other examples in *Seven Types of Ambiguity*, has to do with Empson's main thesis. This thesis is, of course, that beauty derives from ambiguity—in the particular case, the felt possibility and interaction of the *two* readings of "queenlily" (65). But I submit that in this and other examples, as I read it and apparently as Empson read it, *the intended adverbial reading is completely overlooked!* The line is read with "Queenlily" and is charming; it only belatedly occurs to one, if it occurs at all, that the poet meant the adverb—and I feel certain Empson is not maintaining that I was aware of the adverb all along but "unconsciously." What one wonders, in this and many other of Empson's quotations, is whether it is the ambiguity which is the operative factor or *whether the beauty does not derive exclusively from the obscure term of the ambiguity*, the logically "wrong" but possibly analogous symbol.

In all those cases where the poet strains at the limits of the logical and the univocal, and when as a result his figure retains a residue of the logical and so has two readings—the univocal and the analogous—is it not in the latter that he has struck gold? We must be careful not to confuse ambiguity, which means equivocity, with true analogy, simply because both are looked upon as more or less vague. It is always possible, of course, to do what Empson does so well with his obscure metaphors, that is, to cast about for all the different interpretations the line will allow. But does the beauty of the line reside in its susceptibility to two or more possible meanings or in the possibility of a *single* figurational meaning, which is the less analyzable as it is the more beautiful?

I can't help thinking, incidentally, that this hunt for the striking single metaphor in a poet of another time, such as Chaucer or Shakespeare, is a very dangerous game. For both the old poet and his modern reader are at the mercy of time's trick of cancelling the poet's own hard-won figures and setting up new ones of its own. A word, by the very fact of its having been lost to common usage or by its having undergone a change in meaning, is apt to acquire an unmerited potency.

9. Is Obscurity a Virtue?

One is aware of skirting the abyss as soon as one begins to repose virtue in the obscure. Once we eliminate the logical approximation, the univocal figure, as unpoetic and uncreative of meaning—is it not then simply an affair of trotting out words and images more or less at random in the hope of arriving at an obscure, hence efficacious, analogy? And the more haphazard the better, since mindfulness, we seem to be saying, is of its very nature, self-defeating? Such in fact is the credo of the surrealists: "To compare two objects, as remote from one another in character as possible, or by any other method put them together in a sudden and striking fashion, this remains the highest task to which poetry can aspire" (Breton quoted in Richards 1950, 123). There is something to this. If, as so many modern poets appear to do, one simply shuffles words together, words plucked from as diversified contexts as possible, one will get some splendid effects. Words are potent agents, and the sparks are bound to fly. But it is a losing game. For there is missing that essential element of the meaning situation, the authority and intention of the Namer. Where the Namer means nothing or does not know what he means, or the Hearer does not think he knows what he means, the Hearer can hardly participate in a co-intention. Intersubjectivity fails. Once the good faith of the Namer is so much as called into question, the jig is up. There is no celebration or hope of celebration of a thing beheld in common. One is only trafficking in the stored up energies of words, hard-won by meaningful usage. It is a pastime, this rolling out the pretty marbles of word-things to see one catch and reflect the fire of another, a pleasant enough game but one which must eventually go stale.

It is the cognitive dimension of metaphor which is usually overlooked because cognition is apt to be identified with conceptual and discursive knowing. Likeness and difference are canons of discursive thought, but analogy, the mode of poetic knowing, is also cognitive. Failure to recognize the discovering power of analogy can only eventuate in a non-cognitive psychologistic theory of metaphor. There is no knowing; there is no Namer and Hearer; there is no world beheld in common. There is only an interior "transaction between contexts" in which psychological processes interact to the reader's titillation (Richards 1950, 94).

10. Can Poetry Be Judged by Logical Canons?

The peculiar consequences of judging metaphor by discursive categories are especially evident in Professor Richards's method. Lord Kames had criticized the metaphor "steep'd" in Othello's speech:

> Had it pleas'd heaven
> To try me with affliction, had he rain'd
> All kinds of sores, and shames, on my bare head,
> Steep'd me in poverty to the very lips,

by saying that "the resemblance is too faint to be agreeable—Poverty must here be conceived to be a fluid which it resembles not in any manner." Richards goes further: "It is not a case of lack of resemblance but too much diversity, too much sheer oppositeness. For Poverty, the tenor, is a state of deprivation, of desiccation; but the vehicle—the sea or vat in which Othello is to be steep'd—gives an instance of superfluity…." True, disparity as well as resemblance works in metaphor, but Richards says of this instance of disparity: "I do not myself find any defence of the word except this, which seems indeed quite sufficient—as dramatic necessities commonly are—that Othello is himself horribly disordered, that the utterance is part of the 'storm of horrour and outrage.'" Thus, Professor Richards gives "steep'd" a passing mark, but only because Othello is crazy (Richards 1950, 104). He may be right: the figure is extravagant, in a sense "wrong," yet to me defensible even without a plea of insanity. The only point I wish to make is that there is another cognitive ground on which it can be judged besides that of logical rightness and wrongness, univocal likeness and unlikeness. Judged accordingly, it must always be found wanting—an eighteenth century critic would have corrected it. But do the alternatives lie between logical sense and nonsense? Or does such a view overlook a third way, the relation of analogy and its cognitive dimension? In the mode of analogy, "steep'd" is not only acceptable, it is striking. "Steep'd" may be wrong univocally but right analogically. True, poverty is, logically speaking, a deprivation; but in its figuration it is a veritable something, very much a milieu with a smell and taste all its own, in which one is all too easily steep'd. Poverty is defined as a lack but is conceived as a something. What is univocally unlike in every detail may exhibit a figurative proportionality that is more generative of meaning than the cleverest simile.

11. Pointing at and Naming

An unvarying element in the situation is a pointing at by context. There must occur a preliminary meeting of minds and a mutually intended subject before anything can be said at all. The context may vary all the way from a literal pointing-by-finger and naming in the aboriginal naming act, to the pointing context of the poem that specifies the area where the metaphor is to be applied. There is a reciprocal relationship between the selectivity of the pointing and the univocity of the metaphor: the clearer the context and the more unmistakable the pointing, the greater latitude allowed the analogy of the metaphor. The aboriginal naming act is, in this sense, the most obscure and the most creative of metaphors; no modern poem was ever as obscure as Miss Sullivan's naming water "water" for Helen Keller. A perfectly definite something is pointed at and given a name, a sound, or a gesture to which it bears only the most tenuous analogical similarities.

The old debate, started in the *Cratylus,* goes on as lively as ever: what is the relation between the name and the thing, between the word "green" and the color green, between "slice" and slice, "tree" and tree? Most linguists would probably say there is no relation, that the name is purely an arbitrary convention (except in a few cases like "boom"), that any seeming resemblance is false onomatopoeia: no matter how much you might imagine that "slice" resembles and hence expresses the act of slicing, it really does not. But here again, do likeness and unlikeness exhaust the possibilities?

Apparently not. Curtius remarks that:

> despite all change… a conservative instinct is also discernible in language. All the peoples of our family from the Ganges to the Atlantic designate the notion of standing by the phonetic group *sta;* in all of them the notion of flowing is linked with the group *plu*, with only slight modifications. This cannot be an accident. Assuredly the same notion has remained associated with the same sounds through all the millennia, because the peoples felt a certain *inner connection* [emphasis added] between the two, i.e., because of an instinct to express this notion by these particular sounds. The assertion that the oldest words presuppose some relation between sounds and the representations they designate has often been ridiculed. It is difficult, however, to explain the origin of language without such assumptions. (quoted in Cassirer 1953b, 191)

It is this "inner connection" which concerns us. The sounds "plu" and "sta," which could hardly be more different from the acts of flowing and standing, must nevertheless exhibit some mysterious connection that the mind fastens upon, a connection which, since it is not a kind of univocal likeness, must be a kind of analogy.

Given the situation of Naming and Hearing, there can only be one of three issues to an act of pointing at and naming. What is told will either be old, that is, something we already know and know quite overtly; or something new, and if it is utterly new, I can only experience bafflement; or new-old, that is, something that I had privately experienced but which was not available to me because it had never been formulated and rendered intersubjective. Metaphor is the true maker of language.

12. Hopkins's Inscape and the Distanced Metaphor

The creative relationship of "inscape," the distinctive reality as it is apprehended, and the distanced metaphor is illustrated by Hopkins's (1937) nature metaphors. His favorite pursuit in the nature journals is the application of striking (sometimes strained) like-yet-unlike metaphors to nature inscapes. There are some pleasing effects. A bolt of lightning is "a straight stroke, broad like a stroke with chalk and liquid, as if the blade of an oar just stripped open a ribbon scar in smooth water and it caught the light" (150). We are aware that the effect is achieved by applying the notions of water and scars to lightning, the most unwaterlike or unscarlike thing imaginable. But are these metaphors merely pleasing or shocking or do they discover?—discover an aspect of the thing which had gone unformulated before?

Clouds are called variously bars, rafters, prisms, mealy, scarves, curds, rocky, a river (of dull white cloud), rags, veils, tatters, bosses. The sea is "paved with wind," "bushes of foam," "chips of [foam] blew off and gadded about without weight in the air," "straps of glassy spray" (179-81). In these metaphors both the likeness and unlikeness are striking and easily discernible. One has the impression, moreover, that their discovering power has something to do with their unlikeness, the considerable space between tenor and vehicle. Hard things like rocks, bosses, chips, glass, are notably unlike clouds and water; yet one reads "chips of [foam] blew off and gadded about" with a certain sense of validation (181).

If we deviate in either direction, toward a more univocal or accustomed likeness or toward a more mysterious unlikeness, we feel at once the effect of what Richards calls the tension of the bow, both the slackening and tightening of it. When one reads *fleecy clouds* or *woolly clouds*, the effect is slack indeed. Vehicle and tenor are totally interarticulated: clouds are ordinarily conceived as being fleecy; fleecy is what clouds are (just as checkered is what a career is). You have told me nothing. Fleecy cloud, leg of a table, are tautologies, a regurgitation of something long since digested. But "a straight river of dull white cloud" is lively (213). One feels both knowledgeable and pleased. But "a white shire of cloud" is both more interesting and more obscure (140). The string of the bow is definitely tightened. The mind is off on its favorite project, a casting about for analogies and connections. Trusting in the good faith of the Namer, I begin to wonder if he means thus and so—this particular sort of cloud. The only "shire" I know is a geographical area, and what I more or less visualize is a towering cumulus of an irregular shire-shape.

Two levels of analogy-making can be distinguished here. There is the level of metaphor proper, the saying about one thing that it is something else: one casts about to see *how* a cloud can be a shire, and in hitting on an analogy, one validates an inscape of cloud. But there is the more primitive level of naming, of applying a sound to a thing, and of the certification of some sounds as being analogous to the thing without being like it (as in the mysterious analogy between "plu" and flowing, "sta" and standing). Thus "shire" may be applicable to a certain kind of cloud *purely as a sound* and without a symbolized meaning of its own. For as it happens, concrete nouns beginning with *sh* often refer to objects belonging to a class or segmented or sectioned or roughly oblong flattened objects, a "geographical" class: shape, sheath, shard, sheet, shelf, shield, shire, shoal, shovel, shroud, etc. One speculates that the vocable "sh-" is susceptible of this particular spatial configuration. (I easily imagine that the sound "sh" has a flatness or parallelness about it.) This relation is very close to the psychological phenomenon of synesthesia, the trans-sensory analogy in which certain sounds, for example, are characteristically related to certain colors—"blue" to color blue. (Could blue ever be called "yellow"?)

13. Summary

To summarize: the examples given of an accidental blundering into authentic poetic experience both in folk mistakes and in mistaken readings of poetry are explored for what light they may shed on the function of metaphor in man's fundamental symbolic orientation in the world. This "wrongness" of metaphor is seen to be not a vagary of poets but a special case of that mysterious "error" which is the very condition of our knowing anything at all. This "error," the act of symbolization, is itself the instrument of knowing. If we do not take note of it, or try to exorcize it as a primitive residue, we shall find ourselves on the horns of the same dilemma that has plagued philosophers since the seventeenth century. The semanticists, on the one horn, imply that we know as the angels know, directly and without mediation: all that remains is to name what we know, but they do not and cannot say how we know. The behaviorists, on the other, imply that we do not know at all but only respond; but they do not say how they know this. But we do know, not as the angels know and not as dogs know but as men who must know one thing through the mirror of another.

CHAPTER II

THE THING IN THE WORD

There is another property of poetic diction, always present in thought not limited to metaphor, that is closely connected with the phenomenon of the symbolic transformation (Part II, Chapter II). It is the presence in the word of a certain physiognomy—"soul" de Maupassant calls it— that is ordinarily hidden but which is revealed "*au contact d'autres mots.*" It is part of Barfield's (1952) thesis, in fact, that the poet's function is to discover these "souls" and to create new meaning by using them in his own original way (115).

What is this "soul" (compare Max Picard's (1951) description of the word-"soul") and what are the conditions under which in prosaic discourse it is concealed and in poetic diction revealed for our delight?

That such a thing occurs, that by a slight shift of consciousness, a word can take on a poetic quality, is beyond question. A bill of lading listing the items—hemp, tar, sisal, flax, indigo—is poetic or not depending on whether I read it as a shipping clerk or as a lay reader.

1. Business and Technical Words Strongly Articulated by Meaning

The most down-to-earth utilitarian or technical words can by this shift become powerful agents in the creation of new meaning and at the same time be revealed as remarkable structures in themselves. There are Shakespeare's favorite legal and business words, especially in the sonnets: unthrifty (loveliness), (beauty's) legacy, audit, (summer's) lease, sessions, summon up, advocate, plea, bailiff, etc. There are modern scientific words that, because of this peculiar efficacy, are habitually used (and abused?) by modern poets: artery, lymph, neural, pleural, thyroidic, etc.

2. The Savoring of Meaning: The Word-Thing

Are there not then, two moments to the metaphor, though they occur together—two joys, though they are felt as one? There is the cognitive intersubjective joy of discovering and understanding: under the auspices of the like-unlike metaphor, a new something is pointed out and affirmed. But there is a special joy in which the metaphor is beheld and savored in itself and as a separate delectation. Each poet has his favorite word-souls which he uses not only to discover meaning but to share with us as his own darlings: Hopkins has "combe," "dapple," "damson"; Yeats discovered "cars," the brazen cars of Fergus; Faulkner has "annealed," etc. And there are national word-souls whose rare physiognomy has been exposed by a mass shift of consciousness so that they stand available for common use. The word "ruin," though Barfield (1952) does not think it exceptional, seems to me to be one of these. It is a favorite word of poets—or was until the novelists got hold of it. How many novelists, good and bad, have not exploited Milton's discovery of ruin-plus-face, "her ruined face"? (*Paradise Lost* ll. 304-5).

3. A Shift of Context Required to See Word-Thing

Whether this heightened awareness or the seductiveness of the word itself necessarily entails an abandonment of the cognitive function, whether it is a measure of decadence, I am not able to say. But there *is* such a change in awareness. In ordinary discourse, words are used as transparent intentionalities by which the thing is laid hold of. A mother will say, "I punished my child," and there is no doubt about her meaning and certainly no interest in the word "punish." But when Dylan Thomas writes, "Especially when the October wind/ With frosty fingers punishes my hair," we are, for better or worse, in the presence of legerdemain. In the first, "punish" is used in the accustomed context and is invisible: one sees through to its meaning. Thomas plucks it out of its context; it shifts, or we shift, come round and gaze directly at it and its translucent inner workings. It lies revealed to us in all its organic complexity.

A bad novelist might write, is all too likely to write, "the burly man grimaced," and it is good or bad accordingly as we sense he is using "burly" and "grimaced" as the weariest, the cheapest coin available to the hack or actually to convey something he intends. But when Robert Lowell (1943) speaks of the love of the Virgin as a burly love, the soul of the old work-horse "burly" stands revealed for the first time. It is a potent, lumbering sort of thing after all. (Again, I beg to be excused from an esthetic value judgment. This preoccupation of modern poets with dazzling local effects through catachresis may very well be a sorry business compared to the sustained effort of the great poet who tends directly to the incarnate action and trusts metaphor to take care of itself.)

The shift is often from a strong utility context to a sort of cataloguing, a round calling off of names (as in the bill of lading, poetically read). In the market-place and in the mouth of the florist, the word "daffodil" is an intentional agent, through which once thinks of the flower, counts it, buys it, arranges it, etc. But when Perdita in *The Winter's Tale* says

> Daffodils
> That come before the swallow dares,
> And take the winds of March with beauty

she is listing daffodils along with violets, prime-roses, oxlips, and so on, and in effect holding them out for our enjoyment—holding out, not the flower, but the flower-in-the-word. In one of the loveliest lines in the language, whatever else may go into its making (the odd use of the little verb "take" has something to do with it, and the word-things "March" and "swallow," proffered as they are with a rare grace), one ingredient is simply the word "daffodil," not "asphodel," which would be pretty enough, but its corruption, the lovely, golden-headed, daffy daffodil.

4. The Word Is Magically Transformed into Thing

But what is it that one beholds when by the poet's sleight of hand, we are given a quick look into the inner mystery of the word? Is it the word? Or is it the thing? It is not the word—which is after all only a mouthy little sound, almost nothing at all. It is not the thing. I may indeed enjoy daffodils on a hillside, but my enjoyment of Shakespeare's and Wordsworth's "daffodils" is something else again.

It is neither the word nor the thing but the word-thing. What I see when the poet salvages the word from its utility context and holds it up for my gaze is the thing in the word in another mode of existence, *in alio esse*. I look *at* instead of *through* the miraculous transformation by which the poor naked vocable "becomes" the thing, is intentionally transformed into the thing. What I perceive in all its intricate and iridescent reality is the thing itself as it has formed itself within the web of sound. No wonder the poet is seduced. Once he has savored this dangerous delight, it is enough to set him fondling words for life, turning them this way and that in the hope that one will catch this holy fire.

It is perhaps for no other reason that utility and specialty words, "all trades, their gear and tackle and trim," possess such a high poetic potential, for it is they which are most powerfully and unselfconsciously articulated by their meaning. It is the hardworking shop and market word, which, when turned on its side, exhibits a slice of life and not the high-flown Spenserian words of Poesy.

PART V

CONCLUSION

Are we justified in drawing any general conclusions from our modest excursion into semantics? I cannot call it a study of language, for I have left out almost everything that a study of language should treat. I cannot even call it a study of the beginnings of language, for it is not based on genetic psychology or controlled observation—though these are referred to. It is instead a lay reflection on the nature of language. I say "lay" because it is an investigation that anyone can make and that does not depend for its validity on special knowledge or experiments. It is also a phenomenology, for what I have tried to reveal are not underlying principles or theoretical foundations but the essential structure of the symbolic orientation, a structure which is there for all to see.

My aim has been to make a beginning toward a radical anthropology, that is, an objective view of man that will bring into coherence man's double life in the world: his life as an organism in an environment responding to an environment, and his life as the being who makes assertions about the world, who names things, tells truths and lies about them, has beliefs, forms theories. The current sciences that have man as their "datum" are not radical and are therefore in the final analysis incoherent because they either deal with man from one aspect, ignoring the other, or they deal with both without being able to show what one has to do with the other. Thus, objective psychology deals with man as an interacting element and so can say nothing about man's assertory behavior. Other disciplines like symbolic logic, mathematics, semantics, do deal with man's assertory behavior, not by the inductive-empirical method of the sciences, but by a postulational-deductive method, by making "rules" by which symbols are assigned and calculi constructed, and by deducing consequences therefrom. Such *a priori* disciplines can, of course, say nothing about man's assertory behavior as a subject of investigation since they presuppose such behavior and are concerned only with the products of this behavior, the assertions. Still other disciplines deal with man as locus of consciousness (or unconsciousness), some formally-deductively as phenomenology, others empirically-inductively, as psychoanalysis. But neither is able to show a connection between their subject and man as the creature who to a degree knows the world and tells other men and is understood. A hybrid discipline like semiotic brings the two aspects, behavioristic and assertory, willy-nilly together without explaining what one has to do with the other.

Thus we have objective sciences of man as a responding animal or a culture-member, logical sciences of the assertions of man, and subjective sciences of man as a psyche. We have every approach except the one approach necessary to an understanding of man's unique position in the world: *an objective science of man as an asserting organism.*

Such a science finds itself immediately confronted with man as *animal symbolicum*, as the organism who uses symbols. We discover that we can never understand man's orientation to the world in terms either of a responding organism or a solitary consciousness. Instead it is the very condition of his humanity that man participates in a four-term relation. The very condition of his being the creature who knows and speaks is that there be not only an I but a You, not only a thing beheld but a word spoken.

An appreciation of man's fundamental symbolic orientation in the world has important consequences, both for our everyday thinking and for our philosophizing.

It suggests, first and most important of all, a radical therapy of the disease that has afflicted the vision of Western man for three hundred years: Cartesian dualism. We are, whether we know it or not, Cartesians, and our inclination, whether we like it or not, is to see the world as it was split by Descartes and never put back together. We see the world as matter in interaction—with oneself left over as a locus of mind, consciousness, care, marooned in space-time. We recognize sciences of matter and sciences of consciousness, but we do not know what one has to do with the other. "Mind," "consciousness," "soul," tend to dwindle before the assault of the scientific method. Yet the scientist himself remains and anguish remains, and each grows more and more heterogeneous with the world as the Method becomes ever more all-encompassing.

Yet such a view of the world is, after all is said and done, simply false. Man is indeed an organism among other organisms in the world, and he is indeed spirit, but his spirit is achieved mediately, through other organisms, the words they speak and the world they live in. He knows and asserts and is conscious, but his knowing and his asserting and his consciousness are neither the responses of an organism nor the pure intuitions of a psyche; they are achieved through the "other organism" as comrade, through the thing beheld and the word spoken in common. Mind and consciousness are realized through the mediation of matter.

A radical anthropology must take account not only of man as organism and social unit with his responses and his needs and his drives for need-satisfaction. It must take account also of the realities of his basic symbolic orientation to the world. These realities are the bond between man and man, and the relation that they intend between symbol and that which is symbolized. These relations differ from the relations that the scientific method expresses in that, whereas the latter are causal functions, the former are *polar* relations. Thus, the relation between stimulus and response is a determinate function expressible by scientific law. But the relation of I and Thou is polar, admitting of an authentic term (I-Thou) and an inauthentic term (I-It). The relation between a sign and the thing signified is a determinate function, but the relation intended between word and thing is polar, admitting an authentic term (truth) and an inauthentic term (error, magic).

Such an anthropology has the means of dealing with the normative and polar realities of human life, religion/myth, worship/idolatry, truth/error, true/that-which-is. The fundamental act of symbolization is an affirming of the thing to be what it is through the auspices of the symbol. Each symbolic form, whether it be a name-giving, a proposition, a scientific hypothesis, a work of art, an act of worship, is an affirming of what-is. The existence of things, of relations, of laws, of concrete forms, of God, is known and affirmed through the mediation of the symbol.

Philosophically, the main consequences of a semiotic that recognizes the symbol is a transcending of the observer-data split. The intending and assertory activity of a consciousness is brought into coherence with the interaction of the data by the larger unity of the symbolic orientation. This unity suggests a correction of both the phenomenological-existential and biological-naturalist view of the world.

First, it shows that the transcendental ego-consciousness of Kant, of Husserl, of Sartre, is a myth. Consciousness is both genetically and dynamically a we-function. It is not a private realm since it is neither private, being a function of the Thou as well as the I, nor a realm, a state, since it is nothing else than the *act* by which a thing is intended to be what it is under the auspices of the symbol. It is suggested that the ego-consciousness of the phenomenologists is a term of deterioration of the polar relation of consciousness, cognition—magic cognition, true consumption—magic consumption, genuine culture—spurious culture, language-talk (Heidegger's *Rede-Gerede*), and so on. The objective scientific method cannot deal with polar realities without falling into an antimony, as we have seen.

We may express the authentic term of man's symbolic orientation as *a communion that affirms what-is through the mediation of the symbol.*

The communion is not to be understood in the sense of a supposititious goal or happy state of human existence. It rather specifies in the most radical sense possible the very condition under which a man achieves his own consciousness of the world and comes to himself.

The symbol has a fundamentally sacramental function. Like a religious sacrament, it is a sensuous thing that mediates a higher operation. It is both analogical and anagogic: analogical in that it must bear a resemblance to the meaning that it mediates, anagogic because the meaning that it mediates is higher than the symbol itself. Like a sacrament, too, it undergoes a transformation. It is not only the vehicle of meaning; it is also transformed by its meaning toward the end that it carries its meaning within itself in another mode of existence, *in alio esse.*

The symbolic orientation achieves its actuality when it affirms being or, in other words, is a communion.

Secondly, it shows that no amount of objective theorizing about data-elements in interaction can issue in the phenomenon of mind. It is only when the *act* of symbolization is seen to supervene upon the sign-response that knowing, consciousness, make their appearance.

Man is neither a pure consciousness marooned in a world of objects, nor a pure organism, an object among objects. He is instead spirit-in-organism, besouled body, a complex in which spirit achieves itself not in spite of organism, words, and the world, but because of them and through them.

The direction of the book should now be apparent. My conviction is that an honest appraisal of the empirical elements and the genesis and the structure of human meaning must carry one beyond the organismic view of man and toward a philosophic realism. I refer, of course, to realism in the technical sense, as implying a real world, a lawful world, which can to some degree be known and the knowledge communicated to other men. Man is a being in the world. But he is also that being who knows and affirms other beings.

If we look at the work of the two philosophers who are most acutely aware of the seminal role of the symbol in man's orientation, we will find, paradoxically, that in each case, their specific insights into the nature of the symbol run counter to the philosopher's own allegiance. Susanne Langer admits that the symbol-relation cannot be accommodated by orthodox positivism and biological naturalism. Yet she suggests no other anthropology or metaphysic by which it can be understood. The upshot is an incoherent view in which man is seen as the organism who has learned an extraordinary trick that makes no sense biologically. She is driven into the antinomy that the scientific method always encounters when it tries to deal with assertory behavior: she must construe such assertions as myth as false by the true-false criterion of the scientist and true by the immanent criteria of the data.

Ernst Cassirer, on the other hand, tries to fit his symbolic forms into a Kantian mold. Symbols are the "spontaneous creations of the spirit" which regulate and even constitute that which is known. But how can Cassirer remain faithful to the Kantian thesis of the pure ego-consciousness constituting its world, when the very means by which this world is constituted are not just the forms and categories of consciousness but the sensuous symbol, the sound, the gesture, the icon? The symbol is not only something distinct from ego-consciousness, a *something else;* it implies as well a *somebody else*, for whom the symbol is meaningful. If there is no other lesson to be learned from Cassirer's description of *animal symbolicum*, it is surely this: the very condition of symbolization presupposes a real world in which at least four real beings exist and enter into real relations—two organisms, the symbol (not an *a priori* form but a real sound trembling in the air) and something which is symbolized. This latter "something" is, moreover, not entirely accounted for by the symbol. As Cassirer himself said, symbol and thing mutually interpenetrate and inform each other toward the end that the symbol is transformed by the thing and the thing receives the stamp of discreteness of the symbol. Only such a reciprocal relation can account for the polar reality of knowing, with magic cognition at one term, the symbol playing the major role, and true knowledge at the other, the symbol serving as a transparent intentional instrument through which the thing is known.

What is the meaning of the colossal "error" that lies at the very heart of man's knowledge of the world? The "error" is this: that in order to know anything, one must know it through something else. The positivist is scandalized because the semantical pairing, *this is a ball*, lies outside his physico-causal scheme of understanding the world. The idealist is scandalized because the "error" decrees that man may not forsake the incarnate, the concrete, the particular, for the ideal and the universal. He can never get away from the sensuous symbol, the word, the rite, the art form. The critic is scandalized because the great art form is not image or icon, the "like" symbol; it is the analogous symbol, the "wrong" metaphor, the musical discord, the ambiguous narrative. Are we to understand the "error" to mean that man is after all monstrous? Some philosophers and psychiatrists seem to be saying just this: though a few men are capable of scaling the heights of science, we are by and large ruled by emotional, symbolic, and chthonic forces which are either unconscious or irrational.

But is it not rather the case that this "error" is nothing else than the means by which an incarnate spirit knows the world. It knows the world not as an organism does, by responding to it; not as a pure spirit does, by knowing it directly; but *mediately*, through the very thing the world is made of. As for the error itself, the "is" through which a man declares that *this is water* and *water is cool*, this is nothing less than the means for grasping the very act by which the world has come into being and endures: existence.

Far from being the death blow to metaphysics, an awareness of the true nature of language and other symbolic processes provide a fresh access to a philosophy of being. Man is in the world, not merely as an adapting organism but as the creature whose vocation it is to know the truth of being and give testimony of it. His proper mode of existence, not a supposititious goal of life, not a "belief" that may or may not be held, but the very condition of his life as a man, is to live in comradeship with his fellow men and in openness toward the world, as he whose vocation it is, in Heidegger's words, to provide "a clearing for Being."*

* Editors' note: quoted in Collins 1952, 203; see also chapter 5, "Heidegger's Recall of Man to Being."

REFERENCES

Aquinas, Thomas. 1922. *The "Summa Theologica" of St. Thomas Aquinas: Part I*, translated by the Fathers of the English Dominican Province, 177-179. London: Burnes Oates and Washbourne.

Barfield, Owen. 1952. *Poetic Diction: A Study in Meaning*. London, Faber and Faber.

Benedict, Ruth. 1946. *Patterns of Culture.* New York: Pelican Books, Penguin Books.

Bidney, David. 1953. *Theoretical Anthropology*. New York: Columbia University Press.

Blackmur, Richard P. 1952. *Language as Gesture: Essays in Poetry*. New York: Harcourt, Brace.

Bloomfield, Leonard. 1955. "Linguistic Aspects of Science." In *International Encyclopedia of Unified Science* 1(4). Chicago: University of Chicago Press.

Boas, Franz. 1911. "Kwakiutl." *Handbook of American Indian Languages,* Part I, Bulletin 40. Washington: Bureau of American Ethnology, Government Printing Office.

———. 1938. *The Mind of the Primitive Man*. New York: McMillan.

Bowlby, John. 1953. "Critical Phases in the Development of Social Responses in Man." In *New Biology 14*, edited by M. L. Johnson and Michael Abercrombie, 25-32. London: Penguin Books.

Brunswik, Egon. 1952. "The Conceptual Framework of Psychology." In Vol.1, *International Encyclopedia of Unified Science,* edited by Otto Neurath, Rudolf Carnap, and Charles Morris, 655-760. Chicago: University of Chicago Press.

Buber, Martin. 1937. *I and Thou,* translated by Ronald Gregor Smith. Edinburgh: T&T Clark.

———. 1957. "Distance and Relation." *Psychiatry: Journal for the Study of Interpersonal Processes*, 20 (2): 97-104.

———. 1958. *I and Thou*. New York: Scribner's.

Carnap, Rudolf. 1948. *Introduction to Semantics and Formalization of Logic.* Cambridge: Harvard University Press.

Cassirer, Ernst. 1946. *Language and Myth*. Translated by Susanne. K. Langer. New York: Dover.

———. 1953a. *An Essay on Man: An Introduction to a Philosophy of Human Culture.* Garden City, New York: Doubleday Anchor Books.

———. 1953b. *The Philosophy of the Symbolic Forms: Volume One: Language.* New Haven: Yale University Press.

———. 1955. *The Philosophy of the Symbolic Forms: Volume Two: Mythical Thought*, New Haven: Yale University Press.

Chase, Stuart. 1938. *The Tyranny of Words.* New York: Harcourt Brace.

Chisholm, Roderick M. 1954. "Sellars' Critical Realism." *Philosophy and Phenomenological Research* 15 (1): 33-47.

Collins, James. 1952. *The Existentialists.* Chicago: Henry Regnery.

Cornforth, Maurice. 1949. "Logical Empiricism." In *Philosophy for the Future: The Quest of Modern Materialism*, edited by Roy Wood Sellars, V. J. McGill, and Marvin Farber, 495-519. New York: Macmillan.

Crockett, Campbell. 1954. "The Short Puzzling Life of Logical Positivism." *The Modern Schoolman* 31(2): 85-92.

Darwin, Charles. 1936. *The Origin of Species and The Descent of Man.* New York: The Modern Library.

Dawson, Christopher. 1954. "Sociology as a Science." *Cross Currents* 4(2): 124-137.

Dean, Gordon. 1953. "Atomic Miracles We Will See in Ten Years." *Look Magazine*, August 25.

Einstein, Albert. 1934. "Principles of Research." In *Essays in Science*, translated by Alan Harris. New York: Philosophical Library.

Empson, William. 1947. *Seven Types of Ambiguity.* London: Chatto & Windus.

Farber, Leslie H. 1956. "Martin Buber and Psychiatry." *Psychiatry* 19 (2): 109-120.

Feigl, Herbert. 1953. "The Mind-Body Problem in the Development of Logical Empiricism." In *Readings in the Philosophy of Science*, edited by Herbert Feigl and May Brodbeck, 612-626. New York: Appleton-Century-Crofts.

Frankl, Viktor E. 1955. *The Doctor and the Soul.* New York: Alfred A. Knopf.

Friend, Julius and James Feibleman. 1937. *What Science Really Means: An Explanation of the History and Empirical Method of General Science*, London: George Allen and Unwin.

Gray, Louis H. 1939. *Foundations of Language.* New York: Macmillan.

Gurwitsch, Aron. 1955. "The Phenomenological and the Psychological Approach to Consciousness." *Philosophy and Phenomenological Research: A Quarterly Journal*, 15(3): 303-319.

Heidegger, Martin. 1949. *Existence and Being*. Chicago: Henry Regnery.
———. 1953. *Sein und Zeit*. Tübingen: Max Niemeyer Verlag.
Hocking, William E. 1954. "Marcel and the Ground Issues of Metaphysics." *Philosophy and Phenomenological Research,* 14(4): 439-469.
Hopkins, Gerard Manley. 1937. *The Note-Books and Papers of Gerard Manley Hopkins*. Edited by Humphry House. London: Oxford University Press.
———. 1959. *The Journals and Papers of Gerard Manley Hopkins*. Edited by Humphry House and Graham Storey. London: Oxford University Press.
Husserl, Edmund. 1929. "Phenomenology." In *The Encyclopedia Britannica*. 14th ed. Encyclopedia Britannica Company.
———. 1950. *Cartesianische Meditationen and Pariser Vorträge*. The Hague: Martinus Nijhof.
———. 1952. *Ideas: General Introduction to a Pure Phenomenology*. New York: Macmillan Company.
Jaspers, Karl. 1953. *The Origin and Goal of History*. New Haven: Yale University Press.
Jespersen, Otto. 1949. *Language, Its Nature, Development and Origin*. New York: Macmillan.
Jung, Carl Gustav. 1959. "The Archetypes and the Collective Unconscious." In *The Collected_Works of C. G. Jung*, vol. 9, translated by R.F.C. Hull. New York: Bollingen.
Kant, Immanuel. 1929. *Critique of Pure Reason*, translated by Norman Kemp Smith. London: MacMillan.
Kauffman, Walter. 1956. *Existentialism from Dostoevsky to Sartre*. New York: The World Publishing Company.
Keller, Helen. 1928. *The Story of My Life*. Boston: Houghton Mifflin Company.
Kierkegaard, Søren. 1941. *Repetition: An Essay in Experimental Psychology*, translated by Walter Lowrie. New York: Harper and Row.
Klubertanz, George P. 1951. "The Psychologists and the Nature of Man." In Vol. 25, *Proceedings of the American Catholic Philosophical Association: The Nature of Man*, 66-88. Washington D.C.: American Catholic Philosophical Association.
———. 1953. *The Philosophy of Human Nature*. New York: Appleton-Century-Crofts.
Koffka, Kurt. 1935. *Principles of Gestalt Psychology*. New York: Harcourt Brace.

Koppers, Wilhelm. 1952. *Primitive Man and His World Picture.* New York: Sheed and Ward.

Korzybski, Alfred. 1952. *Science and Sanity: An Introduction to Non-Aristotelian Systems and General Semantics*, 3rd ed. Lakeville, Connecticut: The International Non-Aristotelian Library Publishing Company.

Langer, Susanne K. 1951. *Philosophy in a New Key: A Study in the Symbolism of Reason, Rite, and Art.* Mentor Books, New York.

———. 1953. *Feeling and Form: A Theory of Art developed from "Philosophy in a New Key."* New York: Charles Scribner's Sons.

Levy-Brühl, Lucien. 1926. *How Natives Think (Les Functions Mentale Dans Les Societies Inferioures).*Translated by Lilian A. Clare. London: George Allen and Unwinn.

Locke, John. 1824. *An Essay Concerning Human Understanding.* Book 3, Chapter 2, Section 1. New York: Valentine Seaman.

Lowell, Robert. 1943. "On the Eve of the Feast of the Immaculate Conception, 1942." *The Sewanee Review* 51(3), 393-394.

MacIver, Robert. 1947. *The Web of Government.* New York: The MacMillan Company.

Malinowski, Bronislaw. 1953. "The Problem of Meaning in Primitive Tribes." In *The Meaning of Meaning*, edited by C. K. Ogden and I. A. Richards, 296-336. New York: Harcourt Brace.

———. 1954. *Magic, Science, and Religion.* New York: Doubleday Anchor Books.

Marcel, Gabriel. 1951a. *Homo Viator: Introduction to a Metaphysics of Hope*, translated by Emma Craufurd. Chicago: Henry Regnery.

———. 1951b. *The Mystery of Being*, vol. 2 *Faith and Reality.* Translated by Rene Hague. Chicago: Henry Regnery.

Maritain, Jacques. 1948a. *A Preface to Metaphysics: Seven Lectures on Being.* New York: Sheed and Ward.

———. 1948b. *Ransoming the Time*, translated Harry Lorin Binsse. New York: Charles Scribner's Sons.

Mead, George H. 1932. *The Philosophy of the Present.* Edited by A. E. Murphy. Lasalle: Open Court.

———. 1952. *Mind, Self, and Society: From the Standpoint of a Social Behaviorist.* Chicago: University of Chicago Press.

Morris, Charles W. 1946. *Signs, Language, and Behavior.* New York: Prentice-Hall.

———. 1952. "Preface." In *Mind, Self, and Society: From the Standpoint of a Social Behaviorist*, by G. H. Mead. Chicago: University of Chicago Press.

———. 1955. *International Encyclopedia of Unified Science*, vol. 1. Edited by Otto Neurath, Rudolf Carnap, and Charles Morris. Chicago: University of Chicago Press.

Nagel, Ernest. 1953."The Casual Character of Modern Physical Theory." *Readings in the Philosophy of Science*, edited by Herbert Feigl and May Brodbeck, 419-437. New York: Appleton-Century-Crofts.

Nietzsche, Friedrich. 1927. "The Birth of Tragedy." In *The Philosophy of Nietzsche*, 951-1088. New York: Modern Library.

Ogden, C. K., and I. A. Richards. 1953. *The Meaning of Meaning: A Study of the Influence of Language upon Thought and of the Science of Symbolism*. New York: Harcourt and Brace and Company.

Ortega y Gasset, Jose. 1952. *The Revolt of the Masses*. New York : New American Library.

Peirce, Charles S. 1935. *Collected Papers of Charles Sanders Peirce*. Edited by Charles Hartshorne and Paul Weiss. Vol. 6: *Scientific Metaphysics*. Cambridge: Harvard University Press.

———. 1955. "Logic as Semiotic: The Theory of Signs." In *Philosophical Writings of Peirce*, edited by Justus Buchler, 98-119. New York: Dover.

Percy, Walker. 1956. "Symbol as Hermeneutic in Existentialism." *Philosophy and Phenomenological Research* 16 (4): 522-530.

———. 1957. "Semiotic and a Theory of Knowledge." *The Modern Schoolman* 34 (4): 225-246.

Piaget, Jean. 1955. *The Language and Thought of the Child*, translated by Marjorie Gabain. New York: Noonday Press.

Picard, Max. 1951. *The Flight from God*. Chicago: Henry Regnery Company.

Plato. 1892. *Cratylus*. In *Dialogues of Plato*, translated by Benjamin Jowett. Oxford: Clarendon Press.

Reichenbach, Hans. 1956. *The Rise of Scientific Philosophy*. Berkeley: University of California Press.

Richards, I. A. 1950. *The Philosophy of Rhetoric*. New York: Oxford University Press.

Russell, Bertrand. 1914. *Our Knowledge of the External World as a Field for Scientific Method in Philosophy*. LaSalle: Open Court.

Sapir, Edward. 1921. *Language: An Introduction to the Study of Speech*. New York: Harcourt Brace.

———. 1953. "Language." In *Encyclopedia of Social Sciences*, 155-169. New York: Macmillan.

———. 1956. "Culture Genuine and Spurious." In *Selected Writings of Edward Sapir in Language, Culture, and Personality*, edited by David Mandelbaum, 308-331. Berkeley: University of California Press.

Sartre, Jean Paul. 1957. *Being and Nothingness.* Translated by Hazel Barnes. London: Methuen.
Schachtel, Ernest G. 1954. "The Development of Focal Attention and the Emergence of Reality." *Psychiatry: Journal for the Study of Interpersonal Processes* 17 (4): 309-24.
Schütz, Alfred. 1954. "Concept and Theory Formation in the Social Sciences." *Journal of Philosophy* 51 (9): 257-273.
Sellars, Roy Wood, V. J. McGill, and Marvin Farber, eds. 1949. *Philosophy for the Future: The Quest of Modern Materialism.* New York: Macmillan.
Sellars, Roy Wood. 1949. "Materialism and Human Knowing." In *Philosophy for the Future: The Quest of Modern Materialism*, edited by Roy Wood Sellars, V. J. McGill, and Marvin Farber, 75-105. New York: Macmillan.
Standen, Anthony. 1950. *Science is a Sacred Cow.* New York: E. P. Dutton.
Stern, Karl. 1954. *The Third Revolution: A Study of Psychiatry and Religion.* New York: Harcourt, Brace.
Tarski, Alfred. 1944."The Semantic Conception of Truth: And the Foundations of Semantics." *Philosophy and Phenomenological Research*, 4(3): 341-376.
Tate, Allen. 1952. "The Symbolic Imagination: A Meditation on Dante's Three Mirrors." *The Kenyon Review*, 14(2), 256-77.
———. 1953. *The Forlorn Demon.* Chicago: Henry Regnery.
Toynbee, Arnold. 1954. *A Study of History*, vol. 1-10. New York: Oxford University Press.
Veatch, Henry Babcock. 1952. *Intentional Logic.* New Haven: Yale University Press.
———. 1953. "For a Realistic Logic," In *The Return to Reason: Essays in Realistic Philosophy,* edited by John Wild, 177-198. Chicago: Henry Regnery.
Whitehead, Alfred North. 1953. *Science and the Modern World: Lowell Lectures, 1925.* New York: Macmillan.
Wilhelmsen, Frederick D. 1954."The Philosopher and the Myth." *The Modern Schoolman,* 32(1): 39-41.
Wilson, Richard Albert. 1948. *The Miraculous Birth of Language.* New York: Philosophical Library.
Yerkes, Robert M., and Ada W. Yerkes. 1945. *The Great Apes: A Study of Anthropoid Life.* New Haven: Yale University Press.

INDEX